Relevance Ranking for Vertical Search Engines

Relevance Ranking for Vertical Search Engines

Edited by

Bo Long
LinkedIn Inc., Mountain View, CA, USA

Yi Chang
Yahoo! Labs, Sunnyvale, CA, USA

ELSEVIER

AMSTERDAM • BOSTON • HEIDELBERG • LONDON
NEW YORK • OXFORD • PARIS • SAN DIEGO
SAN FRANCISCO • SINGAPORE • SYDNEY • TOKYO
Morgan Kaufmann is an imprint of Elsevier

Acquiring Editor: Steve Elliot
Editorial Project Manager: Lindsay Lawrence
Project Manager: Punithavathy Govindaradjane
Designer: Maria Inês Cruz

Morgan Kaufmann is an imprint of Elsevier
225 Wyman Street, Waltham, MA 02451, USA

Notices
Knowledge and best practice in this field are constantly changing. As new research and experience broaden our understanding, changes in research methods, professional practices, or medical treatment may become necessary.

Practitioners and researchers must always rely on their own experience and knowledge in evaluating and using any information, methods, compounds, or experiments described herein. In using such information or methods they should be mindful of their own safety and the safety of others, including parties for whom they have a professional responsibility.

To the fullest extent of the law, neither the Publisher nor the authors, contributors, or editors, assume any liability for any injury and/or damage to persons or property as a matter of products liability, negligence or otherwise, or from any use or operation of any methods, products, instructions, or ideas contained in the material herein.

Library of Congress Cataloging-in-Publication Data
Relevance ranking for vertical search engines / Bo Long, Yi Chang (Editors).
     pages cm
 Includes bibliographical references and index.
 ISBN 978-0-12-407171-1
 1. Text processing (Computer science) 2. Sorting (Electronic computers) 3. Relevance.
 4. Database searching. 5. Search engines–Programming. I. Long, Bo, editor of compilation.
 II. Chang, Yi (Computer expert)
 QA76.9.T48R455 2014
 025.04–dc23

2013039777

British Library Cataloguing-in-Publication Data
A catalogue record for this book is available from the British Library
ISBN: 978-0-12-407171-1

Printed and bound in the United States of America
14 15 16 17 18   10 9 8 7 6 5 4 3 2 1

Working together
to grow libraries in
developing countries

www.elsevier.com • www.bookaid.org

For information on all MK publications visit our website at *www.mkp.com*

Contents

List of Tables

List of Figures

About the Editors

Bo Long is currently a staff applied researcher at LinkedIn Inc., and was formerly a senior research scientist at Yahoo! Labs. His research interests lie in data mining and machine learning with applications to web search, recommendation, and social network analysis. He holds eight innovations and has published peer-reviewed papers in top conferences and journals including ICML, KDD, ICDM, AAAI, SDM, CIKM, and KAIS. He has served as reviewer, workshop co-organizer, conference organizer, committee member, and area chair for multiple conferences, including KDD, NIPS, SIGIR, ICML, SDM, CIKM, JSM, etc.

Yi Chang is a principal scientist and sciences director in Yahoo Labs, where he leads the search and anti-abuse science group. His research interests include web search, applied machine learning, natural language processing, and social computing. Yi has published more than 60 conference/journal papers, and has served as workshop co-organizer, conference organizer, committee member, and area chair for multiple conferences, including WWW, SIGIR, ICML, KDD, CIKM, etc.

List of Contributors

Jaime Arguello
University of North Carolina at Chapel Hill, Chapel Hill, NC, USA

Jiang Bian
Microsoft Inc., Beijing, P.R. China

Yi Chang
Yahoo! Labs, Sunnyvale, CA, USA

Fernando Diaz
Microsoft Inc., New York, NY, USA

Anlei Dong
Yahoo! Labs, Sunnyvale, CA, USA

David Hanauer
University of Michigan, Ann Arbor, MI, USA

Yoshiyuki Inagaki
Yahoo! Labs, Sunnyvale, CA, USA

Changsung Kang
Yahoo! Labs, Sunnyvale, CA, USA

Yuan Liu
Microsoft Inc., Beijing, P.R. China

Bo Long
LinkedIn Inc., Mountain View, CA, USA

Yuanhua Lv
Microsoft Inc., Mountain View, CA, USA

Qiaozhu Mei
University of Michigan, Ann Arbor, MI, USA

Tao Mei
Microsoft Inc., Beijing, P.R. China

Belle Tseng
Apple Inc., Cupertino, CA, USA

Srinivas Vadrevu
Microsoft Inc., Mountain View, CA, USA

Hongning Wang
University of Illinois at Urbana-Champaign, Urbana, IL, USA

Xuanhui Wang
Facebook Inc., Menlo Park, CA, USA

Kai Zheng
University of Michigan, Ann Arbor, MI, USA

Foreword

As the information available on the Internet continues to grow, Web searchers increasingly run into a critical but not broadly discussed challenge: finding relevant, rich results for highly targeted and specialized queries.

General Web searching has been with us for a long time, has spawned international powerhouse companies like Yahoo! and Google, and is a staple of everyday life for hundreds of millions of people around the world. It is probable that literally billions of generic searches—for general information, celebrities, sports scores, common products, and other items of interest—are well satisfied by the commonly known major search engines whose names are so familiar as to have become part of the vernacular. But since the Internet has become the business- and daily-life critical worldwide resource it is today, increasingly diverse groups of people are relying on it to look for more and more diverse things—things not so easily found by generic Web search engines.

For example, searches focused on travel planning may often have very specific but implicit assumptions about results, such as the expectation of itineraries listed in order of departure or cost. They might also benefit from additional nonobvious information that could be critically helpful, such as changes in checked baggage policies, road construction near relevant airports, or State Department travel warnings. General search engines have no more clue about these things than they do about dosages of medications, celebrity divorces, slugging percentages, and other narrow, domain-specific information; they don't have access to site-specific signals. As a result, the role of so-called "vertical" search engines, which focus on specific segments of online content and deep site-specific information, has quietly increased to become essential to most people looking for key items online.

Somewhat hidden from view but no less important than general Web search technology, vertical search algorithms have been key to helping users find household products they care about, movies they want to see, potential dating partners, their perfect automobiles, well-matched insurance policies, and thousands of other things for which generalized text processing algorithms are not well tuned and cannot make the right judgments of relevance for results.

In this context, the term *vertical* is usually taken to connote in-depth treatment of fairly narrow domains, e.g., medical information, rather than broad ranges of information that meet a very wide range of needs (as you will see, for the purposes of this book, *vertical* can also refer to a limited range of search result types, such as entities or measurements or dates, or specific types of information access modalities, such as mobile search). What sets vertical search apart from more general, broad-based search is the fact that relatively specific domain knowledge can be leveraged to find the right pieces of information. Further, an understanding of a more limited set of information-seeking tasks (for example, looking for specific kinds of football statistics for your fantasy team) can also play an important role in satisfying narrower information needs. With fewer but very common tasks carried out by users, it may be easier to infer a user's intent for a particular vertical search, which could dramatically improve the quality and value of the results for the user.

In addition to the opportunity to provide highly relevant and richer results to information seekers, vertical search engines that focus on specific segments of online content have shown great potential to offer advertisers more contextually relevant, better-targeted audiences for their ads. Given the dependence of the Internet search industry on advertising, this makes vertical search an economically central part of the Internet's future. There is no doubt that vertical search is starting to play a role of which the significance was probably never imagined in the early days of Internet searching.

As with other forms of search, the heart of successful vertical search is relevance ranking. Specialized understanding of the domain and sophisticated ranking algorithms is critical. Algorithms that work hard to infer a user's intention when doing a search are the ones that are successful. The ability to use the right signals and successfully compare various aspects of a query and potential retrieved results will make or break a search engine. And that is the focus of this book: introducing and evaluating the critical ranking technology needed to make vertical searching successful.

Although there exist many books on general Web search technology, this new volume is a unique resource, dedicated to vertical search technologies and the relevance ranking technology that makes them successful. The book takes a comprehensive view of this area and aims to become an authoritative source of information for search scientists, engineers, and other interested readers with a technical bent. Despite many years of research on algorithms and methods of general Web search, vertical search deserves its own dedicated study and in-depth treatment because of the unique nature of its structures and applications. This volume provides that focused treatment, covering key issues such as cross-vertical searching, vertical selection and aggregation, news searches, object searches, image searches, and medical domain searches.

The authors represented in this book are active researchers who cover many different aspects of vertical search technology and who have made tangible contributions to the progress of what is clearly a dynamic research frontier. This ensures that the book is authoritative and reflects the current state of the art. Nevertheless—and importantly—the book gives a balanced treatment of a wide spectrum of topics, well beyond the individual authors' own methodologies and research specialties.

The book presents in-depth and systematic discussions of theories and practices for vertical search ranking. It covers the obvious major fields as well as recently emerging areas for vertical search, including news search ranking, local search ranking, object search ranking, image search ranking, medical domain search ranking, cross-vertical ranking, and vertical selection and aggregation. For each field, the book provides state-of-the-art algorithms with detailed discussions, including background, derivation, and comparisons. The book also presents extensive experimental results on various real application datasets to demonstrate the performance of various algorithms as well as guidelines for practical use of those algorithms. It introduces ranking algorithms for various vertical search ranking applications and teaches readers how to manipulate ranking algorithms to achieve better results in real applications. Finally, the book provides thorough theoretical analysis of various algorithms and problems to lay a solid foundation for future advances in the field.

Vertical search is still a fairly young and dynamic research field. This volume offers researchers and application developers a comprehensive overview of the general concepts, techniques, and applications of vertical search and helps them explore this exciting field and develop new methods and applications. It may also serve graduate students and other interested readers with a general introduction to the state of the art of this promising research area. It uses plain language with detailed examples, including case studies and real-world, hands-on examples to explain the key concepts, models, and algorithms used in vertical search ranking. I think that overall you will find it quite readable and highly informative.

Although not widely known, vertical search is an essential part of our everyday lives on the Internet. It is increasingly critical to users' satisfaction and increasing reliance on online data sources, and it provides extraordinary new opportunities for advertisers. Given recent growth in the application of vertical search and our increasing daily reliance on it, you hold in your hands the first guidebook to the next generation of information access on the Internet. I hope you enjoy it.

—Ron Brachman
Chief Scientist and Head, Yahoo! Labs
Yahoo!, Inc.

Introduction

1.1 Defining the Area

In the past decade, the impact of general Web search capabilities has been stunning. However, with exponential information growth on the Internet, it becomes more and more difficult for a general Web search engine to address the particular informational and research needs of niche users. As a response to the great need for deeper, more specific, more relevant search results, vertical search engines have emerged in various domains. By leveraging domain knowledge and focusing on specific user tasks, vertical search has great potential to serve users highly relevant search results from specific domains.

The core component of vertical search is *relevance ranking*, which has attracted more and more attention from both industry and academia during the past few years. This book aims to present systematic study of practices and theories for vertical search ranking. The studies in this book can be categorized into to two major classes. One class is single-domain-related ranking that focuses on ranking for a specific vertical, such as news search ranking and medical domain search ranking. However, in this book the term *vertical* has a more general meaning than topic. It refers to specific topics such as news and medical information, specific result types such as entities, and specific search interfaces such as mobile search. The second class of vertical search study covered in this book class is multidomain-related ranking, which focuses on ranking involving multiple verticals, such as multiaspect ranking, aggregating vertical search ranking, and cross-vertical ranking.

1.2 The Content and Organization of This Book

This book aims to present an in-depth and systematic study of practices and theories related to vertical search ranking. The organization of this book is as follows.

Chapter 2 covers news vertical search ranking. News is one of the most important of Internet users' online activities. For a commercial news search engine, it is critical to provide users with the most relevant and fresh ranking results. Furthermore, it is necessary to group the related news articles so that users can browse search results in terms of news stories rather than individual news articles. This chapter describes a few algorithms for news search engines, including ranking algorithms and clustering algorithms. For the ranking problem, the main challenge is achieving appropriate balance between topical relevance and freshness. For the clustering problem, the main challenge is how to group related news articles into clusters in a scalable mode. Chapter 2 introduces a few news search ranking approaches, including a learning-to-rank approach and a joint learning approach from clickthroughs. The chapter then describes a scalable clustering approach to group news search results.

Chapter 3 studies another important vertical search, the medical domain search. With the exponential growth of electronic health records (EHRs), it is imperative to identify effective means to help medical clinicians as well as administrators and researchers retrieve information from EHRs. Recent research advances in natural language processing (NLP) have provided improved capabilities for automatically extracting concepts from narrative clinical documents. However, before these NLP-based tools become widely available and versatile enough to handle vaguely defined information retrieval needs by EHR users, a convenient and cost-effective solution continues to be in great demand. In this chapter, we introduce the concept of medical information retrieval, which provides medical professionals a handy tool to search among unstructured clinical narratives via an interface similar to that of general-purpose Web search engines, e.g., Google. In the latter part of the chapter, we also introduce several advanced features, such as intelligent, ontology-driven medical search query recommendation services and a collaborative search feature that encourages sharing of medical search knowledge among end users of EHR search tools.

Chapter 4 is intended to introduce some fundamental and practical technologies as well as some major emerging trends in visual search ranking. The chapter first describes the generic visual search system, in which three categories of visual search are presented: i.e., *text-based*, *query example-based* and *concept-based* visual search ranking. Then we describe the three categories in detail, including a review of various popular algorithms. To further improve the performance of initial search results, visual search re-ranking of four paradigms will be presented: 1) *self-reranking*, which focuses on detecting relevant patterns from initial search results without any external knowledge; 2) *example-based reranking*, in which the query examples are provided by users so that the relevant patterns can be discovered from these examples; 3) *crowd-reranking*, which mines relevant patterns from crowd-sourcing information available on the Web; and 4) *interactive reranking*, which utilizes user interaction to guide the reranking process. In addition, we also discuss the relationship between learning and visual search, since most recent visual search ranking frameworks are developed based on machine learning technologies. Last, we conclude with several promising directions for future research.

Chapter 5 introduces *mobile search ranking*. The wide availability of Internet access on mobile devices, such as phones and personal media players, has allowed users to search and access Web information while on the go. The availability of continuous fine-grained location information on these devices has enabled mobile local search, which employs user location as a key factor to search for local entities (e.g., a restaurant, store, gas station, or attraction) to overtake a significant part of the query volume. This is also evident by the rising popularity of location-based search engines on mobile devices, such as Bing Local, Google Local, Yahoo! Local, and Yelp. The quality of any mobile local search engine is mainly determined by its ranking function, which formally specifies how we retrieve and rank local entities in response to a user's query. Acquiring effective ranking signals and heuristics to develop an effective ranking function is arguably the single most important research problem in mobile local search. This chapter first overviews the ranking signals in mobile local search (e.g., distance and customer rating score of a business), which have been recognized to be quite different from general Web search. We next present a recent data analysis that studies the behavior of mobile local search ranking signals using a large-scale query log, which reveals interesting heuristics that can be used to guide the exploitation of different signals to develop effective ranking features. Finally, we also discuss several interesting future research directions.

Chapter 6 is about *entity ranking*, which is a recent paradigm that refers to retrieving and ranking related objects and entities from different structured sources in various scenarios. Entities typically have associated categories and relationships with other entities. In this chapter, we introduce how to build a Web-scale entity ranking system based on machine = learned ranking models. Specifically, the entity ranking system usually takes advantage of structured knowledge bases, entity relationship graphs, and user data to derive useful features for facilitating semantic search with entities directly within the learning-to-rank framework. Similar to generic Web search ranking, entity pairwise preference can be leveraged to form the objective function of entity ranking. More than that, this chapter introduces ways to incorporate the categorization information and preference of related entities into the objective function for learning. This chapter further discusses how entity ranking is different from regular Web search in terms of presentation bias and the interaction of categories of query entities and result facets.

Chapter 7 presents learning to rank with multiaspect relevance for vertical searches. Many vertical searches, such as local search, focus on specific domains. The meaning of relevance in these verticals is domain-specific and usually consists of multiple well-defined aspects. For example, in local search, text matching and distance are two important aspects to assess relevance. Usually, the overall relevance between a query and a document is a tradeoff among multiple aspect relevancies. Given a single vertical, such a tradeoff can vary for different types of queries or in different contexts. In this chapter, we explore these vertical-specific aspects in the learning-to-rank setting. We propose a novel formulation in which the relevance between a query and a document is assessed with respect to each aspect, forming the multiaspect relevance. To compute a ranking function, we study two types of learning-based approaches to estimate the tradeoff among these aspect relevancies: a label aggregation method and a model aggregation method. Since there are only a few aspects, a minimal amount of training data is needed to learn the tradeoff. We conduct both offline and online bucket-test experiments on a local vertical search engine, and the experimental results show that our proposed multiaspect relevance formulation is very promising. The two types of aggregation methods perform more effectively than a set of baseline methods including a conventional learning-to-rank method.

Chapter 8 focuses on *aggregated vertical search*. Commercial information access providers increasingly incorporate content from a large number of specialized services created for particular information-seeking tasks. For example, an aggregated Web search page may include results from image databases and news collections in addition to the traditional Web search results; a news provider may dynamically arrange related articles, photos, comments, or videos on a given article page. These auxiliary services, known as *verticals*, include search engines that focus on a particular domain (e.g., news, travel, sports), search engines that focus on a particular type of media (e.g., images, video, audio), and application programming interfaces (APIs) to highly targeted information (e.g., weather forecasts, map directions, or stock prices). The goal of *aggregated search* is to provide integrated access to all verticals within a single information context. Although aggregated search is related to classic work in distributed information retrieval, it has unique signals, techniques, and evaluation methods in the context of the Web and other production information access systems. In this chapter, we present the core problems associated with aggregated search, which include sources of predictive evidence, relevance modeling, and evaluation.

Chapter 9 presents recent advances in *cross-vertical ranking*. A traditional Web search engine conducts ranking mainly in a single domain, i.e., it focuses on one type of data source, and effective modeling relies on a sufficiently large number of labeled examples, which require an expensive and time-consuming labeling process. On the other side, it is very common for a vertical search engine to conduct ranking tasks in various verticals, which presents a more challenging ranking problem, that of *cross-domain ranking*. Although in this book our focus is on cross-vertical ranking, the proposed approaches can be applied to more general cases, such as cross-language ranking. Therefore, we use a more general term, cross-domain ranking, in this book. For cross-domain ranking, in some domains we may have a relatively large amount of training data, whereas in other domains we can only collect very little. Theretofore, finding a way to leverage labeled information from related heterogeneous domain to improve ranking in a target domain has become a problem of great interest. In this chapter, we propose a novel probabilistic model, pairwise cross-domain factor (PCDF) model, to address this problem. The proposed model learns latent factors (features) for multidomain data in partially overlapped heterogeneous feature spaces. It is capable of learning homogeneous feature correlation, heterogeneous feature correlation, and pairwise preference correlation for cross-domain knowledge transfer. We also derive two PCDF variations to address two important special cases. Under the PCDF model, we derive a stochastic gradient-based algorithm, which facilitates distributed optimization and is flexible to adopt various loss functions and regularization functions to accommodate different data distributions. The extensive experiments on real-world data sets demonstrate the effectiveness of the proposed model and algorithm.

1.3   The Audience for This Book

The book covers major fields as well as recently emerging fields for vertical search. Therefore, the expected readership of this book includes all the researchers and systems development engineers working in these areas, including, but not limited to, Web search, information retrieval, data mining, and specific application areas related to vertical search, such as various specific vertical search engines. Since this book is self-contained in its presentation of the material, it also serves as an ideal reference book for people who are new to the topic of vertical search ranking. Consequently, in addition, the audience also includes anyone with interest or who works in a field requiring this reference book. Finally, this book can be used as a reference for a graduate course on advanced topics of information retrieval or data mining, since it provides a systematic introduction to this booming new subarea of information technology.

1.4   Further Reading

As a newly emerging area of information retrieval and data mining, vertical search ranking is still in its infant stage; currently there is no dedicated, premier venue for the publication of research in this area. Consequently, related work in this area, as the supplementary information to this book for further readings, may be found in the literature of the two parent areas.

In information retrieval, related work may be found in the premier conferences, such as the annual Association for Computing Machinery (ACM) Special Interest Group on Information Retrieval (SIGIR) conference, the International World Wide Web Conference (WWW), and the ACM, the International Conference on Information and Knowledge Management (ACM CIKM). For journals, the premier journals in the information retrieval area, including *Information Retrieval, Foundations and Trends in Information Retrieval* (FTIR), may contain related work in vertical search ranking.

In data mining, related work may be found in the premier conferences, such as the ACM International Conference on Knowledge Discovery and Data Mining (KDD), the Institute of Electrical and Electronics Engineers (IEEE), International Conference on Data Mining (ICDM), and the Society for Industrial and Applied Mathematics (SIAM) International Conference on Data Mining (SDM). In particular, related work may be found in the workshop dedicated to the area of relational learning, such as the Statistical Relational Learning workshop. The premier journals in the data mining area, including *IEEE Transactions on Knowledge and Data Engineering* (TKDE), *ACM Transactions on Data Mining* (TDM), and *Knowledge and Information Systems* (KAIS), may contain related work in relational data clustering.

News Search Ranking

2

2.1 The Learning-to-Rank Approach

The main challenge for ranking in news search is how to make appropriate balance between two factors: Relevance and freshness. Here relevance includes both topical relevance as well as news source authority.

A widely adopted approach in practice is to use a simple formula to combine relevance and freshness. For example, the final ranking score for a news article can be computed as

$$\mathbf{score}_{rank} = \mathbf{score}_{relevance} e^{-\beta t} \qquad (2.1)$$

where $\mathbf{score}_{relevance}$ is the value representing the relevance between query and news article, t is news article age and $e^{-\beta t}$ is a time decay term, for which the older a news article is, the more penalty the article will receive for its final ranking. The parameter β is used to control the relative importance of freshness in the final ranking result. In the literature of information retrieval, *document* is usually used to refer to a candidate item in ranking tasks. In this chapter, we use the terms *document* and *news article* equally because the application here is to rank news articles in a search.

The advantage of such a heuristic approach to a relevance and freshness combination is its efficiency in real practice, for which only the value of the parameter β needs to be tuned by using some ranking examples. Furthermore, the appropriate β value often leads to good ranking results for many queries, which also makes this approach effective.

The drawback of this approach is that it is incapable of further improving ranking performance, because such a heuristic rule is too naive to handle more complicated ranking cases. For example, in (2.1), time decay is represented by the term $e^{-\beta t}$, which is totally dependent on the document age. In fact, an appropriate time decay factor should also rely on the nature of the query, since different queries have different time sensitivities: If a query is related to breaking news, such as an earthquake, that has just happened and has extensive media reports on casualty and rescue, then freshness should be very important because even a document published only one hour ago could be outdated. On the other hand, if a query is for an event that happened weeks ago, then relevance is more important in ranking because the user would like to find the most relevant and comprehensive reports in the search results.

2.1.1 Related Works

Many prior works have exploited the temporal dimension in searches. For example, Baeza-Yates *et al.* [22] studied the relation among Web dynamics, structure, and page quality and demonstrated that PageRank is biased against new pages. In T-Rank Light and T-Rank algorithms [25], both activity (i.e., update rates) and freshness (i.e., timestamps of most recent updates) of pages and links are taken into account in link analysis. Cho *et al.* [66] proposed a page quality ranking function in order to alleviate the problem of popularity-based ranking, and they used the derivatives of PageRank to forecast future PageRank values for new pages. Nunes [269] proposed to improve Web information retrieval in the temporal dimension by combining the temporal features extracted from both individual documents and the whole Web. Pandey *et al.* [276] studied the tradeoff between new page exploration and high-quality page exploitation, which is based on a ranking method to randomly promote some new pages so that they can accumulate links quickly.

Temporal dimension is also considered in other information retrieval applications. Del Corso *et al.* [94] proposed the ranking framework to model news article generation, topic clustering, and story evolution over time, and this ranking algorithm takes publication time and linkage time into consideration as well as news source authority. Li *et al.* [221] proposed a TS-Rank algorithm, which considers page freshness in the stationary probability distribution of Markov chains, since the dynamics of Web pages are also important for ranking. This method proves effective in the application of publication search. Pasca [277] used temporal expressions to improve question-answering results for time-related questions. Answers are obtained by aggregating matching pieces of information and the temporal expressions they contain. Furthermore, Arikan *et al.* [20] incorporated temporal expressions into a language model and demonstrated experimental improvement in retrieval effectiveness.

Recency query classification plays an important role in recency ranking. Diaz [98] determined the newsworthiness of a query by predicting the probability of a user clicking on the news display of a query. König *et al.* [204] estimated the clickthrough rate for dedicated news search results with a supervised model, which is to satisfy the requirement of adapting quickly to emerging news event.

2.1.2 Combine Relevance and Freshness

Learning-to-rank algorithms have shown significant and consistent success in various applications [226,184,406,54]. Such machine-learned ranking algorithms learn a ranking mechanism by optimizing particular loss functions based on editorial annotations. An important assumption in those learning methods is that document relevance for a given query is generally stationary over time, so that, as long as the coverage of the labeled data is broad enough, the learned ranking functions would generalize well to future unseen data. Such an assumption is often true in Web searches, but it is less likely to hold in news searches because of the dynamic nature of news events and the lack of timely annotations.

A typical procedure is as follows:

- Collect query-URL pairs.
- Ask editors to label the query-URL pairs with relevance grades.
- Apply a learning-to-rank algorithm to the train ranking model.

Traditionally, in learning-to-rank, editors label query-URL pairs with relevance grades, which usually have four or five values, including *perfect, excellent, good, fair,* or *bad.* Editorial labeling information is used for ranking model training and ranking model evaluation. For training, these relevance grades are directly mapped to numeric values as learning targets.

For evaluation, we desire an evaluation metric that supports graded judgments and penalizes errors near the beginning of the ranked list. In this work, we use DCG [175],

$$DCG_n = \sum_{i=1}^{n} \frac{G_i}{\log_2(i+1)}, \tag{2.2}$$

where i is the position in the document list, and G_i is the function of relevance grade. Because the range of DCG values is not consistent across queries, we adopt the NDCG as our primary ranking metric,

$$NDCG_n = Z_n \sum_{i=1}^{n} \frac{G_i}{\log_2(i+1)}, \tag{2.3}$$

where Z_n is a normalization factor, which is used to make the NDCG of the ideal list be 1. We can use $NDCG_1$ and $NDCG_5$ to evaluate the ranking results.

We extend the learning-to-rank algorithm in news searches, for which we mainly make two modifications due to the dynamic nature of the news search: (1) training sample collection and (2) editorial labeling guideline.

2.1.2.1 *Training Sample Collection*

The training sample collection has to be near real time for news searches by the following steps:

1. Sample the *latest* queries from the news search query log.
2. *Immediately* get the candidate URLs for the sampled queries.
3. *Immediately* ask editors to do judgments on the query-URL pairs with relevance and freshness grades.

We can see that all the steps need to be accomplished in a short period. Therefore, the training sample collection has to be well planned in advance; otherwise, any delay during this procedure would affect the reliability of the collected data. If queries are sampled from an outdated query log or if all of the selected candidate URLs are outdated, they cannot represent the real data distribution. If editors do not label query-URL pairs on time, it will be difficult for them to provide accurate judgments, because editors' judgments rely on their good understanding of the related news events, which becomes more difficult as time elapses.

2.1.2.2 *Editorial Labeling*

In a news search, editors should provide query-URL grades on both traditional relevance and freshness. Although document age is usually available in news searches, it is impossible to determine a document's freshness based solely on document age. A news article published one day ago could either be very fresh or very old, depending on the nature of the related news event. So, we ask editors to provide subjective judgments on document freshness, which can have a few different grades, such as the following:

- Very fresh: latest documents (promote grade: 1)
- Fresh (promote grade: 0)
- A little bit outdated (demote grade: −1)
- Totally outdated and useless (demote grade: −2)

For ranking model training, we combine relevance grade and recency grade for a new grade as learning target. An example of such a grade combination is shown in the list. If the document is very fresh, we promote one grade from its original relevance grade. For example, if a document has a *good* grade on relevance and a *fresh* grade on freshness, its final grade is *excellent*, which is one grade higher than it is relevance grade, *good*. If the document is fresh, we neither promote nor demote. If the document is a little bit outdated, we demote one grade from its original relevance grade. If the document is totally outdated and useless, we demote two grades.

For ranking model evaluation, we can compute DCG values based on either the combined grades or the relevance grade and freshness grade separately.

To evaluate freshness in isolation, we also include a freshness metric based on DCG, called DCF:

$$\mathrm{DCF}_n = \sum_{i=1}^{n} \frac{F_i}{\log_2(i+1)}, \tag{2.4}$$

where i is the position in the document list, and F_i is the freshness label (1 or 0). A query may have multiple very fresh documents—for example, when multiple news sources simultaneously publish updates to some ongoing news story. Note that DCF is a recency measurement that is independent of overall relevance. Therefore, when we evaluate a ranking, we should first consider demoted NDCG, which represents the overall relevance, then inspect the value of the DCF. We also define normalized discounted cumulative freshness (NDCF) in the same way as for NDCG in Eq. 2.3.

2.2 Joint Learning Approach from Clickthroughs

Given the highly dynamic nature of news events and the sheer scale of news reported around the globe, it is often impractical for human editors to constantly keep track of the news and provide timely relevance and freshness judgments. To validate this conjecture, we asked editors to annotate the news query log for the day of August 9, 2011, immediately one day after, and then demoted the news search results based

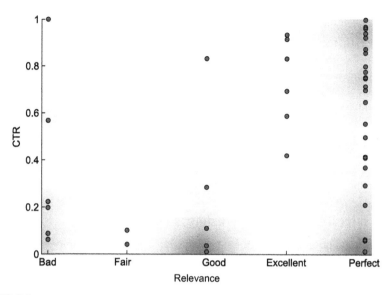

FIGURE 2.1

Scatter plot of CTR versus editor's relevance judgments.

on their judgments using the method from Dong *et al.* [106]. The relation between observed CTR and the demoted grades is visualized by a scatter plot in Figure 2.1.

From Figure 2.1, we observe that the clicks are not strictly correlated with the demoted grades; the average Pearson correlation between them across the queries is 0.5764 with a standard deviation 0.6401. The main reason for this inconsistency is the hard demotion rule: Users might have different demotion preferences for different queries, and it's almost impossible for an editor to predefine the combination rules, given the plurality of possibilities. As a result, the uncertainty from this heuristically derived ranking grade will limit the performance of subsequent learning-to-rank algorithms.

Suppose that, when a user submits a query to a news search engine and gets a list of ranked news documents, she would first judge the usefulness of each document by her underlying sense of relevance and freshness and give it an overall impression grade based on her preference for relevance and freshness at that particular time. Once she has such impressions in mind, she would deliberately click the documents most interesting to her and skip all the others.

Inspired by this example, we proposed to model the users' click behavior in news searches as a direct consequence of examining the relevance and freshness aspects of the returned documents. Besides, for different queries, users' relative emphasis on these two aspects can vary substantially, reflecting the searching intention for the specific news event. Therefore, a good ranking function should be able to infer such a tradeoff and return the *optimally combined* ranking results for individual queries.

However, we cannot explicitly obtain users' relevance/freshness judgments and the preferences for these two aspects, since their evaluation process is not directly observable from the search engine. Fortunately, users' click patterns are recorded, from which we can assume that the clicked documents are more meaningful to them than the unclicked ones [188]. Therefore, we model relevance and freshness as two latent factors and assume that a linear combination of these two, which is also latent, generates the observed click preferences.

To better determine the temporal property of the news documents and detect the recency preference imposed for the query, we design a set of novel temporal features from click statistics and content-analysis techniques. In the following sections, we introduce the proposed model and temporal features in detail.

2.2.1   Joint Relevance and Freshness Learning

The basic assumption of our proposed model is that a user's overall impression assessment by combining relevance and freshness for the clicked URLs should be higher than the unclicked ones, and such a combination is specific to the issued query. Therefore, our method falls into the pairwise learning-to-rank framework.

Formally, we have N different queries, and for the n-th query we observed M different URL click preference pairs $(U_{ni} \succ U_{nj})$, in which U_{ni} is clicked but U_{nj} is not. We denote X_{ni}^R and X_{ni}^F as the relevance and freshness features for U_{ni} under query Q_n, and S_{ni}^R and S_{ni}^F are the corresponding relevance and freshness scores for this URL given by the relevance model $g_R(X_{ni}^R)$ and freshness model $g_F(X_{ni}^F)$, respectively. In addition, we denote α_n^Q as the relative emphasis on freshness aspect estimated by the query model $f_Q(X_n^Q)$, i.e., $\alpha_n^Q = f_Q(X_n^Q)$, based on the features X_n^Q describing query Q_n. To make relevance/freshness scores comparable across all the URLs, we require $0 \leq \alpha_n^Q \leq 1$. As a result, the user's latent assessment Y_{ni} about the URL U_{ni} for a particular query Q_n is assumed to be a linear combination of its relevance and freshness scores:

$$Y_{ni} = \alpha_n^Q \times S_{ni}^F + \left(1 - \alpha_n^Q\right) \times S_{ni}^R \tag{2.5}$$

Since we have observed the click preference $(U_{ni} \succ U_{nj})$, we can safely conclude that $Y_{ni} > Y_{nj}$.

Based on the previous discussion, we characterize the observed pairwise click preferences as the joint consequences of examining the combined relevance and freshness aspects of the URLs for the query. For a given collection of click logs, we are looking for a set of optimal models (g_R, g_F, f_Q), which can explain as many of the observed pairwise preferences as possible. As a result, we formalize this problem as an optimization task,

$$\min_{f_Q, g_R, g_F, \xi} \frac{1}{2}(\|f_Q\| + \|g_R\| + \|g_F\|) + \frac{C}{N} \sum_{n=1}^{N} \sum_{i,j} \xi_{nij} \tag{2.6}$$

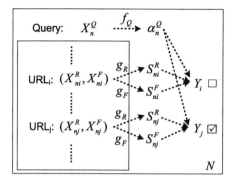

FIGURE 2.2

Intuitive illustration of the proposed Joint Relevance and Freshness Learning (JRFL) model. The user-issued query and the corresponding returned URLs are represented by their features on the left part. Dashed-arrow lines in the middle indicate the assumed user's judging process before she clicks. The check boxes on the right record the clicked URLs.

$$\text{s.t. } \forall (n, i, j), \quad URL_{ni} \succ URL_{nj}$$
$$Y_{ni} - Y_{nj} > 1 - \xi_{nij}$$
$$0 \leq f_Q(X_n^Q) \leq 1 \tag{2.7}$$
$$\xi_{nij} \geq 0,$$

where Y_{ni} and Y_{nj} are defined in Eq. 2.5, the nonnegative slack variables $\{\xi_{nij}\}$ are introduced to account for noise in the clicks, $\|\cdot\|$ is the functional norm (to be defined later) describing complexity of the models, and C is the tradeoff parameter between model complexity and training error.

Figure 2.2 depicts the intuition behind the proposed Joint Relevance and Freshness Learning (JRFL) model. From the figure, we can clearly notice the difference between our proposed JRFL and other classic pairwise learning-to-rank algorithms, e.g., RankSVM [184] and GBRank [406]. A classic pairwise learning-to-rank algorithm uses only one scoring function to account for all the observed click preferences, where different ranking criteria cannot be easily incorporated. Besides, even though the RankSVM model shares a similar object function as JRFL, they are still quite different: JRFL simultaneously learns a relevance model and a freshness model and utilizes a query-specific model to leverage these two aspects to explain the observed click patterns. Neither RankSVM nor GBRank deal with such query-specific multi-criteria ranking. Besides, in previous studies [106,83], S_{ni}^R and S_{ni}^F for each URL were already known so that they tuned α_n^Q directly for each type of query. In our problem, all those factors are latent and estimated automatically from the click logs.

In our previous description, we didn't specify the forms of the relevance model $g_R(X^R)$, freshness model $g_F(X^F)$, and query model $f_Q(X^Q)$. Although many alternatives exist, we choose linear functions for all these models to simplify the exposition and derive efficient model estimation procedures. Other types of functions can also be employed, although numerical approximation is unavoidable in general when optimizing their model parameters.

Formally, we use three linear models:

$$g_R\left(X_{ni}^R\right) = w_R^\mathsf{T} X_{ni}^R \tag{2.8}$$

$$g_F\left(X_{ni}^F\right) = w_F^\mathsf{T} X_{ni}^F \tag{2.9}$$

$$f_Q\left(X_n^Q\right) = w_Q^\mathsf{T} X_n^Q \tag{2.10}$$

where the bias factor b in linear functions is excluded by introducing the dummy feature 1.

As a result, the proposed JRFL model defined in Eq. 2.6 can be instantiated as:

$$\min_{w_R, w_F, w_Q, \xi} \frac{1}{2}(\|w_Q\|^2 + \|w_R\|^2 + \|w_F\|^2) + \frac{C}{N}\sum_{n=1}^{N}\sum_{i,j}\xi_{nij} \tag{2.11}$$

$$\text{s.t.} \quad \forall(n,i,j), \quad U_{ni} \succ U_{nj}$$
$$w_Q^\mathsf{T} X_n^Q \times w_F^\mathsf{T}\left(X_{ni}^F - X_{nj}^F\right)$$
$$+ \left(1 - w_Q^\mathsf{T} X_n^Q\right) \times w_R^\mathsf{T}\left(X_{ni}^R - X_{nj}^R\right) > 1 - \xi_{nij}$$
$$0 \le w_Q^\mathsf{T} X_n^Q \le 1$$
$$\xi_{nij} \ge 0.$$

Thanks to the associative property of linear functions, the optimization problem defined in Eq. 2.11 can be divided into two subproblems: relevance/freshness model estimation and query model estimation. Each is a convex programming problem. (Note that Eq. 2.11 itself is nonconvex.) Therefore, we can utilize the coordinate descent algorithm to iteratively solve the two convex programs, as shown in Figure 2.3.

The interaction between the relevance/freshness models and the query model is clearly stated in the optimization process: In relevance/freshness model estimation, the query-specific preference weight acts as a tuning factor, which increases or decreases the features in these two models to represent the searching intention. Once we have the relevance/freshness models, we tune the query model to preserve as many click preferences as possible based on the current relevance/freshness predictions.

Since each update step is convex, our coordinate optimization is guaranteed to decrease the object function in Eq. 2.11 monotonically and therefore converges to a local optimum.

2.2.2 Temporal Features

We use 95 basic text matching features, such as query term matched in title, matched position in document, and source authority score, from a subset of features employed

---

Algorithm: Coordinate Descent for JRFL

Input: A collection of click preferences

$$L = \left\{ \left[X_n^Q, ((X_{ni}^R, X_{ni}^F) \quad \succ \right. \right.$$
$$\left. \left. (X_{nj}^R, X_{nj}^F)), \ldots, ((X_{nk}^R, X_{nk}^F) \succ (X_{nl}^R, X_{nl}^F)) \right] \right\};$$

Input: Tradeoff parameter C,
Input: Maximum iteration step S,
Input: Relative convergency bound ϵ,
Output: Learned   model   parameters   of (w_R, w_F, w_Q),
Step 0: Randomly initialize (w_R, w_F, w_Q) and set $i = 0$,
Step 1: Update relevancy/freshness models:

$$(w_R^{(i+1)}, w_F^{(i+1)}) \leftarrow \underset{w_R, w_F, \xi}{\text{argmin}} \frac{1}{2}(\|w_R\|^2 + \|w_F\|^2) + \frac{C}{N}\sum_{n=1}^{N}\sum_{i,j} \xi_{nij}$$

with respect to the constraints listed in Eq. 2.11 by fixing the query model o $w_Q^{(i)}$,
Step 2: Update query model.

$$w_Q^{(i+1)} \leftarrow \underset{w_Q, \xi}{\text{argmin}} \frac{1}{2}\|w_Q\|^2 + \frac{C}{N}\sum_{n=1}^{N}\sum_{i,j} \xi_{nij}$$

with respect to the constraints listed in Eq. 2.11 by fixing the relevancy/freshness models to $(w_R^{(i+1)}, w_F^{(i+1)})$,
Step 3: Compute object function value defined in Eq. 2.11 $\rightarrow obj$ and increase $i = i + 1$,
Step 4: *if* the relative change in *obj* is greater than ϵ and i is smaller than S, go to **Step 1**; else return $(w_R^{(i)}, w_F^{(i)}, w_Q^{(i)})$

FIGURE 2.3

Coordinate descent for JRFL.

in Yahoo! News search engine as our URL relevance features. To capture the temporal property of the news documents and queries, we propose a set of novel time-sensitive features as our URL freshness features and query features, which are summarized in Table 2.1.

Table 2.1 Temporal features for URL freshness and query model.

Type	Feature
URL freshness	$\mathbf{age}_{pubdate}(URL|Query) = timestamp(Query) - pubdate(URL)$
	$\mathbf{age}_{story}(URL|Query) = timestamp(Query) - pubdate_{extracted}(URL)$
	$\mathbf{LM@1}(URL|Query, t) = \max\limits_{d\in Corpus(q-t)[t-1day,t]} \log p(URL|d)$
	$\mathbf{LM@5}(URL|Query, t) = \max\limits_{d\in Corpus(q-t)[t-5days,t-2days]} \log p(URL|d)$
	$\mathbf{LM@ALL}(URL|Query, t) = \max\limits_{d\in Corpus(q-t)[-\infty,t-6days]} \log p(URL|d)$
	$\mathbf{t\text{-}dist}(URL|Query) = \dfrac{\mathbf{age}_{pubdate}(URL|Query)-mean[\mathbf{age}_{pubdate}(URL|Query)]}{dev[\mathbf{age}_{pubdate}(URL|Query)]}$
Query model	$\mathbf{q\_prob}(Query|t) = \log \dfrac{Count(Query|t)+\delta_q}{\sum_q Count(Query|t)+\delta}$
	$\mathbf{u\_prob}(User|t) = \log \dfrac{Count(User|t)+\lambda_u}{\sum_q Count(User|t)+\lambda}$
	$\mathbf{q\_ratio}(Query|t) = \mathbf{q\_prob}(Query|t) - \mathbf{q\_prob}(Query|t-1)$
	$\mathbf{u\_ratio}(User|t) = \mathbf{u\_prob}(User|t) - \mathbf{u\_prob}(User|t-1)$
	$\mathbf{Ent}(Query|t) = -p(Query|t)\log p(Query|t)$
	$\mathbf{CTR}(Query|t) = mean\left[CTR(URL|Query,\ t)\right]$
	$\mathbf{pub\_mean}(Query|d) = mean_{URL\in Corpus(Q|t)}\left[\mathbf{age}_{pubdate}(URL|Query)\right]$
	$\mathbf{pub\_dev}(Query|d) = dev_{URL\in Corpus(Q|t)}\left[\mathbf{age}_{pubdate}(URL|Query)\right]$
	$\mathbf{pub\_frq}(Query|t) = \log \dfrac{Count(URL|d)+\sigma_u}{\sum_{URL} Count(URL|t)+\sigma}$

2.2.2.1 *URL Freshness Features*

Publication age $\mathbf{age}_{pubdate}(URL|Query)$: The URL's publication timestamp is used to identify the document's freshness property.

However, for a news search, the freshness of news content is more important. Therefore, we propose to identify the given news document's freshness quality from a content analysis perspective.

Story age $\mathbf{age}_{story}(URL|Query)$: We use the regular expressions defined in [106] to extract the mentioned dates in the news content, calculate their distances to the given query within the document, and select the one with the minimal distance as the extracted story timestamp to infer the corresponding story age.

Story coverage $\mathbf{LM@\{1,5,ALL\}}(URL|Query, t)$: Content coverage is an important character of freshness for a news document. Newer stories should cover more content that has not been mentioned by the previous reports. For a given query with a list of candidate news articles at a particular time, we first collect all the previous news articles associated with this query in our query log and build language models [199,400] for each of these documents. Then we separate those language models into three sets: models with documents published one day before, published two to five days before, and all the rest, and we treat the candidate URLs as queries to calculate the maximum generation probability given by all the models in these three sets accordingly.

Relative age **t-dist**(URL|Query): From a user's perspective, since the news search engine has already displayed **age**$_{pubdate}$(URL|Query), the document's relative freshness within the returned list is more meaningful for the user. To capture this signal, we shift each URL's **age**$_{pubdate}$(URL|Query) value within the returned URL list by the mean value in this list and scale the results by the corresponding standard deviation.

2.2.2.2 *Query Freshness Features*

The query features are designed to capture the latent preference between relevance and freshness.

Query/User frequency **q_prob**(Query|t) and **u_prob** (User|t): The frequency of a query within a fixed time slot is a good indicator for a breaking news query. We calculate the frequency of the query and unique users who issued this query within a time slot prior to the query time.

Frequency ratio **q_ratio**(Query|t) and **u_ratio**(User|t): The relative frequency ratio of a query within two consecutive time slots implies the change of users' interest. A higher ratio indicates an increasing user interest in this news event.

Distribution entropy **Ent**(Query|t): The distribution of a query's issuing time is a sign of breaking news; a burst of searching occurs when a particular news event happens. We utilize the entropy of query issuing time distribution to capture such burstiness. A multinomial distribution $p(Query|t)$ with fixed bin size (e.g., 2 hours per bin) is employed to approximate the query's temporal distribution within the day.

Average CTR **CTR**(Query|t): CTR is another signal representing the freshness preference of the query. When breaking news happens, people tend to click more returned URLs. We calculate the average CTR over all the associated URLs within a fixed time slot prior to the query time.

URL recency **pub_mean**(Query|d), **pub_dev**(Query|d) and **pub_frq**(Query|d): The recency of URLs associated with the query can be treated as a good profile of this query's freshness tendency. When the URLs associated with one particular query in a fixed period are mostly fresh, it indicates that the query itself is highly likely to be a breaking news query. We calculate the mean and standard deviation of the associated URLs' **age**$_{pubdate}$(URL|Query) features and the frequency of the URLs created in that specific period.

2.2.3 Experiment Results

This section validates our JRFL model empirically with large-scale click datasets and editorial annotations. We begin by describing the datasets used.

2.2.3.1 *Datasets*
2.2.3.2 *Click Datasets*

We collected real search sessions from the Yahoo! News search engine over a two-month period, from late May to late July 2011. To unbiasedly compare different ranking algorithms, we also set up a random bucket to collect exploration clicks from a small portion of traffic at the same time. In this random bucket, the top four URLs were randomly shuffled and displayed to the real users. By doing such random shuffling, we were able to collect user click feedback on each document without positional bias; such feedback can be thought of as a reliable proxy on information utility of documents [218]. As a result, we collected only the top four URLs from this random bucket.

In addition, we also asked editors to annotate the relevance and freshness in the August 9, 2011, query log immediately one day after, according to the editorial guidance given by Dong *et al.* [106].

Simple preprocessing is applied on these click datasets: (1) filtering out the sessions without clicks, since they are useless for either training or testing in our experiments; (2) discarding the URLs whose publication time is after the query's issuing time (caused by errors from news sources); and (3) discarding sessions with fewer than two URLs.

2.2.3.3 *Preference Pair Selection*

We decide to train our model on the normal click data because such clicks are easier to collect without hurting the search engine's performance. However, this kind of click is known to be heavily positional biased [8]. To reduce the bias for training, we followed Joachims *et al.*'s method to extract preferences from clicks [188]. In particular, we employed two click heuristics:

1. "*Click $\succ$ Skip Above*": For a ranked URL list $\{U_1, U_2, \ldots, U_m\}$ and a set C containing the clicked URLs, extract a preference pair $U_i \succ U_j$ for all pairs $1 \le j < i$ with $U_i \in C$ and $U_j \notin C$.
2. "*Click $\succ$ Skip Next*": For a ranked URL list $\{U_1, U_2, \ldots, U_m\}$ and a set C containing the clicked URLs, extract a preference pair $U_i \succ U_{i+1}$ for all $U_i \in C$ and $U_{i+1} \notin C$.

In addition, to filter out noisy and conflicting preferences, we defined three rules: (1) filter out the preference pairs appearing fewer than five times; (2) calculate Pearson's χ^2 value [65] on all the pairs and order them according to their χ^2 value; and (3) if both $U_i \succ U_j$ and $U_j \succ U_i$ are extracted, discard the one with a smaller χ^2 value.

After these selection steps, we were able to keep the top 150,000 preference pairs from some portion of normal clicks we collected in Section 2.2.3.2. Besides, for testing purposes, we randomly selected 500,000 query-URL pairs from original normal click set (not including the URLs used for generating the click preference pairs) and 500,000 from the random bucket clicks. To guarantee the quality of the freshness annotation, we asked the editors to finish the annotation in one day. As a result, we have only about 13,000 query-URL pairs annotated out of that day's query log. As a summary, we list the datasets for our experiments in Table 2.2.

Table 2.2   Evaluation corpus.

	#(Q,t)	**#(Q,U,t)**	**#URL Pairs**
Training preferences	75,236	230,351	150,000
Normal clicks	59,062	500,000	–
Random clicks	127,474	500,000	–
Editorial judgment	1,404	13,091	–

2.2.3.4 *Temporal Feature Implementation*

For most of our temporal features, we had to specify a time slot for the implementation; for example, the *Query/User frequency* **q_prob**(Query|t) and **u_prob**(User|t) are both calculated within a predefined time slot. In the following experiments, we set such a time slot to be 24 hours, and accordingly all the necessary statistics were collected from this time window. Once the features were generated, we linearly scaled each of them into the range $[-1, 1]$ to normalize them.

2.2.3.5 *Baselines and Evaluation Metrics*

Since the proposed JRFL model works in a pairwise learning-to-rank manner, we employed two classic pairwise learning-to-rank algorithms, RankSVM [184] and GBRank [406], as our baseline methods. Because these two algorithms do not explicitly model relevance and freshness aspects for ranking, we fed them with the concatenation of all our URL relevance/freshness and query features. In addition to compare the models trained on clicks with those trained on editorial judgments, we also used Dong *et al.*'s freshness-demotion-trained GBRank model [106] as our baseline and denoted it "FreshDem."

To quantitatively compare different ranking algorithms' retrieval performance, we employed a set of standard evaluation metrics in information retrieval. In click data, we treat all the clicked URLs as relevant and calculate the corresponding *Precision at 1* (P@1), *Precision at 2* (P@2), *Mean Average Precision at 3* (MAP@3), *Mean Average Precision at 4* (MAP@4), and *Mean Reciprocal Rank* (MRR). Definitions of these metrics can be found in standard texts (e.g., [21]). In the editorial annotation dataset, we treated the grade "Good" and above as relevant for precision-based metrics, and we used *discounted cumulative gain* (DCG) [176] as an evaluation metric.[1]

2.2.4 Analysis of JRFL

2.2.4.1 *Convergency*

We first demonstrate the convergency of the coordinate descent algorithm for the JRFL model as described in Figure 2.3, which is the necessary condition for applying the proposed model in real ranking problems. We randomly divided the training

---

[1] According to Yahoo!'s business rule, the reported metrics are normalized accordingly; therefore only the relative improvement makes sense.

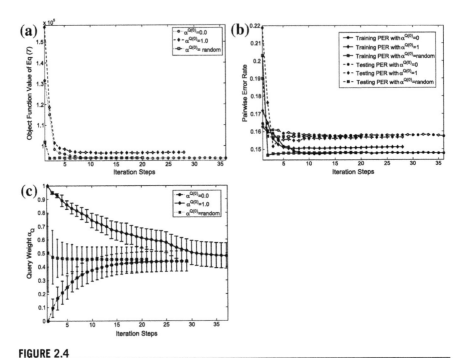

FIGURE 2.4

Scatter plot of CTR versus JRFL's prediction. (a) Object function value update. (b) Pairwise error rate (PER) update. (c) Query weight α^Q update.

preference pairs into two sets, one with 90,000 pairs for training and the rest with 60,000 for testing. We fixed the tradeoff parameter C in JRFL to be 5.0 (we also tried other settings for this parameter; smaller C would render us fewer iterations to converge, but the tendency of convergency is the same), relative convergency bound ϵ to be 10^{-5}, and maximum iteration step S to be 50 in the coordinate descent algorithm. To study if the algorithm's convergence is sensitive to the initial state, we tried three starting points: (1) fixing the initial query weights $\alpha^{Q(0)}$ to 1.0 (freshness only); (2) fixing $\alpha^{Q(0)}$ to 0.0 (relevance only); and (3) setting it uniformly between 0 and 1 by directly setting all the query weights accordingly at step 0. We visualize the training process by illustrating the updating trace of object function defined in Eq. 2.11, pairwise error rate on both training and testing set, and the mean/standard deviation of the updated query weights during the iterative optimization in Figure 2.4.

As demonstrated in Figure 2.4, the proposed model converges during the coordinate descent optimization process, and such convergency does not depend on the initial state. From Figure 2.4(c), we can observe that the optimal query weight setting for this training set is usually around 0.4546 ± 0.0914. Hence, the random initialization converges fastest compared with two other settings, since the initial state given by random is closest to this optimal setting.

In addition, it should be emphasized that, although the average of the converged value of α^Q is less than 0.5, it does *not* necessarily indicate that freshness is less

Table 2.3   Feature weights learned by JRFL.

Feature	Type	Top Three Features
URL freshness	Neg	**age**$_{\text{pubdate}}$(URL|Query) **LM@5**(URL|Query, t) **t-dist**(URL|Query)
	Pos	**q_ratio**(Query|t) **pub_frq**(Query|t) **q_prob**(Query|t)
Query model	Neg	**Ent**(Query|t) **pub_dev**(Query|d) **pub_mean**(Query|d)

important than relevance in general for the news search task, because the scales of the outputs of our freshness and relevance models may not be comparable. Therefore, only the order among the queries given by such learned query weights represents their relative emphasis on relevance and freshness aspects.

Another phenomena we observe in Figure 2.4(a) and (b) is that even though the object function decreased quickly after the first several iterations, the pairwise error rate needed more iterations to reach its optimal value. Furthermore, during these updates, there were some inconsistent updates between the object function value and the pairwise error rate; whereas the object function value always decreased with more iterations, the pairwise error rate did not show the same monotonic behavior. This inconsistency is expected because our object function in Eq. 2.11 is a relaxed one; we do *not* directly minimize the pairwise error rate, which is computationally intractable, but we are trying to reduce the *prediction gap* between the misordered pairs.

Table 2.3 gives the top three positive and negative features from the newly proposed URL freshness features and query features, ordered by the learned weights. The weights in the linear model reflect the features' relative contribution to the final ranking decision. Because we have only six URL freshness features, and the learned weights for them are all negative, we only list the top three negative ones in this table.

The weights learned by the corresponding models are reasonable and consistent with our design: For URL freshness features, the smaller the values of *Publication age* **age**$_{\text{pubdate}}$(URL\|Query), *Story coverage* **LM@5**(URL\|Query, t), and *Relative age* **t-dist**(URL\|Query) are, the more recent the news article is; and for the query features, the larger the values of *query frequency* **q_prob**(Query\|t) and *URL recency* **pub_frq**(Query\|d), and the smaller the values of *Distribution entropy* **Ent**(Query\|t), *URL recency* **pub_mean**(Query\|d), and **pub_dev**(Query\|d) are, the more users and news reports start to focus on this event, and therefore the freshness aspect becomes more important.

2.2.4.2 *Relevance and Freshness Learning*

Since our JRFL model does not rely on explicit relevance/freshness annotations, it is important to evaluate how well our relevance and freshness models can estimate each

Table 2.4   Performance of individual relevance and freshness estimations.

	P@1	MAP@3	DCG@5
Relevance GBRank	0.9655	0.3422	14.6026
JRFL relevance	0.8273	0.2291	14.7962
Freshness GBRank	0.9823	0.4998	18.8597
JRFL freshness	0.9365	0.3106	19.8228

aspect separately. We separately used the relevance and freshness annotations on the August 9, 2011, query log as the test bed and utilized two GBRank models trained on Dong *et al.*'s relevance and freshness annotation dataset accordingly (44,641 query-URL pairs) [106]. Because [106]'s dataset does not contain the corresponding click information, those two GBrank models were trained without new query features. Our JRFL was trained on all the extracted click preference pairs.

We observe mixed results in Table 2.4: The relevance and freshness modules inside JRFL have worse ranking performance than the purely relevance/freshness trained GBRank models at the top positions (lower P@1 and MAP@3), but they have similar cumulative performance, i.e., DCG@5 for both aspects. The reason for this result is that the JRFL model has to account for the tradeoff between relevance and freshness imposed by the queries during training. The most relevant or recent documents might not be treated as good training examples if their other aspects were not desirable. However, the purely relevance/freshness trained GBRank models do not have such constraints and can derive patterns to put the most relevant/recent documents at the top positions separately. As a result, those two GBRank models' performance can be interpreted as *upper bounds* for each individual ranking criterion (freshness/relevance) in this dataset. When we reach the lower positions, those two types of ranking algorithms give users quite similar utilities, i.e., under the DCG@5 metric. In addition, we want to emphasize that such result is already very encouraging, since the JRFL model successfully infers the relevance and freshness *solely from the clicks*, which confirms the soundness of our assumption in this work that users' click behavior is the joint consequence of examining the relevance and freshness of a news article for the given query. By properly modeling such relationships, we can estimate the relevance and freshness from the clickthroughs to a certain extent.

2.2.4.3 *Query Weight Analysis*

There is no direct way for us to evaluate the correctness of the inferred query weights, since such information is not observable in the search log. Therefore, in this experiment, we investigate it in an indirect way. As we discussed in the previous discussion, the order among the queries given by such weight reflects the query's relative emphasis over the freshness aspect. Therefore, we ranked the queries in our training set according to the learned weights and list the top 10 (freshness-driven) and bottom 10 (relevance-driven) queries in Table 2.5.

Table 2.5   Query intention analysis by the inferred query weight.

Freshness Driven	Relevance Driven
7-Jun-2011, china	5-Jul-2011, casey anthony trial summary
6-Jul-2011, casey anthony trial	9-Jul-2011, nascar qualifying results
24-Jun-2011, nba draft 2011	8-Jul-2011, burbank 100 years parade
28-Jun-2011, libya	10-Jul-2011, gas prices summer 2011
9-Jun-2011, iran	10-Jul-2011, bafta film awards 2011
6-Jun-2011, pakistan	2-Jul-2011, green lantern cast
13-Jun-2011, lebron james	9-Jul-2011, 2011 usga open leaderboard
29-Jun-2011, greece	3-Jul-2011, lake mead water level july 2011
27-May-2011, joplin missing	5-Jul-2011, caylee anthony autopsy report
6-Jun-2011, sarah palin	4-Jul-2011, aurora colorado fireworks 2011

At first glance, it may be surprising to note that most of the top-ranked *freshness-driven* queries are the names of some countries and celebrities, e.g., "iran," "libya," and "lebron james." But that is also quite reasonable: For those kind of queries, these results are actually ambiguous, since there would be many candidate news reports related to different aspects of these queries. But when users issue such types of "ambiguous" queries in news search engines, they should be most interested in the recent updates about these countries and celebrities. We went back to check the most-clicked URLs of these queries, and the clicks confirmed our assumption: The most-clicked URLs for query "libya" were about the recent progress of the Libyan war; news articles covering the latest diplomatic affairs between the United States and Iran got the most clicks for the query "iran."

Another interesting finding from the learned query weights is that the length of queries is much longer than the freshness-driven queries. To validate this observation, we selected the top 500 *relevance-driven* and the top 500 *freshness-driven* queries to calculate the corresponding query length distributions comparing to the length distribution of all the queries; Table 2.6 shows the results . These results are consistent with our intuition: When users are seeking specific information, they tend to put more constraints (i.e., longer queries) to describe their information need; in contrast, when users are making a recency search, they usually do not have a predetermined mindset about the events, so they often issue broad queries (i.e., shorter queries) about entities of their interest to see what is happening recently to those entities. Apparently, our query weight model is consistent with this intuition and is able to distinguish these two typical searching scenarios. In addition, this also reminds us that query length is a good feature to indicate the preference for the freshness aspect.

Table 2.6   Query length distribution under different query categories.

Freshness Driven	Relevance Driven	All
1.446 ± 0.804	3.396 ± 1.309	2.563 ± 1.203

2.2.5 Ranking Performance

To validate the effectiveness of the proposed JRFL model in real news search tasks, we quantitatively compare it with all our baseline methods on random bucket clicks, normal clicks, and editorial judgments. All the click-based learning algorithms are trained on all 150,000 click preferences. Since all these models have several parameters to be tuned (e.g., the tradeoff parameter C in both RankSVM and JRFL), we report their best performance on the corresponding testing set according to the MAP@4 metric in the following results and perform a t-test to validate the significance of improvement (against the second best performance).

First, we performed the comparison on the random bucket clicks because such clicks are more trustable than normal clicks due to the removal of positional biases.

From the results in Table 2.7, we find that the proposed JRFL model achieves encouraging improvement over the second-best GBRank model, especially on MAP@4, where the relative improvement is over 5.88%. This improvement confirms that properly integrating relevance and freshness can indeed improve the user's search satisfaction.

Now we perform the same comparison on the normal click set, and we can observe similar improvement of JRFL over other ranking methods, as shown in Table 2.8. Besides, from the results on both of these two click datasets, we can clearly observe that the click-preference-trained models generally outperform the freshness-demotion-trained GBRank model: JRFL's improvement on P@1 against the freshness-demotion-trained GBRank model is 16.2% and 58.6% on the random bucket click set and normal click set, respectively.

Table 2.7   Comparison of random bucket clicks.

Model	FreshDem	RankSVM	GBRank	JRFL
P@1	0.3413	0.3706	0.3882	**0.3969***
P@2	0.3140	0.3372	0.3477	**0.3614***
MAP@3	0.5301	0.5601	0.5751	**0.6012***
MAP@4	0.5859	0.6090	0.6218	**0.6584***
MRR	0.5899	0.6135	0.6261	**0.6335***

Table 2.8   Comparison of normal clicks.

Model	FreshDem	RankSVM	GBRank	JRFL
P@1	0.3886	0.5981	0.5896	**0.6164***
P@2	0.2924	0.4166	0.4002	**0.4404***
MAP@3	0.4991	0.7208	0.6849	**0.7502***
MAP@4	0.5245	0.7383	0.7024	**0.7631***
MRR	0.5781	0.7553	0.7355	**0.7702***

On the editorial annotation dataset, to compare different models' performance, we mapped the separately annotated relevance and freshness grades into one single grade by the freshness demotion strategy in Dong *et al.*'s work [106].

From this result, we find that the freshness-demotion-trained GBRank model did not achieve the best performance on such "grade-demoted" testing sets either. This might be caused by the time gap between different annotations: [106]'s annotations were generated more than one year previously (February to May 2009). The out-of-date annotation might contain inconsistent relations between queries and documents, as in the new annotations. Besides, we also notice that the margin of improvement from JRFL becomes smaller compared to the click-based evaluations. In the following, we perform some case studies to find out the reasons for the diminished improvement (see Table 2.9).

In Table 2.10, we illustrate one case of inferior ranking result for the query "afghanistan" from JRFL. We list the top four ranked results from JRFL, together with the editorial relevance and freshness grades. (We have had to truncate some of the URLs because they are too long to be displayed.)

The freshness weight inferred by JRFL for this query is 0.7694, which is biased to freshness aspect. However, all those URLs' freshness grades are "Excellent" so that, in the demoted final grades, the "ground-truth" ranking depends only on the relevance aspect. The predicted relevance score differences get diminished by this biased

Table 2.9 Comparison of editorial annotations.

Model	FreshDem	RankSVM	GBRank	JRFL
P@1	0.9184	0.9626	**0.9870**	0.9508
P@2	0.9043	0.9649	**0.9729**	0.9117
MAP@3	0.3055	0.3628	0.3731	**0.4137**
MAP@4	0.4049	0.4701	**0.4796**	0.4742
MRR	0.9433	0.9783	**0.9920**	0.9745
DCG@1	6.8975	7.9245	**8.1712***	7.2203
DCG@5	15.7175	17.2279	17.7468	**18.9397***

Table 2.10 Case study: Degenerated ranking results by JRFL for query "afghanistan."

URL	Relevance	Freshness
http://www.cbsnews.com/video/watch/?id=7376057nXXX	Good	Excellent
http://news.yahoo.com/afghanistan-helicopter-crash-why-army-used-chinook-half-180000528.html	Excellent	Excellent
http://news.yahoo.com/whatever-happened-civilian-surge-afghanistan-035607164.html	Excellent	Excellent
http://www.msnbc.msn.com/id/44055633/ns/world_news-south_and_central_asia/XXX	Perfect	Excellent

freshness weight in JRFL; the JRFL predicted relevance score difference between the best document in "ground-truth" (last row in the table) versus JRFL ordering (first row in the table) is 0.44, whereas the corresponding freshness score difference is -0.31. As a result, JRFL gives an arguably "bad" ranking result for this query.

In addition, we want to revisit the relationship between the predicted orders given by JRFL and CTR, as we did in Figure 2.1. This time we draw the scatter plot between the JRFL predicted ranking scores and CTRs on the same set of URLs as shown in Figure 2.1.

The monotonic relationship between the predicted ranking and CTRs is much more evident than the one given by the demoted grades: URLs with lower CTRs concentrate more densely in the area with lower prediction scores, and the average Pearson correlation between the predicted ranking score and CTR across all the queries is 0.7163, with standard deviation 0.1673, compared to the average of 0.5764 and standard deviation of 0.6401 in the demoted grades (see Figure 2.5).

In this work, we proposed a joint learning framework, Joint Relevance Freshness Learning, for modeling the topical relevance and freshness, and the query-specific relative preference between these two aspects based on the clickthroughs for the news search task. Experiments on large-scale query logs and editorial annotations validate the effectiveness of the proposed learning method. We only instantiated the proposed joint learning framework by linear models, but many alternatives exist. It would be meaningful to employ other types of nonlinear functions to enhance JRFL.

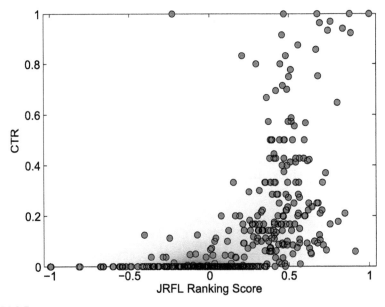

FIGURE 2.5

Scatter plot of CTR versus JRFL's prediction.

For example, using logistic functions can naturally avoid the range constraints over query weights in optimization. Besides, in our current setting, the preference between relevance and freshness is assumed to be only query-dependent. It would be interesting to extend this to user-dependent, i.e., personalized, search. By defining a proper set of user-related features, or profiles, the proposed JRFL can be easily applied in such user-centric retrieval environments. What is more, the proposed model can also be flexibly extended to other retrieval scenarios, where usefulness judgment is beyond pure topical relevance, such as opinions in blog searches and distance in location searches.

2.3 **News Clustering**

Clustering of search results provides a unified view of the search results by grouping together similar documents. This allows the user to examine all the related categories of the search results without having to go through hundreds of items. Clustering becomes more important in the context of a domain such as news because there could be thousands of related articles for a given query. Most of these news articles are related, however, and if we group the articles in terms of related stories, then the number quickly reduces to a handful. This makes it easier for the user to browse the search results in terms of news stories rather than individual news articles. Furthermore, news sites re-publish articles from different sources to provide comprehensive coverage of a particular topic. This further exacerbates the problem by increasing the redundancy in the search results. Instead of leaving the search result organization to the user, a clustered representation of search results provides an overview to explore a topic.

The news search also has another component of recency, which introduces additional complexities. Although two articles are very related in terms of document content, if they are far apart in the time axis, they might correspond to a repetitive event, such as *California earthquake*. Even though such events occur multiple times, they correspond to different clusters because they are totally independent events and the user may be interested in looking at them individually.

Most of the work on search result clustering focused more on salient feature extraction and utilizing this information to cluster the search results [153,56]. However, the salient features do not provide the complete picture about the document. Sometimes the most important information about the news article is buried deep in the document body. Later we provide experimental evidence that shows that the body of the document provides a great boost in the performance of the clustering system. Other approaches [153,56] utilize standard clustering algorithms such as a hierarchical agglomerative clustering (HAC) algorithm and partitional algorithms such as K-means. In [396], the clustering problem is modeled as phrase extraction from documents and then uses a suffix tree-based clustering algorithm to group documents that contain common phrases. However, we show that the query information is vital in clustering the search results, and we also show how to utilize this information in the clustering algorithm.

Other research related to clustering the search results focuses on utilizing various matrix factorization techniques [272,271] such as singular value decomposition, non-negative matrix factorization [211], local nonnegative matrix factorization [220], and concept decomposition [97]. These clustering algorithms focus on extracting quality descriptions for the clusters by finding the labels with matrix factorization on the word features from snippets of search results. Although the descriptions may be important in Web search results clustering, they do not play a vital role in news search results, since the most representative document can be used to show the summary of the cluster. Another algorithm called DisCover [207] clusters search results by maximizing the coverage and distinctiveness of the clusters.

Another line of work is related to using named entities to browse the clusters of search results [349]. However, this work mainly focuses on extracting the named entities from search results, organizing them into clusters using the named entities. Other related work [135] identifies discriminative, ambiguous, and common terms by constructing a relational graph of terms and using them to cluster Web search results.

It is clear that the named entities that occur in the body of the documents are valuable for producing quality clusters of search results. However, it is expensive to process the entire documents to cluster the search results in real time as it impacts the user experience. In this work we propose a scalable clustering technique that can provide a fast execution time without sacrificing accuracy by utilizing the body features in terms of offline clusters that provide a prior of the document relatedness of search results. The offline clusters are obtained by a process that is run offline. We also handle incremental clustering for documents that arrive continuously.

In fact, the offline clusters that are obtained by clustering the entire corpus provide a useful representation, and the search results can be organized into clusters by using this information alone. Some of the existing work exactly follows these methodologies. However, such organization would have a fixed granularity of clustering, which may not be desirable for all queries. Some queries can be broad and require a higher level of clustering hierarchy; other queries can be very specific and require a fine level of clustering hierarchy. If the offline clusters alone are used to organize the search results, the granularity of the clustering cannot be adjusted according to query. However, the solution we provide overcomes this problem by applying a clustering algorithm on the search results in real time by utilizing the offline clusters as features.

The contributions of our work are twofold:

- We provide a unified framework for scalable online clustering and detail the architecture of the system that describes each of the three components: offline clustering, incremental clustering, and real-time clustering.
- We propose novel techniques to cluster search results in real time by incorporating the query information in the clustering algorithm itself.

The section that follows presents the overall architecture of our system. Sections 2.3.2, 2.3.3, and 2.3.4 discuss various clustering algorithms corresponding to offline, incremental, and real-time clustering that we used in this work. Section 2.3.5 presents the experimental results for our algorithms.

2.3.1 **Architecture of the System**

To cluster the search results in real time, we need just the top-ranked search results. However, the user would like to browse all the related articles in relation to a particular news story, which might not be covered in the top-ranked news results. To address this issue, we rely on offline clustering that clusters the entire news corpus. We utilize the offline clusters as an additional source of information in real-time clustering, which helps its performance as well. However, this offline batch processing of documents, especially news articles, does not work efficiently, because news articles arrive continuously every second. To address this issue, we also incorporate incremental clustering solutions to address the streaming data clustering problem. Figure 2.6 shows the architecture of our system that describes individual components that address these needs.

The offline batch clustering algorithm will be run on a regular basis, multiple times a day, on the news corpus, which we limit to a full month of news articles. This clustering algorithm assigns a cluster ID to every document that is present to the algorithm. The incremental clustering algorithm works in a streaming fashion, assigning cluster IDs to documents that arrive in the interim time before the next offline batch clustering is run. This is a continuous process that assigns cluster IDs to documents based on the existing batch clustering algorithm output. Thus each document in the corpus at any given time will have at least a cluster ID from either the offline clustering algorithm or the incremental clustering algorithm. The real-time clustering algorithm, which is run when a query is issued, is executed at runtime utilizing these cluster IDs for each of the documents in the corpus. This real-time clustering groups the search results into clusters and provides the final presentation of clustered search results.

In following sections describe the offline clustering, incremental clustering, and real-time clustering components in detail.

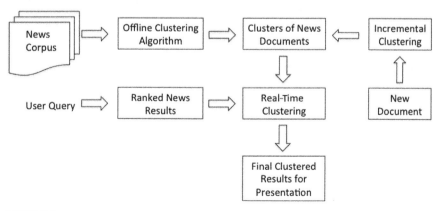

FIGURE 2.6

The architecture of the news search result clustering.

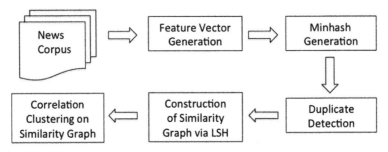

FIGURE 2.7

Overview of the offline clustering system.

2.3.2 Offline Clustering

Our offline clustering system draws from the work of [338]. In this method, the similarity between all pairs of articles is first computed via *locality sensitive hashing* (LSH). While we also use the LSH method to determine the pairwise similarities, we then construct a similarity graph on the corpus, wherein a pair of articles has an edge if the similarity between the two meets a threshold. A correlation clustering algorithm is then run on top of the similarity graph to produce the final clustering. Note that it is essential to define a good similarity measure while constructing the graph. False edges cause different story clusters to be merged, whereas missing edges cause stories to be split. Figure 2.7 shows the main components of our clustering system. Now let's look in detail the design of each component.

2.3.2.1 *Feature Vector Generation*

The good performance of our system is heavily dependent on the underlying similarity function that is used to construct the similarity graph. As mentioned earlier, a poorly designed similarity function can either merge different stories or split a story into many clusters. Note that we use the term *story* to represent the set of news articles that are about the same news story and hence should belong to the same cluster. News articles have several important information sources associated with them that can be used to define a custom similarity function. The different types of features that were extracted are:

- *Term frequency-inverse document frequency* (TF-IDF). A unigram-based feature vector was constructed using the TF-IDF values for the words in a news article after stop-word removal and stemming.
- *Wikipedia topics.* Wikipedia topics was extracted from the news article using the technique described in [389]. The set of Wikipedia topics was then assigned an "aboutness score," which represents how important that topic is to the article. The ranked list was then used as features, with the feature values corresponding to the aboutness scores.

- *Part-of-speech tagging.* The news article was also tagged with a part-of-speech tagger, and unigrams were extracted from nouns, adjectives, and verbs and used as features. Term frequencies were used as feature values.

In addition to these feature vectors, we also made use of presentation cues associated with the article to emphasize certain phrases or unigrams, such as the fact that a phrase appears in the title or abstract or is italicized. Thus, the different features mentioned previously were assigned a score based on their presentation in the news article. The features from the three different channels were then combined through a simple aggregation of weights assigned to unigrams from each channel. The feature vector was then unit normalized before being used to compute the cosine similarity. Another important feature that was used is that of time. News articles typically have a timestamp associated with them. Given two articles published on days t_1 and t_2, the cosine similarity on the custom feature space was weighted by $\exp(-|t_1 - t_2|/7)$. The intuition behind this weighting function is that the closer the date of publication of the two articles, the more likely they are to be similar. Since we believe that a story cluster typically should not contain any articles that are apart by more than a week, we decrease the similarity between such pairs even more.

Although it is trivial to compute the feature spaces and compare all pairs of articles within a small set, such pairwise comparison becomes computationally expensive for larger corpora. A corpus with 100,000 articles requires 10,000,000,000 such comparisons. However, once an article has been mapped into its feature space, the chances of a pair of completely unrelated articles sharing any useful features is quite low. It is then unnecessary to explicitly compute the pairwise similarity between such pairs. We use the LSH to eliminate unnecessary similarity computations. An important component of the LSH method is the generation of Minhash signatures for each article.

2.3.2.2 *Minhash Signature Generation*

The min-wise independent permutations locality-sensitive hashing scheme (Minhash) signatures are a succinct representation of each article, computed such that the probability that two articles have the same Minhash signature is equal to the Jaccard similarity between the two [171]. To compute the Minhash signature for each article, we first represent it as a feature vector in the custom feature space described in Section 2.3.2.1. We then construct a length-100 Minhash signature using the technique detailed in [338]. However, the randomized nature of the Minhash generation method requires further checks to increase the chances of uncovering all pairs of related articles and removing articles that were brought together by chance. Thus, we resort to LSH to reduce chance pairings. Prior to performing LSH, the Minhash signatures can also be quickly used to detect exact duplicates.

2.3.2.3 *Duplicate Detection*

Given each article and its 100-length Minhash signature, we use these signatures to identify articles that are duplicates of each other. If an article is a duplicate of another, it is unnecessary to include both in the clustering process. One article per group of duplicates is sufficient to determine the cluster memberships of the rest. Given that a typical news corpus has a number of duplicates due to different publishers reprinting the same story from a news agency such as the Associated Press, identifying such groups and using only the unique documents for clustering provide significant computational savings. If two articles have the same Minhash value in each of the 100 slots, they are highly likely to be duplicates and are marked as such. Thus, the articles are grouped by their Minhash signatures and a representative is chosen for each group to participate in the clustering process. Once the representative article has been assigned to a cluster, we then propagate that cluster membership to all of its duplicates as a post-processing step after clustering.

2.3.2.4 *Locality-Sensitive Hashing*

Although the Minhash technique allows us to represent each article by a length-100 signature and enables duplicate detection, we still need a $O(N^2)$ comparison to determine the similarity between all pairs of articles. However, as mentioned earlier, documents that are unrelated are likely to have a very low similarity, the value of which need not be explicitly computed. Locality-sensitive hashing can be used to quickly eliminate pairs of articles that share very few features from the pairwise similarity computation. We use the method detailed in [338] for LSH. For each article we construct a shorter LSH signature by concatenating a smaller set (2) of Minhash signatures. This process is repeated 200 times. Thus, documents that contain at least a few words in common are likely to agree in at least one of the LSH signatures. Only those pairs of articles with at least one common LSH signature need to have their similarity computed. The particular settings of our LSH method, 200 LSH signatures of length 2, were obtained by offline experimentation on a smaller dataset. The current parameter settings enabled us to uncover ~96% of all pairs of similar documents as a full-blown pairwise comparison. Pairwise similarity is computed on all the documents sharing an LSH signature. Note that cosine similarity is computed on the unit-normalized vectors represented in the custom feature space and not on the Minhash signatures. The cosine similarity thus computed is further weighted with the time information, as explained in Section 2.3.2.1. Only those pairs of articles whose similarity exceeds a user-defined threshold are recorded. A similarity graph is then constructed using the output of the LSH process. Each article is represented as a node in the graph, and an edge exists between two nodes if its similarity exceeds the threshold. The edges are also weighted by the cosine similarity measure.

2.3.2.5 *Correlation Clustering*

The similarity graph is then fed into a correlation clustering algorithm based on the work to partition the graph into clusters. Correlation clustering is also a randomized algorithm that attempts to minimize a cost function based on the number of dissimilar pairs in the same cluster and the number of similar pairs in different clusters. We modified the original algorithm to allow the weight on the edges that are cut or formed, as clustering proceeds, to participate in the cost function. The algorithm is sensitive to the initialization data point. So we start multiple correlation clustering algorithms multiple times with different random seeds and identify the one with the lowest cost as the final clustering solution. An important characteristic of the correlation clustering approach is that it does not require the specification of the number of clusters. This feature is important because it is not easy to guess the number of clusters in an evolving corpus, in which a major news event can trigger multiple stories over a few days.

2.3.2.6 *Evaluation*

To evaluate the performance of the offline clustering system in terms of the quality of the clusters produced, editorial tests were conducted. We first constructed a corpus of news articles collected over a week. The size of this corpus is ~700,000. Pairwise similarities were then computed between all pairs of articles in the corpus. Roughly ~5,000 article pairs were sampled by stratified random sampling, with the stratification done on the similarity measure. Pairs of articles were then presented to the editors and were labeled as follows:

- *Must-link.* Includes pairs of articles that are duplicates, pairs in which one article summarizes or paraphrases the content in the other, and pairs covering the same news event but with different text.
- *Maybe-linked.* When the two articles are about the same set of entities but in two different news stories, the pair is labeled maybe-linked.
- *Cannot-link.* When the two articles in the pair are about unrelated news stories, it is marked as unrelated.

The clustering system was then run on the same corpus, and we compute the fraction of times pairs of articles appear in the same cluster for each label. Note that this number should be high for must-links and low for cannot-links. The maybe-linked label is the gray area where it is not entirely wrong to show the two articles in the same cluster, but for better user experience one would want to keep this number low as well. The results of the clustering system are shown in Table 2.11. As we can see, the offline clustering system performs well.

2.3.3 Incremental Clustering

The offline clustering phase produces a set of clusters of similar/relevant documents. These clusters are then taken as groundtruth for constructing a classifier for incremental clustering. The incremental clustering refers to the task of assigning a new document that has just arrived at the system to a cluster it is *most likely* to be associated with.

Table 2.11   Performance of offline clustering system.

Label	Editor Pairs	# in Same Clus.	% in Same Clus.
Must-link	1,958	1,504	77.0%
Maybe-linked	1,327	293	22.0%
Cannot-link	1,436	40	2.8%

Since offline clustering is usually scheduled to run at the interval of a couple of hours, it is likely the case that news that has just broken after the offline clustering phase does not belong to any of the existing clusters. Here we describe three simple classifiers with strategies to reduce the potential impact of this scenario:

- *Static.* A standard classifier that must be retrained on the latest set of documents at a shorter time interval.
- *Semiadaptive.* A classifier that is capable of creating a new class for news articles that are not "close enough" to any of the existing clusters. The closeness here is a value that requires careful tuning.
- *Fully adaptive.* A classifier that is not only capable of creating new classes but also updating itself to cope with the evolution of the news in the existing clusters. That said, the classifier is also able to remove classes corresponding to "submerging" stories. Compared to the semiadaptive classifier, this classifier is more flexible but also more likely to suffer from suboptimality because it is sensitive to the order of the news articles that arrived at the system.[2]

The three types of classifiers we've described roughly cover the whole spectrum of incremental clustering. The choice of a specific classifier depends on the computational and time constraints we are confined to; as long as offline clustering can be carried out more frequently, the static classifier is perhaps the best choice, since it is simple to implement, is easy to deploy, and requires no maintenance effort. Otherwise, semi- or fullyadaptive classifiers, which are harder to maintain, can be used instead.

2.3.4 Real-Time Clustering

It is vital to adjust the granularity of clustering at the query time. For example, the query "earthquake" in a news search engine returns clusters of news stories where each cluster represents a news story discussing an earthquake that occurred in a particular location. Thus, all the results related to a Chile earthquake may be grouped into a single cluster. However, a related query such as "chile earthquake" might return detailed news stories that are all related to a particular Chile earthquake. In this case, the news stories may be discussing the damages caused by the earthquake, donation-related information, and the incredible force of the earthquake, all of which depict various aspects of "Chile earthquake."

Thus adjusting the granularity in real-time clustering is very important, and we propose three novel techniques to handle this task, as described in the following sections. Each of the methodologies shows how to modify the similarity measure in a standard clustering algorithm that can be used to cluster the top documents retrieved by a news search engine. In our experiments we used hierarchical agglomerative clustering (HAC) to incorporate these similarity measures and compared the proposed similarity measures with the standard cosine similarity.

---

[2] This cause of suboptimality is also commonly seen in online learning.

2.3.4.1 *Meta Clustering and Textual Matching*

This approach relies on the output of the offline clustering output and textual matching features among the query and the documents. The similarity measure in this clustering can be formulated as:

$$\text{sim}(q, d_1, d_2) = \sum_{i=1}^{K} w_i c_i + \frac{\text{bm25}(q, d_1 \cap d_2)}{\text{bm25}(q, d_1) + \text{bm25}(q, d_2)}$$

where

- K is the number of offline clustering algorithms
- w_i is the weight for the clustering algorithm i
- $c_i = 1$ if the clustering algorithm i puts d_1 and d_2 in the same cluster
- $c_i = 0$ if the clustering algorithm i puts d_1 and d_2 in different clusters
- $d1 \cap d2$ is the overlap of documents d_1 and d_2

The first term in this equation is the term corresponding to the offline clustering weights. This is similar to ensemble cluster learning or meta clustering that is a simple combination of various clustering solutions from the offline clustering assignments. The second term in the equation relies on the textual matching features among the query and the documents. We use BM25 [292] as a proxy for textual matching between the query and the document. Given a query q and a document d, a BM25 score can be computed as:

$$BM25F(d) = \sum_{t \in q \cup d} \frac{\bar{x}_{d,t}}{K_1 + \bar{x}_{d,t}} w_t^{(1)}$$

$$\bar{x}_{d,t} = \frac{x_{d,t}}{1 + B(\frac{|d|}{|avgdl|} - 1)}$$

where $w_t^{(1)}$ is the usual relevance weight of the term t in the document, which can often be the inverse document frequency, $x_{d,t}$ is the frequency of the term t in the document d, and $\bar{x}_{d,t}$ is the weighted term frequency that can be further broken into fields that can, in turn, have individual weights. The term frequency is normalized with the document length with $avdl$, which is average document length in the corpus, so that long and short documents are treated in the same manner. K_1 and B are parameters in this score, for which we used standard weights in our experimental setting.

2.3.4.2 *Contextual Query-Based Term Weighting*

In this *QrySim* methodology, we modify the weights of the term vectors to account for the context around the query in the document. We want to weigh the terms that appear closer to the query higher than the terms that appear farther from the query.

Our postulation is that terms that occur closer to the query terms are more important in real-time query-dependent clustering than those that occur far from the query terms. This can be validated from considering a piece of anecdotal evidence. Consider a query "earthquake" where the user might be interested in research about recent earthquakes that happened, so the important terms for clustering in this case would be locations such as "Haiti," "Chile," "Japan," etc., all of which occur close to the term "earthquake." However, if the query is "Chile Earthquake," the important terms for clustering might be different, such as "Rescue," "death toll," "donations," etc. Finding the representative terms for each query might be difficult, but a good approximation for finding them is to look for the context around the query.

We first construct the query position vector for each document, which lists the positions where the entire query occurs together in the document. We experimented with various n-grams of the query (unigrams and bigrams) as a proxy for the entire query to increase the coverage, but we found that using the entire query to build the position vector works well in practice. With this position vector, we parse each document and assign the weight for each term as the distance of the term from the closest query occurrence, i.e.,

$$F'_t = F_t * \frac{1}{\sqrt{d_{min}}}$$

where F_t is the original frequency/term weight of the term t and d_{min} is the closest distance of the term t to the query occurrence in the document.

With these new weights to each of the terms, we construct a new term vector for each document and use them in computing the similarity measure for clustering, which weights higher the terms that appear closer to the query terms.

2.3.4.3 *Offline Clusters as Features*

Although the body provides vital information to the clustering algorithm, the feature space increases dramatically if all the body features are used in the real-time clustering algorithm. Since the real-time clustering algorithm needs to be executed at runtime after the query is issued, this poses latency issues, since the clustering algorithm needs to compute a similarity measure between the documents that operate on this huge feature vector. Thus, it is expensive to use all the body features in the real-time clustering algorithm. To address this problem, we propose to utilize the offline cluster IDs as additional features to the online clustering algorithm. In computing the similarity measure for the real-time clustering, these offline cluster IDs can be used to determine the closeness of two documents based on whether they have similar offline cluster IDs. For this purpose, a document can have multiple IDs from either different algorithms or with the same algorithm, with different granular settings such as coarse and fine. We utilize the standard HAC for the real-time clustering algorithm with the standard cosine similarity and the regular term features and use the Jaccard similarity to compute the similarity in the offline cluster IDs.

Thus the final similarity measure between two documents in this setting is as follows:

$$Sim = \alpha * CosineSim + (1 - \alpha) * Jaccard$$

where $CosineSim$ is the cosine similarity computed on the bag of words, $Jaccard$ is the Jaccard similarity measure between the vector of offline cluster IDs for two documents, and α is the tradeoff parameter between the two similarity measures, which we set to 0.5 in our experiments. The Jaccard similarity between two documents can be computed as

$$\text{Jaccard}(C_1, C_2) = \frac{C_1 \cap C_2}{C_1 \cup C2}$$

where C_1 and C_2 are vectors of offline cluster IDs of two documents that correspond to output from various clustering algorithms or the same clustering algorithm with various granular settings.

2.3.4.4 *Performance Analysis*

In this section, we provide a short analysis to estimate the number of computational operations required by using the entire body features, compared with using just the offline clusters as an approximation. We performed this analysis on an editorially evaluated dataset containing 300 queries and approximately 25,000 news documents. The clustering features contain words from three sections of the news documents, including title, abstract, and body. The number of unique body features is 20 times more than the features contained in both title and abstract. Therefore we observe a far greater number of unique features in the body, thus increasing the total number of operations in computing the similarity between documents if the body features are included in the computation. Hence we gain $20x$ savings in terms of number of operations if we do not use the body features and use the offline clusters as a proxy for these features.

2.3.5 Experiments

In this section we present the experimental evaluation of our techniques on the Yahoo! news corpus and search engine. The results we present evaluate the end product of the entire system that we presented, which is real-time clustering. Thus we present several experimental evaluations to determine the quality of the clustering output on the search results given a query. In the following subsections, we first describe the experimental data we used, present various evaluation metrics, and finally show the results to evaluate various techniques we described.

2.3.5.1 *Experimental Setup*

We scrape the Yahoo! News search engine with a list of random queries sampled from the query log and collect the top 100 news search results returned by the ranking algorithm. Each of these search results corresponds to an individual news article. Our goal is to group these search results into clusters that refer to related news stories. Since the news articles are coming through feeds from news sources, we have access to the individual fields, such as publication time, URL, title, abstract, and body of the news article. We extract several features from these news articles, including simple term features, unigram and bigram features, and named entity-based features. To extract named entities from the text of news articles, we use a dictionary-based maximum entropy-based tagger [29].

All of the search results for a given query are editorially grouped into related clusters by incrementally going through them one by one. For example, the first document is assigned to cluster A. If the second document is similar to cluster A, it too is assigned to cluster A; if it is not similar, it is assigned to a new cluster, B. In this manner, all the top-100 results are grouped into clusters. We define a cluster to be a news story. For example, the documents in the same cluster are referring to the same news story. If the story is a developing story, we require the related news articles to be in the same cluster, unless they talk about a significantly different news story. With this criterion for clustering the news articles, all documents within the same cluster correspond to the same news story from various news sources such as *New York Times* and *The Wall Street Journal*.

The offline clustering algorithms were run on the entire corpus of news documents within a one-month timeframe, comprising millions of news articles that correspond to U.S./English documents. Offline clustering algorithms utilize 600,000 features comprising unigram and bigram features and named entity-based features. For real-time clustering evaluation, we editorially labeled top-100 results into clusters for a set of 300 queries. The features used for real-time clustering algorithms were chosen to be a subset of the features used in offline clustering algorithms, comprising 12,000 features.

2.3.5.2 *Evaluation Metrics*

We utilize the following extrinsic metrics to evaluate our clustering algorithms that compare the performance of a given clustering solution to the editorial solution:

- *Precision.* If C is the number of clusters to be evaluated, L is the number of categories (from editorial judgments), and N is the total number of documents (100 per query), precision can be computed as the weighted average of maximal precision values:

$$\text{Precision} = \sum_i \frac{|C|}{N} \max_j \text{Precision}(C_i, L_j)$$

$$\text{Precision}(C_i, L_j) = \frac{|C_i \cap L_i|}{|C_i|}$$

- *Recall.* Recall, also referred to as inverse purity, focuses on the cluster with maximum recall for each category. Recall can be defined as:

$$\text{Recall} = \sum_i \frac{|L_i|}{N} \max_j \text{Precision}(L_i, C_j)$$

- *F-measure.* Standard F-measure can be computed from treating the precision and recall values equally.
- Q_4. This is an information-theoretic validity measure that characterizes how well the cluster labels assigned to the objects by a clustering algorithm agree

with their (manually assigned) class labels by the number of bits required to encode/compress the class labels of the objects, given knowledge of their cluster labels. This code length corresponds to a special encoding scheme inspired by the *minimum description length* principle [288,144]. The form of the measure that gives the bits per object to do this encoding is Q_3. The measure-form Q_4 is simply a normalized form of Q_3, designed to vary between zero (no information about class labels contained in cluster labels) and one (perfect clustering).

$$Q_3(C, K) = \frac{1}{n} \sum_{k=1}^{|K|} \left[\log \left(\frac{v(k)}{\{v(c, k)\}} \right) + \log \left(\frac{v(k) + |C| - 1}{|C| - 1} \right) \right],$$

where $\begin{pmatrix} v(k) \\ \{v(c, k)\} \end{pmatrix} = \frac{v(k)!}{\prod_{c=1}^{|C|} v(c,k)!} = $ multinomial coefficient

$$\begin{aligned} Q_4(C, K) &= \frac{\max_K Q_3(C, K) - Q_3(C, K)}{\max_K Q_3(C, K) - \min_K Q_3(C, K)} \\ &= \text{normalized } Q_3(C, K) \end{aligned}$$

These measures are refinements of the measures Q_0 and Q_2 derived in [104]. These refinements remove a form of redundancy known as *incompleteness* from Q_0 and Q_2. The details of the refinements are discussed in [105]. We chose to include Q_4 in our set of clustering-accuracy metrics because it satisfies a set of desirable properties, which are not all satisfied by more traditionally used metrics based on pairwise agreement/disagreement. These properties are listed in [104], and the fact that they are not all satisfied by traditional measures is demonstrated there as well.

- *Jaccard.* This is a simple Jaccard coefficient computed on the pairs of documents. It is computed as the number of pairs of documents that are supposed to be together, and the algorithm actually put them together over all of the number of pairs of documents.

$$\text{Jaccard} = \frac{\text{SS}}{\text{SS} + \text{SD} + \text{DS}}$$

where SS is the number of pairs that belong to the same algorithmic cluster and editorial class, SD is the number of pairs that belong to the same algorithmic cluster and different editorial class, and DS is the number of pairs that belong to a different algorithmic cluster and the same editorial class.

- *Rand.* This statistic relies on counting pairs of documents and their assignments into appropriate clusters and categories. Essentially it is the ratio of the number of pairs of documents that got correctly assigned into categories to the total number of pairs of documents

$$\text{Rand} = \frac{\text{SS} + \text{DD}}{\text{SS} + \text{SD} + \text{DS} + \text{DD}}$$

2.3.5.3 *Evaluating Meta Clustering and Textual Matching*

Table 2.12 shows the performance of various offline clustering algorithms applied directly on the editorial dataset for real-time clustering. It can be seen that the best

Table 2.12 Results with various simple offline clustering algorithms and the real-time clustering algorithm, which includes the meta-clustering algorithm.

Algorithm	Precision	Recall	F-Measure	Rand
Minhash clustering	0.77	0.92	0.84	0.66
Subspace clustering	0.83	0.90	0.86	0.69
K-means (k=20)	0.89	0.93	0.91	0.63
K-means (k=25)	0.95	0.96	0.95	0.71
Meta clustering	0.95	0.96	0.95	0.71
Meta clustering + textual matching	0.97	0.96	0.96	0.75

Table 2.13 Real-time clustering results with QrySim similarity measure that boosts the weights to the terms that occur close to the query term over the standard similarity measure (OrigSim) with equal weights to all terms.

Metric	OrigSim	QrySim	Gain	T-Test	%Times
				p-Value	OrigSim Is Better
Q_4	0.724	0.731	0.96%	0.06	62%
Jaccard	0.258	0.260	0.74%	0.07	62%
Rand	0.564	0.571	1.27%	0.02	96%

offline clustering algorithm is K-means, with 25 clusters, which achieves an F-measure of 0.95. A meta-clustering algorithm that is simply a combination of various clustering algorithms achieves the same performance as the best offline algorithm, whereas that utilizing the query information improves on this result because it incorporates additional information in terms of query.

2.3.5.4 *Results with QrySim*

Table 2.13 shows results with the *QrySim* method described in Section 5.2. HAC is used as a clustering algorithm for these results. We compared the standard cosine similarity with the *QrySim* similarity measure where we emphasize the weights on the terms that are close to the query. The *QrySim* method clearly outperforms the standard similarity measure, as shown in the results.

2.3.5.5 *Results with Offline Clusters as Features*

Next, we present experimental results by evaluating the efficacy of using offline clusters as features in real-time clustering. In this setting, we used the Minhash offline clustering algorithm to cluster a big corpus of news documents and used HAC to cluster the top-100 search results by using the offline cluster IDs as features.

The baseline feature set includes simple features such as bag of words, and we experimented with three variations of the Minhash clustering algorithm with various number of hash functions for the offline clustering algorithm as additional features.

We also utilize the structured fields in the news articles, such as title, abstract, and body, as individual features. The results are shown in Table 2.14.

We also experimented with various granularity settings for the offline clustering algorithm mentioned in Section 2.3.2 and their usefulness as features in the real-time clustering algorithm. Table 2.15 shows the results with various combinations of such granularity settings as features in the real-time clustering algorithm. The results show that the redundancy in the clustering algorithms is helpful to achieve maximum accuracy in real-time clustering. We can also observe a trend that the accuracy decreases as we go from coarse to fine granularity in the clustering algorithm.

The experimental results indicate that the meta clustering that combines various offline clustering algorithms is as good as the best clustering algorithm, but the real-time query-based clustering can be improved upon by utilizing the query information. We also show how to utilize the offline cluster information in the real-time

Table 2.14 Q_4 values with the real-time clustering algorithm with various combinations of features. The baselines include features with title and abstract and a single offline clustering algorithm. Although the combined feature set with all the features is the best one, the features with the offline clusters and title and abstract features are comparable to the ones that include body features.

Algorithm Description	Avg Q4
Best single offline clustering algorithm	0.7340
Title + abstract features only	0.7584
Title + abstract + best offline set of clusters	0.7801
Title + abstract + body features	0.8157
Title + abstract + body + best offline set of clusters	0.8208

Table 2.15 Q_4 values with the real-time clustering algorithm and various granularity settings of offline clusters as features. The baseline feature set includes just title and abstract features. The numbers 1, 2, 3 refer to different settings of the offline clustering algorithm at different granularity settings, specifically varying from coarse to fine representation of clusters. It can be observed that the best accuracy is obtained by combining all the configurations, and individual cluster IDs themselves provide inferior performance.

Offline Cluster Sets	Avg Q4
(1,2,3)	0.78009
(1,2)	0.77686
(1,3)	0.77444
(1)	0.77418
(2)	0.77130
(2,3)	0.77036
(3)	0.76155

clustering by using them as features; this shows an improvement in both accuracy and the performance of the system.

SUMMARY

This chapter introduced the algorithms for both ranking problems and clustering problems for news search engines. For ranking problems, although we can follow the learning-to-rank framework, it is important to consider the freshness factor that plays a critical role in user experience. We proposed a few unique aspects for this task, such as data collection, data sampling, editorial judging, and evaluations metrics. We also deep-dived into a real user search log to get a better understanding of user behavior and better modeling. For clustering problems, we presented a system that involves clustering the entire news corpus with an offline clustering algorithm and handling the incoming streaming data with incremental clustering algorithm. The output from the offline and incremental clustering algorithms is then utilized for improving the real-time query-based clustering.

Medical Domain Search Ranking

3

INTRODUCTION

Each patient visit to an outpatient care facility or hospital stay in an inpatient ward generates a great volume of data, ranging from physiological measurements to clinician judgments and decisions. Such data are not only important for reuse in current and later care episodes, they are also critical in supporting numerous secondary-use scenarios, including epidemic surveillance, population health management, and clinical and translational research [299,102]. It is widely believed that effective and comprehensive use of patient care data created in day-to-day clinical settings has the potential to transform the healthcare system into a self-learning vehicle to achieve better care quality, lower costs, and faster and greater scientific discoveries [157,115,128].

The launch of the health IT incentive program established through the American Recovery and Reinvestment Act of 2009 has stimulated widespread adoption of health IT systems in the United States, electronic health records (EHRs) in particular [37]. Medical professionals' everyday interactions with such systems have in turn led to the exponential growth of rich, electronically captured data at the patient level, providing great promise for large-scale computational reuse. However, the increasing availability of electronic data does not automatically warrant the increasing availability of information [67]. A majority of clinical documents continue to exist in an unstructured, narrative format in the EHR era [260,352,52]; these documents are extremely difficult to process due to many characteristics unique to narrative medical data, such as frequent use of nonstandard terminologies and acronyms [340,365]. Recent studies have also shown that the quality of data stored in EHRs, compared to the quality of data recorded in paper forms, has deteriorated considerably due to the inappropriate use of electronic documentation features such as automated fill-in and copy-and-paste [160,149,369]. As a result, onerous, costly, and error-prone manual chart reviews are often needed in order to reuse the data in direct patient care or to prepare it for secondary-use purposes [159].

It is therefore imperative to identify effective means to help clinicians, as well as administrators and researchers, retrieve information from EHRs. Recent research advances in natural language processing (NLP) have provided improved capabilities for automatically extracting concepts from narrative clinical documents [411,353]. However, until these NLP-based tools become widely available and versatile enough to handle vaguely defined information retrieval needs of EHR users, a convenient and cost-effective solution continues to be in great demand. In this chapter, we introduce the concept of medical information retrieval, which provides medical professionals a handy tool to search among unstructured clinical narratives via an interface similar to that of general-purpose Web search engines such as Google. In the latter part of the chapter, we also introduce several advanced features, such as intelligent, ontology-driven medical search query recommendation services and a collaborative search feature that encourages sharing of medical search knowledge among end users of EHR search tools.

This chapter focuses on information retrieval systems for electronic health records in a clinical setting, to be distinguished from information retrieval systems for biomedical literature, such as PubMed, and those for consumer-oriented health information, such as MedlinePlus. Interested readers can refer to Hersh, 2009 [158], for information retrieval systems of biomedical literature and consumer-oriented information.

The chapter is organized as follows: In Section 3.1, we discuss the current research on EHR search engines and introduce a homegrown EHR search engine, EMERSE, which has been widely used at the University of Michigan Health Systems. Results of analyzing the search behaviors of EMERSE users are summarized in Section 3.2, which motivate the approaches to enhance the performance of EHR search. In Section 3.3, we describe effective approaches to enhance the relevance ranking of EHR search engines, which is a summary of the experiences of the TREC medical record track and the next generation of EMERSE. In Section 3.4, we present an alternative approach that leverages the collective intelligence instead of the machine intelligence to enhance medical record search.

3.1   Search Engines for Electronic Health Records

Clinicians and researchers routinely search medical records, but today they are doing so in a highly inefficient manner. Many of them simply go through each document manually and read through each clinical note to find the information they are looking for, a simple procedure known as *chart review* or *chart abstraction*. The tedious effort of manual search sometimes returns no results, either because the information was not there at all or because it was overlooked. An automatic search engine becomes essential in the modern setting of retrieving electronic health records.

Although there are multiple search engines to assist with searching medical literature or health-related Web pages [51,241,40,240,252,108,170,242], adoption of search engines for EHRs remains limited. This may, in part, be due to a lack of understanding of the information needs of clinicians and researchers compared to those of the general population. Additional factors limiting the widespread adoption of EHR search engines include the complex medical information contained in clinical documents and the inadequacy of standard search engines to meet users' needs [270]. As a result, customized solutions are required. Even with such solutions, obtaining the proper approvals from a medical information technology department to integrate and support such a system and meeting all regulatory and privacy requirements are ongoing challenges that also limit the number of investigators who are able to work with such protected data in the clinical environment.

Only a few medical record search engines have been reported, and even among those it is difficult to know what level of adoption or usefulness has been achieved. The StarTracker system at Vanderbilt University was discussed in a brief report from 2003 [143]. At the time, it was available to 150 pilot users. It was reported to have been used successfully for cohort identification of clinical studies and to help with physician evaluation of clinical outcomes.

Columbia University also has a search engine, CISearch, that has been integrated with its locally developed EHR, WebCIS, since 2008 [263]. Supporting the notion that the information needs of an EHR search engine differ from those of standard search engines, the CISearch tool limits searches to a single patient at a time, and the system does not rank documents but rather displays the results in reverse chronological order, which is a common data view in medical record systems. The system was reported to have incorporated a limited number of document types, including discharge summaries, radiology reports, and pathology reports.

Other research systems have also been reported to support searching clinical documents, although these are not explicitly labeled as search engines [238]. An example is the STRIDE system at Stanford University, which has been shown to be of benefit for clinical decision making [126]. Additionally, the Informatics for Integrating Biology and the Bedside (i2b2) Workbench tool has been modified to handle searching free text notes [417].

At the University of Michigan we have had a search engine in our production environment since 2005. The Electronic Medical Record Search Engine (EMERSE) was developed to support users with an efficient and accurate means of querying our repository of clinical documents [145]. As of April 2013, we had over 60 million clinical documents and reports from approximately 2 million patients. EMERSE is used for a wide variety of information retrieval tasks, including research (e.g., cohort identification, eligibility determination, and data abstraction), quality improvement and quality assurance initiatives, risk management, and infection control monitoring.

From a technical perspective, EMERSE utilizes Apache Lucene to index and retrieve documents, but the Web application itself has been modified substantially to meet the needs of medical search. For example, stop words are not removed from the index, since many are themselves important acronyms. Examples include AND (axillary node dissection), ARE (active resistance exercise), and IS (incentive spirometry). Additionally, two indices are maintained of all documents: a standard lowercased index for the default case-insensitive searches and a case-sensitive index so users can distinguish medical terms from potential false positives. An example is the need to distinguish ALL (acute lymphoblastic leukemia) from the common word *all*.

EMERSE contains a large vocabulary of synonyms and related concepts that are presented to users to expand their search queries. For example, searching for "ibuprofen" would bring up suggestions that include brand names such as "Advil" and "Motrin" as well as common misspellings derived from our search logs, including "ibuprofin" and "ibuprophen." As of April 2013, the synonym list contained 45,000 terms for about 11,000 concepts. From prior experimental work on intelligent query expansion, supported by the National Library of Medicine, we have learned that users often want fine-grained control over the terms used in their searches, since this can help them refine the search to meet their specific information needs. Incorporating other information sources from the Unified Medical Language System (UMLS), such as the [103], could further enhance users' ability to expand their search queries. Assessing the relevance of documents at the concept level is a crucial practice in EHR information retrieval, which we will elaborate on in Section 3.3.

There are many aspects of clinical documents that make information retrieval challenging. These include the use of ambiguous terminology, known as *hedge phrases* (e.g., "the patient possibly has appendicitis"), as well as negation (e.g., "there is no evidence of appendicitis in this patient"). EMERSE provides a mechanism for handling negation that is easy for users to implement, but that deviates from standard practices for "typical" search engines. Negation can be achieved by adding *exclude* phrases, which are phrases that contain a concept of interest but in the wrong context. These phrases are notated with a minus sign in front of them, which tells the system to ignore those specific phrases but not the overall document itself. Thus, one can look for "complications" but ignore "no complications occurred." Indeed, this was recently done for the Department of Ophthalmology as part of a quality assurance initiative to identify post-operative complications. The term "complication" or "complications" was searched and a collection of approximately 30 negated phrases were excluded. This greatly reduced the false-positive rate for the searches and allowed the department to conduct an efficient and accurate search for potential complications.

The EMERSE system also provides a framework to encourage the collaborative sharing and use of queries developed by others [405]. Saved searches, called *bundles*, can be created by any user and either shared or kept private. Many users have shared their bundles, and many bundles have been used by a wide variety of users. This paradigm allows users with specific medical expertise to share their knowledge with other users of the system, allowing those with less domain expertise to benefit from those with more. Bundles also provide a means for research teams to standardize their searches across a large group to ensure that the same processes are applied to each medical record [92]. We believe social search features an important functionality of the next generation of medical search engines. More details about the collaborative search component of EMERSE are provided in Section 3.4.

Studies have been carried out to assess various aspects of EMERSE. In addition to the collaborative search feature already described, we analyzed the EMERSE query logs to derive insights about users' information-seeking habits [381]. Results of this query log analysis shed light on many important issues of medical search engines, which are elaborated in Section 3.2. Another study looked at how well eligibility determination for a psychiatric study could be carried out using traditional manual chart reviews in the EHR (which often requires clicking individually on each document to read through it) compared to using EMERSE [309]. Using EMERSE was far more efficient than the manual processes, yet the accuracy was maintained.

Another study looked into the feasibility of using a tool such as EMERSE to collect data for the American College of Surgeons, National Surgical Quality Improvement Program (ACS NSQIP) [146]. EMERSE was used to identify cases of post-operative myocardial infarction pulmonary embolus, a process that is traditionally performed manually. Utilizing the negation components of EMERSE was essential in these tasks to rule out false-positive results. Overall the system worked well, and it even identified cases that had been missed during the old standard manual review process. For myocardial infarction, sensitivity and specificity of 100.0% and 93.0%, respectively, were achieved. For pulmonary embolus, the sensitivity and specificity were 92.8% and 95.9%, respectively.

In the next section, we discuss the analysis of EHR search engine users' search behaviors, especially users of EMERSE. The results of these analyses motivate various important approaches to enhancing the performance of EHR search engines.

3.2 Search Behavior Analysis

One might initially think that clinicians (physicians and nurses) would be the primary users of an EHR search engine. However, this is only partly true, according to the results of a survey of EMERSE users. EMERSE users cover nearly all medical disciplines, ranging from primary care fields such as general pediatrics, family medicine, and general internal medicine to subspecialties such as neurosurgery, urology, and gastroenterology. Among the users who responded to an EMERSE survey, only 7% are full-time practicing clinicians; the others are cancer registrars, infection control specialists, quality assurance officers, pharmacists, data managers, and other research-oriented individuals, including medical fellows, residents, students, and even undergraduates working on research projects within the University of Michigan Health System.

According to the survey, EMERSE users were using the search engine for various kinds of tasks. Two-thirds used the search engine to determine medication use for patients. Nearly as many users reported using EMERSE for assisting with clinical trials. Other uses included detection of adverse events, determining eligibility for clinical studies, infection surveillance, internal quality assurance projects, study feasibility determination, billing/claims abstraction, and risk management review. As a comparison, researches of the Columbia University's EHR search engine revealed that searches for laboratory or test results and disease or syndromes constituted the majority of the search purposes.

The availability of longitudinal collection of search logs of EHR search engines made it possible to quantitatively analyze EMERSE users' search behaviors. Natarajan *et al.* analyzed the query log of an EHR search engine with 2,207 queries [263]. They found that among these queries, 14.5% were navigational queries and 85.1% were informational. Searching for laboratory results and specific diseases were users' predominant information needs. In 2011, Yang *et al.* analyzed a much larger collection that consisted of 202,905 queries and 35,928 user sessions recorded by the EMERSE search engine over four years [381]. The collection represented the information-seeking behavior of 533 medical professionals. Descriptive statistics of the queries, a categorization of information needs, and temporal patterns of the users' information-seeking behavior were reported [381]. The results suggest that information needs in medical searches are substantially more complicated than those in general Web searches.

Specifically, the frequency of medical search queries does not follow a power-law distribution, as that of Web search queries does. A medical search query contains five terms on average, which is two times longer than the average length of a Web search query. Users of the EHR search engine typically start with a very short query (1.7 terms on average) and end up with a much longer query through a search session. A session of EHR search is considerably longer than a session of Web search, in terms of both the time period (14.8 minutes on average) or the number of queries (5.64 on average). All of these points suggest that it is substantially more difficult for users to compose an effective medical search query than a general Web search query.

In what aspects are the medical search queries more difficult? It is reported that more than 30% of the query terms are not covered by a common English dictionary, a medical dictionary, or a professional medical ontology, compared to less than 15% of terms in Web searches. Furthermore, 2,020 acronyms appeared 55,402 times in the EMERSE query log, where 18.9% of the queries contain at least one acronym [381].

The low coverage of query terms by medical dictionaries not only implies the substantial difficulty of developing effective spell-check modules for EHR search, but it also suggests the need to seek beyond the use of medical ontologies to enhance medical information retrieval. One possible direction leads towards deeper corpus mining and natural language processing of electronic health records.

Moreover, the categorization of medical search queries is substantially different from those in Web searches. The well-established categorization of information needs in Web searches into *navigational*, *informational*, and *transactional* queries does not apply to medical search [45]. This calls for a new categorization framework for medical search queries. Yang *et al.* suggests one possible categorization that discriminates high-precision information needs from high-recall information needs [381]. In that work, a clinical ontology is used to categorize the semantics of queries into a few high-level medical concepts (see Table 3.1). According to their results, around 28% of the queries are concerned with *clinical findings*, which include subcategories such as diseases and drug reactions. Furthermore, 12.2% of the queries are concerned with *pharmaceutical or biological products*, followed by *procedures* (11.7%) and *situation with explicit context* (8.9%). In addition 10.4% of the EMERSE queries cannot be described by any of the categories. It is an interesting question to ask to what extent such a semantic categorization is useful in enhancing the performance of an EHR search engine.

All the findings from the analysis of real users suggest that medical search queries are in general much more sophisticated than Web search queries. This difficulty imposes considerable challenges for users to accurately formulate their search strategies. There is an urgent need to design effective mechanisms to assist users in

Table 3.1   Distribution of categories of medical concepts in EMERSE queries.*

Category	Coverage (%)
Clinical finding	28.0
Pharmaceutical/biological products	12.2
Procedures	11.7
Unknown	10.4
Situation with explicit context	8.9
Body structure	6.5
Observable entity	4.3
Qualifier value	3.7
Staging and scales	3.2
Specimen	2.2
Physical object	2.2
Event	1.7
Substance	1.5
Linkage concept	1.0
Physical force	0.6
Environment or geographical location	0.6
Social context	0.5
Record artifact	0.4
Organism	0.3
Special concept	0.03

*Queries submitted to EMERSE are categorized into the top 19 medical concepts in the ontology structure of SNOMED-CT [327], a standard clinical terminology.

formulating and improving their queries. These findings motivate many important directions for improving EHR search engines. Now let's discuss three particular directions: relevance ranking, query recommendation, and collaborative search.

3.3 Relevance Ranking

Conventional search engines for medical records (e.g., EMERSE) do not provide the functionality of ranking matched results as is commonly done by Web search engines. This largely contributes to the uniqueness of the information needs in medical search. Indeed, when users search for medical records, the concept of a "hit" is different where there are usually no "best document" or "most relevant" records to rank and display. Instead, the final "answer" depends heavily on the initial question and is almost always determined after the user views a *collection* of documents for a patient, not a single document.

The heavy dependence on manual reviewing is largely due to the uncertainty and ambiguity that is inherent in medical records. Consider an example: A clinician is trying to identify patients diagnosed with asthma. The diagnosis of asthma for a young child can be difficult. When a child with difficulty breathing is on an initial clinic visit, the clinical note may mention terms such as *wheezing, coughing, reactive airway disease*, and, perhaps, *asthma*. However, this does not mean that the patient actually *has* asthma, because many children may develop wheezing during an upper respiratory viral infection. Observations of documented recurrent episodes have to be done before one might conclude that a child truly has asthma, and one should also take into account the prescribed medications and the changes in the patient's condition based on the use of those medications. Therefore, a single medical record mentioning asthma, regardless of how frequently it is mentioned in the document, cannot truly provide a confident diagnosis. Therefore, in conventional EHR searches, the requirement of a high recall is usually more important than a high precision. The ranking of search results is not critical, since all the retrieved records will be manually reviewed by the users.

It was not until recently that designers of EHR search engines started to adopt relevance ranking in the retrieval architecture. On one hand, the volume of electronic records is growing rapidly, making it difficult for users to manually review all the documents retrieved. On the other hand, the recent development of natural language processing for EHRs has made it possible to handle negation [261], uncertainty [147], and ambiguity [63] to a certain degree. Relevance ranking has become appealing in many scenarios of medical record search, especially in scenarios with a need for high precision, such as identifying patients for clinical trials. In the next section we examine the effort of a medical record search challenge organized by the Text REtrieval Conference (TREC), followed by an implementation we adopt for the next generation of the EMERSE search engine.

3.3.1 Insights from the TREC Medical Record Track

The Text REtrieval Conference (TREC), organized by the U.S. National Institute of Standards and Technology (NIST) every year since 1992, provides a standard testbed to evaluate particular information retrieval (IR) tasks. In 2011 and 2012, TREC organized a new track called the Medical Record Track that provides an IR challenge task to identify cohorts of patients fitting certain criteria from electronic health records, which are similar to those specified for participation in clinical studies [359].

The task in both years used a collection of electronic health records from the University of Pittsburgh NLP repository, which consisted of 93,551 de-identified clinical reports collected from multiple hospitals, including radiology reports, history and physicals, consultation reports, emergency department reports, progress notes, discharge summaries, operative reports, surgical pathology reports, and cardiology reports [359]. These clinical reports were aggregated into 17,264 visits, each of which corresponds to the single stay at a hospital of an individual patient. Query topics (35 in 2011 and 50 in 2012) of the track represent different case definitions, which vary widely in terms of linguistic complexity. Both the selection of the query topics and the relevance assessments were carried out by physicians who were also students in the Oregon Health & Science University (OHSU) Biomedical Informatics Graduate Program.

It is reported that the majority of the participating teams employed some sort of domain-specific vocabulary normalization, concept extraction, and/or query expansion [359]. This largely attributes to the informal and ambiguous language used in health records. Indeed, a given medical entity is usually referred to by a wide variety of acronyms, abbreviations, and informal designations [359]. A typical method used by the participating teams is to identify and normalize medical terms in text and map the terms to concepts in the UMLS metathesaurus using MetaMap. Some participants also map these UMLS concepts to entities in some controlled medical vocabularies, such as SNOMED-CT or MeSH, which allows the system to navigate through different granularities of concepts in the queries and documents and to expand the queries using related concepts in the ontology.

It is also worth mentioning that many other information sources were used for query expansion. These sources included domain specific taxonomy such as the International Classification of Diseases (ICD) codes, term relations mined from the EHR corpus, and various external sources such as encyclopedias, biomedical literature, and Wikipedia, as well as the open Web.

It is also important to note that medical records frequently use negated expressions to document the absence of symptoms, behaviors, and abnormal diagnostic results [359]. Results from the participating teams suggest that it is an effective practice to specifically handle negations in EHR retrieval, which is in contrast to many other ad hoc information retrieval tasks.

A team from Cengage Learning achieved top performance in the TREC 2011 medical track [202]. The key techniques they applied included information extraction and query expansion. Specifically, medical terms that appeared in the UMLS were extracted from the queries and the documents, together with a limited collection of demographical information. Three methods of query expansion were explored, one through UMLS-related terms, one through a network of terms built from UMLS, and the other through terms from in-house medical reference encyclopedias. It is worth mentioning that they conducted a specific treatment in information extraction to detect negations and uncertainty. Furthermore, 256 and 130 rules were used to detect negation uncertainty, respectively. Medical terms associated with a negated or uncertain expression were excluded from the index. Such a treatment was reported to have improved the average precision by 5%.

In the TREC 2012 medical track, a team from the University of Delaware achieved the top performance [414]. It is reported that they mainly explored three effective directions: (1) aggregating evidence of relevance at different granularities, i.e., at the level of individual medical reports and at the level of patient visits; (2) query expansion through a variety of large-scale external sources; and (3) applying machine learning methods to combine classical IR models and different types of features. A Markov random field (MRF) was employed to model the proximity dependency of terms.

To summarize, it is a common practice to enhance relevance ranking in medical records searches by introducing concept-level relevance assessment and query expansion. In the next subsection, we discuss our practice of the two directions in the next generation of the EMERSE search engine.

3.3.2 Implementing and Evaluating Relevance Ranking in EHR Search Engines

We built a proof-of-concept prototype of the next generation of EHR search engine (referred to as EHR-SE), which features a concept-level relevance ranking and a component of query recommendation. As a proof of concept, we adopted straightforward query recommendation and relevance ranking algorithms. Under the same architecture, we could apply more sophisticated query suggestion methods and/or relevance ranking methods.

In general, the new EHR search engine advances EMERSE and other existing full-text search engines for medical records by assessing document relevance and recommending alternative query terms at the level of medical concepts instead of at the level of individual words. A document is retrieved because one of the medical concepts implied by its terms matches the concepts in the query. Relevant documents are ranked based on how well the concepts in the documents match the concepts in the query, through classical retrieval methods extended to the concept level. For example, when the query is looking for patients with "hearing loss," documents containing "difficulty of hearing" or "deaf" will also be retrieved and ranked highly.

As a proof of concept, we adopted the same corpus of electronic health records used in the TREC medical record track. Medical terms and concepts were extracted from the reports in two ways. First, medical terms were identified and mapped to the metathesaurus concepts in the UMLS by MetaMap, with a numerical score from 0 to 1000 representing the confidence in the match. Second, we also extracted medical terms that were frequently searched by EMERSE users and mapped them to an empirical synonym set (ESS), which was constructed through mining the search log of EMERSE. The medical records were then indexed by either the medical terms in the metathesaurus or the synonyms in the EES using the Lemur toolkit, denoted as indexes M and E, respectively.

With the new representation of an individual document or a query as a set of medical terms, the relevance score of a document, given a query, can be calculated based on a classical vector space retrieval model known as the method:

$$Score(d, q) = \sum_{t \in q \cup d} \frac{1 + \ln[1 + \ln(c(t, d))]}{(1 - s) + s \frac{|d|}{avdl}} \cdot c(t, d) \cdot \ln \frac{N + 1}{df(t)}. \qquad (3.1)$$

In Equation 3.1, t, d, and q denote a medical term, a medical document, and a query, respectively; $c(t, d)$ denotes the frequency of the term t appearing in the document; $|d|/avdl$ denotes the length of the document normalized by the average length of documents in the collection, and $df(t)$ denotes the document frequency of t (i.e., the number of documents containing the term t). We modified the formula such that (1) the set of synonyms under the same concept are treated as a single term; (2) the metrics are calculated from both of the indexes (the metathesaurus index M and the ESS index E) and then combined; and (3) the metrics consider the case that a term may be contained in multiple metathesaurus concepts of ESS subsets.

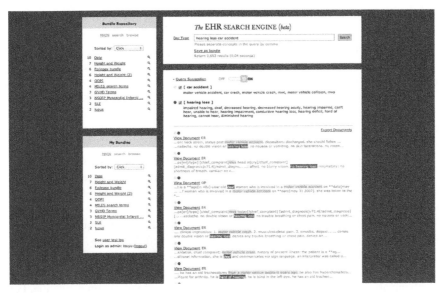

FIGURE 3.1

Snapshot of the new EHR Search Engine (EHR-SE). Medical terms in the query are expanded with synonyms under the same medical concepts. A user can choose to turn on or turn off the query suggestions. The retrieved results are ranked in the lower-right panel with the matched concepts highlighted. The left panel provides a functionality of social search so that the users can store, share, and adopt effective queries.

The analysis of the query log of EMERSE showed that the performance of medical record searches still suffers from the low quality of queries entered by end users and the tremendous amount of redundant effort on exploring similar queries across users [4]. It is difficult even for clinicians with years of training to form adequate queries that lead to desirable search results due to the complexity of the domain and the information needs [5]. Two techniques that have been deployed in commercial search engines could be helpful to this issue in the medical context: (1) query recommendations, which provide alternative query terms based on the "wisdom" of data mining algorithms; and (2) social searches, which select and promote efficient queries among users based on the "wisdom of the crowd."

The new EHR-SE is featured with a component of recommending alternative query concepts to users. When a user submits a query q, the same process for document preprocessing is applied to identify the medical terms in the query and match them to concepts. For each medical term t extracted from the query, the query recommendation algorithm simply generates all synonyms of the term that are either under the same metathesaurus concepts, $M(t)$, or belong to the same synonym subset in ESS, $E(t)$. The union of $M(t)$ and $E(t)$ is presented to expand the original query. A particular example of the query expansion is shown in Figure 3.1, a snapshot of the real EHR-SE system.

The effectiveness of this proof-of-concept system was evaluated with a carefully designed user study. 33 participants were recruited, representing different departments and divisions in the University of Michigan Health System.

We assigned standardized scenarios to each participant to simulate the real information needs in medical record search.

In each scenario, a participant could explore the system with as many queries as necessary. After obtaining satisfactory search results, each participant answered three questions with a score from 1 to 5 and provided narratives to describe their perceptions of the system performance.

Overall, the participants gave very positive feedback on the system performance. The overall evaluation score suggested that the performance of the system when automatic query recommendation was turned on was significantly better than the performance when the service was turned off.

In summary, concept-level relevance assessment and automatic query expansion play an important role in relevance ranking of medical record searches. In this way, the challenge introduced by the sophistication of the medical domain and the information needs are alleviated to a certain degree. However, there are still quite a few barriers to solving all the problems with automatic query expansion or recommendation. For example, findings from the TREC medical record track suggest that automatic query expansion for some query types may cause query drifts, which hurt retrieval performance [359]. In a recent paper summarizing the failure analysis of the TREC medical record track, the authors listed a few common causes of retrieval errors, including irrelevant chart references to medical terms; variation of the uses and spellings of terminology; ambiguity of different conditions with similar names; ambiguity among past, present, and future conditions or procedures, and imperfect treatments of negations and uncertainties [112].

In the long run, most of these barriers may be overcome with more advanced natural language processing techniques for electronic health records. An alternative approach to helping users formulate the effective queries, however, may go beyond machine intelligence and require the utilization of social intelligence. The following section describes our exploration of collaborative searches, which allows users to disseminate search knowledge in a social setting.

3.4 Collaborative Search

An intelligent search engine does not solve all problems of information retrieval for medical records; its performance depends highly on the quality of search queries that users are able to construct. From our analysis of the EMERSE query log, it seems that average users often do not have adequate knowledge to construct effective and inclusive search queries, given that users usually revise their queries multiple times through a search session and frequently adopt system-generated or socially disseminated suggestions.

One way to address this issue that has drawn increasing attention is the concept of *social information seeking* or *collaborative search*. Such a process enables users to collaboratively refine the quality of search queries as well as the quality of information resources. Examples include the Yahoo! Search Pad,[1] Microsoft SearchTogether,[2] and various social bookmarking sites. A common goal of these approaches is to encourage users to record the queries they found effective and share such search knowledge with other users.

Can this concept be applied to facilitate information retrieval for medical records? We implemented a "collaborative search" feature in EMERSE that allows users to preserve their search knowledge and share it with other users of the search engine. Through this feature, a user can create, modify, and share so-called "" that contain collections of keywords and regular expressions to describe that user's information needs [8]. For example, a commonly used search term bundle, named "Cancer Staging Terms," contains as many as 202 distinct search terms, such as "gleason," "staging workup," and "Tmic" [405]. Analysis of the EMERSE query log shows that as many as 27.7% of the search sessions ended up adopting a search bundle created by other users.

There are two ways for an EMERSE user to share a search bundle that user created. She may share it to the public, so that all EMERSE users can view and adopt the bundle. She may also share it exclusively to a list of users who can benefit from the bundle, according to her own assessment. Our survey found that 34.3% of all bundles were shared privately, and 20.5% of the bundles were shared publicly, with the rest not shared at all. About 41.9% of the EMERSE users were involved in collaborative search activities (either shared or adopted a bundle) based on either privately shared bundles (24.8%) or publicly shared bundles (26.8%).

To better describe the effect of the collaborative search feature, a social network analysis was conducted that quantified the utility of search bundles in enhancing the diffusion of search knowledge [405].

Figure 3.2 presents a network of search bundles created and adopted by users associated with different departments in the University of Michigan Health System. Clearly, the interdepartmental bundle-sharing activities (red links) played important roles in disseminating the search knowledge from one department to another. The potential of this feature was far from being fully realized, however, given that a larger number of bundles were still used only internally in a department [405].

Figure 3.3 presents a different view of the diffusion of search knowledge by including the users in the network.

To quantify and compare the effectiveness of publicly shared bundles and privately shared bundles in the diffusion of search knowledge, analysis was conducted on a few creator-consumer networks, the nodes of which represent EMERSE users, and a (directed) edge connects the creator of a bundle to the consumer of the bundle [405]. Overall, a creator-consumer network established through collaborative search

---

[1] www.ysearchblog.com/2009/07/07/unveiling-yahoo-search-pad/.
[2] http://research.microsoft.com/en-us/um/redmond/projects/searchtogether/.

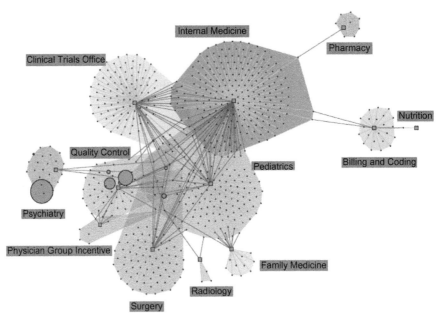

FIGURE 3.2

Network of search bundles presenting the diffusion of search knowledge across departments. Every circle node is a search bundle, sized proportionally to its frequency of use. Every rectangle node refers to a department, with colored convex hulls encompassing all search bundles created by the same department. Every red edge connects a bundle to the departments of the users who "borrowed" them in search; every gray edge connects a bundle to the department of the user who created it. (For interpretation of the references to color in this figure legend, the reader is referred to the web version of this book.)

presents a high average degree, a high clustering coefficient, and a small average shortest path compared to random networks of the same size. This indicates that the collaborative search feature has successfully facilitated the diffusion of search knowledge, forming a small-world network of search users. Between privately shared bundles and publicly shared bundles, the latter seems to be slightly more effective, with the combination of the two types of bundles significantly more effective than either individual type.

Our work also compared the search knowledge diffusion networks with a hypothetical social network of users constructed by connecting users who had ever typed in the same queries [405]. Such an analysis revealed a big potential gain if we had a better mechanism of collaborative search. The hypothetical network was featured with much fewer singletons, a much higher average degree, and a much shorter average shortest path length. The findings of this study suggest that although the collaborative search feature had effectively improved search-knowledge diffusion in medical record search, its potential was far from being fully realized.

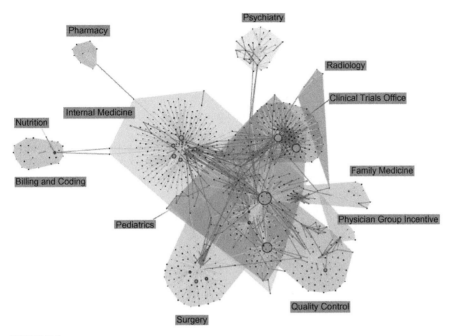

FIGURE 3.3

Network of users and bundles presenting the diffusion of search knowledge. Every circle node is a user, sized proportionally to the number of search bundles he has created. Orange edges connect users in the same department. Every other (rectangle) node is a search bundle. A colored convex hull encompasses all users and search bundles created by the users in the same department. Every red edge connects a bundle to the users who "borrowed" them in search; every gray edge connects a bundle to the user who created it.

3.5 Conclusion

Information retrieval of medical records in a clinical setting is especially challenging in various ways. The sophistication of the domain knowledge, the unique linguistic properties of the medical records, the complex information needs, and the barriers due to patient privacy protection have together limited the effectiveness of search engines for electronic health records. In this chapter we presented recent findings from the experience with our in-house EHR search engines and the TREC medical record track, which shed light on several effective practices for improving medical records search. Specifically, we highlighted three key approaches: concept-level relevance ranking, automatic query expansion, and collaborative search.

There remain many challenging issues in effective information retrieval for medical records. A more accurate and robust natural language processing pipeline for medical records should largely improve the performance of EHR search engines. Such a pipeline should provide powerful tools for medical concept extraction, acronym resolution, word disambiguation, and negation and uncertainty detection.

An even more urgent task is to better understand the information needs and search behaviors of the users of EHR search engines. In analogy to the query log analysis in Web search, which has long been proven a successful approach to enhancing the performance of Web search engines, better models and techniques utilizing the observations of search behaviors are anticipated to significantly enhance the effectiveness of EHR search engines.

Finally, this chapter pointed out a potentially high-return approach, collaborative search, that is an alternative to the methods based on machine intelligence. With such an approach, the users of medical record search engines are enabled to preserve, disseminate, and promote search knowledge that leads to satisfactory search results. A promising future direction of medical information retrieval will be incentive-centered designs that better engage users with the collaborative search features.

Visual Search Ranking

INTRODUCTION

With rapid advances in data capturing, storage devices, networks and social communication technologies, large-scale multimedia data has become available to the general public. Flickr [123], the most popular photo-sharing site on the Web, reached 5 billion photo uploads in 2011, with thousands of photos uploaded every minute (about 4.5 million daily). As of 2011, Facebook held more than 60 billion photos shared by its communities [117]. YouTube streamed more than 1 billion videos per day worldwide in 2012 [390].

Such explosive growth and widespread accessibility of visual content have led to a surge in research activities related to visual searches. The key problem is to retrieve visual documents (such as images, video clips, and Web pages containing images or videos) that are relevant to a given query or users' search intent from a large-scale database. Unlike text search, visual search is a more challenging task because they require the semantic understanding of visual content. There are two main issues in creating an efficient visual search mechanism. One is how to represent queries and index visual documents. The other is how to map the representations of queries and visual documents and find the relevance between queries and visual documents. In the last decade, visual search has attracted much attention, though it has been studied since the early 1990s (then referred to as content-based image/video retrieval [214,217,297]). All previous research has aimed at addressing our two stated issues.

This chapter introduces the basic techniques for visual search ranking. We first briefly introduce the generic visual search system, and then we categorize the approaches to video search ranking. Specifically, we present several basic techniques for video search ranking: (1) text-based search ranking, which leverages query keywords and documents' textual features; (2) query example-based search ranking, which examines query examples because they may provide rich information about the user's intent; and (3) concept-based search ranking, which utilizes the results from concept detection to aid search. Due to the great success of text document retrieval, most popular image and video search engines only rely on the surrounding text associated with the images or videos. However, visual relevance cannot be merely judged by text search techniques, since the textual information is usually too noisy to precisely describe visual content, or it could even be unavailable. To address this problem, visual search reranking has received increasing attention in recent years.

Therefore, we present the current approaches to visual search reranking as well. In addition, we discuss search models by using machine learning techniques, including classification-based ranking and learning to rank. We conclude this chapter with a list of promising directions for future research.

4.1 Generic Visual Search System

A typical visual search system consists of several main components, including query preprocessing, visual feature extraction, semantic analysis, (e.g., text, visual, and concept searches), search models, and reranking. Figure 4.1 shows a generic visual search framework. Usually the query in a visual search system consists of a piece of textual query (e.g., "find shots in which a boat moves past") and probably a set of query examples (e.g., images or video keyframes/clips). Query preprocessing is mainly used to obtain more accurate text-based search results based on a given speech recognition transcript, the closed captions available from a program channel, or the recognized captions embedded in video frames through optical character recognition (OCR). Visual feature extraction is used to detect a set of low-level visual features (global, local, and region features) to represent the query examples. Query analysis is used to map the query to some relevant high-level concepts with pretrained

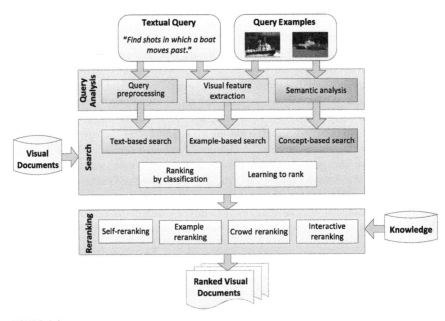

FIGURE 4.1

A generic visual search system.

classifiers (e.g., "boat," "water," "outdoor") for concept-based search. These multi-modal queries are fed into individual search models, such as text, concept, and visual-based searches, respectively. Based on these initial search results as well as some knowledge, a reranking module is applied to aggregate the search results and reorder the initial document list to improve search performance. Learning-based search, a popular method that includes classification and learning to rank, has attracted the attention of researchers' published works in recent years. Therefore we further discuss related works on learning-based visual search.

4.2 Text-Based Search Ranking

Due to the great success of text search, most popular image and video search engines, such as Google [141], Yahoo! [377], and Bing [32], build on text search techniques by using text information associated with media content. The text search module aims to retrieve a number of top-ranked documents based on the similarity between query keywords and documents' textual features. The textual features can be extracted from a number of information sources such as speech recognition transcripts, closed captions (CC), and video OCR. Unless the textual features are unavailable in some visual documents (such as surveillance videos), they are usually the most reliable sources to handle semantic queries in visual search systems. In this section, we describe several key components of the text-based search module, including text search models, query preprocessing approaches, and text sources.

4.2.1 Text Search Models

In a visual search system, the text search is often explored to generate the initial ranked results, which are used in achieving multimodal fusion or reranking. Thus nearly all existing text-based information retrieval (IR) models can be explored. The classic IR models can be classified into three kinds of model, i.e., set-theoretic, algebraic, and probabilistic models. In set-theoretic models, the documents are represented as sets of words or phrases. Similarities are usually derived from set-theoretic operations on these sets. Standard Boolean model [208], extended Boolean model [137] and fuzzy model [125,195,394] are some popular set-theoretic models. Algebraic models represent documents and queries as vectors, matrices, or tuples. The similarity of the query vector and document vector is represented as a scalar value. Vector space model [301], generalized vector space model [351,371], latent semantic indexing [93,109], and neural networks models [287] are some common algebraic models. Probabilistic models treat the process of document retrieval as a probabilistic inference. Similarities are computed as probabilities that a document is relevant to a given query. Binary independence model [289,295], language models [245,250], and divergence-from-randomness model [9] are some of the main probabilistic models. Probabilistic theorems like the Bayes theorem are often used in these models [29]. A more complete survey of text retrieval models can be found in [205,307].

4.2.2 Textual Query Preprocessing

Using textual queries in practical visual search engines is generally the most popular way to express users' intent; however, the user-supplied queries are often complex and subjective, so it is unreliable to use them directly. The following steps are the typical preprocessing in generic visual search systems.

4.2.2.1 Query Expansion

Query expansion is used as a term for adding related words to a query in order to increase the number of returned documents and improve recall accordingly. Typically, all the keywords in each query should first be extracted, and then for each keyword the synonyms and acronyms are automatically selected [360]. In addition, content-based [162,225] and conceptual suggestions [163] have been proven effective in visual content search during the past decade.

4.2.2.2 Stemming Algorithm

A *stemming algorithm*, a procedure to reduce all words with the same stem to a common form, is useful in many areas of computational linguistics and information retrieval work, for example, "stemmer," "stemming," and "stemmed" can be reduced to "stem." The first ever published stemmer was written by J. B. Lovins in 1968 [236]. This paper was one of the first of its kind and had great influence on later work in this area. A later stemmer was written by Martin Porter [282] and was very widely used, becoming the standard algorithm for English stemming. More details of Porter's stemmer and the other stemming algorithms can be found in [310].

4.2.2.3 Stopword Removal

All *stopwords*—for example, common words such as "a" and "the"—are removed from multiple-word queries to increase search performance. To remove the stopwords, a list of stopwords for a language is useful. Making a list of stopwords can be done by sorting through the vocabulary of a text corpus for words used with great frequency and going down the list, picking off words to be discarded. Given a query like "find shots of one or more people reading a newspaper" (a typical query in TRECVID search tasks [350]), the key terms ("people," "read," and "newspaper" in this example) are retained after stemming (such as converting "reading" to "read") and removing stopwords (such as "a" and "of").

4.2.2.4 N-Gram Query Segmentation

The query strings are segmented into term sequences based on the *N*-gram method [46] before being input to the search engine. For our "find shots of one or more people reading a newspaper" example, if it has three levels of *N*-gram (i.e., *N* is from 1 to 3), seven total query segments will be generalized as (1) uni-gram: *people, read*, and *newspaper*; (2) bi-gram: *people read, people newspaper*, and *read newspaper*; and (3) tri-gram: *people read newspaper*. These segments were submitted to the search engine as different forms of the query, and the relevance scores of visual documents retrieved by different query segments can be aggregated with different weights, which can be set empirically [225]. The higher gram a query segment has, the higher the weight that should be assigned.

4.2.2.5 *Part-of-Speech Tagging*

In corpus linguistics, *part-of-speech tagging* (POS tagging, or POST), also called *grammatical tagging* or *word-category disambiguation*, is the process of marking a word in a text (corpus) as corresponding to a particular part of speech, based on both its definition as well as its context, i.e., its relationship with adjacent and related words in a phrase, sentence, or paragraph. Some current major algorithms for part-of-speech tagging include the Viterbi algorithm [191], Brill Tagger [43], Constraint Grammar [200], and the Baum-Welch algorithm [366] (also known as the forward-backward algorithm). Many machine learning methods have also been applied to the problem of POS tagging. Methods such as support vector machine (SVM) [75], maximum entropy classifier [28], Perceptron [127], and nearest-neighbor [42] have all been tried, and most can achieve accuracy above 95%. A simplified method is to identify query terms as nouns, verbs, adjectives, adverbs, and so on. For a long and complex query [225,255], we can label the query topic with POS tags and extract the terms with noun or noun phrase tags as the "targeted objects," since the noun and noun phrases often describe the centric objects that the query is seeking. For example, given a query "find shots of one or more people reading a newspaper," "people" and "newspaper" will be tagged as nouns and extracted as the targeted objects in the query.

4.2.3 **Text Sources**

The text data in visual document collection are not always generated from a single source alone. Instead, a lot of visual document corpora, such as broadcast news, are associated with multiple text sources that can be extracted via manual annotation as well as some well-established automatic techniques such as audio signal processing or visual appearance analysis [378]. Given the many retrieval sources available, it is interesting to study the distinctive properties for each type of text information and what kinds of text sources can most contribute to retrieval. Generally speaking, the text sources processed in multimedia corpora span the following dimensions:

- Automatic speech transcripts (ASRs), which are converted from raw audio signals by speech recognizers
- Closed captioning (CC), which contains accurate spoken text written by a person, but usually no time markers for individual words
- Video optical character recognition (VOCR) extracted from the text visible on the screen
- Production metadata such as titles, tags, and published descriptions of the visual documents (e.g., surrounding text on Web pages)

4.3 Query Example-Based Search Ranking

Query example-based search, often called query by example (QBE), aims to use query example image/video data (e.g., video clips and keyframes), given by the user on input, to find visual documents in the database that are most visually, semantically, or perceptually similar to the query examples. The setting of using query examples is very similar to the traditional content-based visual retrieval (CBVR), where a user is required to provide a visual example [87]. The typical query-by-example (QBE) systems are often built based on a vector space model in which both documents and queries are represented by a set of visual features, and the similarity between two documents is measured through a distance metric between their feature vectors. In the remainder of this section, we discuss these two intrinsic elements in QBE systems, i.e., visual features and distance metrics.

4.3.1 Low-Level Visual Features

As stated earlier, QBE systems rely on multiple visual features to describe the content of visual documents. These features can be categorized into three types according to the pixels used: *global*, *region*, and *local features*. Global features are extracted over the entire image or subimage based on grid partition; regional features are computed based on the results of image segmentation, which attempts to segment the image into different homogenous regions or objects; and local features focus on robust descriptors invariant to scale and orientation based on local maxima.

4.3.1.1 *Global Feature*

In published research on the subject, there are three main types of (low-level) visual features that have been applied: color-based features, texture-based features, and shape-based features [378].

Color has been an active area of research in image retrieval, more than in any other branch of computer vision [138]. Color-based features have also proven to be the most effective features in TRECVID evaluation video search tasks [255]. This is because color features maintain strong cues that capture human perception in a low dimensional space, and they can be generated with less computational effort than other advanced features. Most of them are independent of variations of view and resolution, and thus they possess the power to locate target images robustly [138,378].

The simplest representation of color-based features is the *color histogram*, where each component in the color histogram is the percentage of pixels that are most similar to the represented color in the underlying color space [118,321]. Another type of color-based image feature is called *color moment*, which computes only the first two or three central moments of color distributions in the image [323,330], with other information discarded. The aim is to create a compact and effective representation in image retrieval. Other than these independent color representations, Pass *et al.* [278] developed color coherence histograms (CCHs) to address the matching problems of standard color histograms. They include both spatial information along with color density information in a single representation. Other color-based features include color coherence, color correlogram, and so on.

Texture-based features aim to capture the visual characteristics of homogeneous regions that do not come from the presence of a single color or intensity [322]. These regions may have unique visual patterns or spatial arrangements of pixels, and the gray levels or color features in a region may not sufficiently describe them. The basic texture features include Tamura, multi-resolution simultaneous auto-regressive model (MRSAR), Gabor filter, and wavelet transform [124,320].

To capture the information of object shapes, a huge variety of shape-based features have been proposed and evaluated [68,215,254,395]. Shape features can be either generated from boundary-based approaches that use only the outer contour of the shape segments or generated from region-based approaches that consider the entire shape regions [298]. Typical shape features include normalized inertia [62], moment invariants, Fourier descriptors [124], and so on.

Using global features, an image can be represented by a single vector corresponding to a unimodality or a set of vectors and weights corresponding to multimodal features and their importance.

4.3.1.2 *Region Features*

The region features are similar to global features except that they are computed over a local region with homogeneous texture rather than the whole image. Therefore, an image is often segmented into several regions and represented as a set of visual feature vectors, each of which represents one homogenous region. The underlying motivation of region-based image representation is that many objects such as "cat," "tiger," and "plane" usually appear at a small portion of image. If a satisfying segmentation could be achieved, i.e., each object could be segmented as a homogenous and distinctive region, region-based representation would be very useful. The most widely used features for describing a region include color moment [62], color correlogram [121], wavelet transform texture, and normalized inertia [62].

4.3.1.3 *Local Features*

Local invariants such as salient points from which descriptors are derived, traditionally used for stereo matching and object recognition, are being used in image similarity. For example, the algorithm proposed by Lowe [237] constructs a scale-space pyramid using difference-of-Gaussian (DoG) filters and finds the local 3D maxima (i.e., salient point) on the pyramid.

A robust scale-invariant feature transform (SIFT) descriptor is computed for each point. An image is thus represented by a set of salient points and 128 dimensional SIFT features, or a histogram of code words built on a large visual vocabulary [318].

4.3.2 **Distance Metrics**

The other intrinsic element of QBE is the distance metric between query examples and indexed visual documents. Therefore, a large number of distance metrics have been proposed and tested in past research. In the rest of this section, we discuss several common distance metrics under the assumption that only one query image is available.

Let $f_q(i)$ denote the i-th feature of the query example and $f_c(i)$ denote the i-th feature of the indexed visual document to be compared, where $i = 1, \ldots, M$. The most widely adopted similarity is computed based on Minkowski-form distance, defined by

$$\mathbf{D}_{L_p}(\mathbf{I}_q, \mathbf{I}_c) = \left\{ \sum_{i=1}^{M} |f_q(i) - f_c(i)|^p \right\}^{1/p}. \tag{4.1}$$

For $p = 2$, this yields the Euclidean distance. The histogram intersection is a special case of L1 distance, defined as

$$\mathbf{D}_{HI}(\mathbf{I}_q, \mathbf{I}_c) = \frac{\sum_{i=1}^{M} \min(f_q(i), f_c(i))}{\sum_{i=1}^{M} f_c(i)}. \tag{4.2}$$

It has been shown that histogram intersection is fairly sensitive to the changes of image resolution, occlusion, and viewing point [124]. A distance robust to noise is the Jeffery distance (JD), which is based on the Kullback-Leibler (KL) divergence given by

$$\mathbf{D}_{KL}(\mathbf{I}_q, \mathbf{I}_c) = \sum_{i=1}^{M} f_q(i) \log \frac{f_q(i)}{f_c(i)}. \tag{4.3}$$

Although it is often intuited as a distance metric, the KL divergence is not a true metric since it is not symmetric.

The JD is defined as

$$\mathbf{D}_{JD}(\mathbf{I}_q, \mathbf{I}_c) = \sum_{i=1}^{M} \left\{ f_q(i) \log \frac{f_q(i)}{m_i} + f_c(i) \log \frac{f_c(i)}{m_i} \right\}, \tag{4.4}$$

where $m_i = \frac{f_q(i) + f_c(i)}{2}$. In contrast to KL divergence, JD is symmetric and numerically stable in comparing two empirical distributions.

Hausdorff distance [87] is another matching method that is symmetrized by further computing the distance with image $\mathbf{I}_q$ and $\mathbf{I}_c$ reversed and choosing the larger one of the two distances

$$\mathbf{D}_H(\mathbf{I}_q, \mathbf{I}_c) = \max(\max_{i} \min_{j} d(f_q(i), f_c(j)), \ \max_{j} \min_{i} d(f_c(j), f_q(i))), \tag{4.5}$$

where $d(,)$ can be any form of distance such as L1 and L2 distances. The Mahalanobis distance metric deals with the case that each dimension of the vector is dependent and has different importance, given by

$$\mathbf{D}_M(\mathbf{I}_q, \mathbf{I}_c) = \sqrt{(\mathbf{f}_q - \mathbf{f}_c)^T \mathbf{C}^{-1} (\mathbf{f}_q - \mathbf{f}_c)}, \tag{4.6}$$

where $\mathbf{C}$ is the covariance matrix of the feature vectors. The preceding distance measures are all derived from a linear feature space that has been noted as the main challenge in measuring perceptual or semantic image distance.

Manifold ranking replaces traditional Euclidean distance using the geodesic distance in a nonlinear manifold [408]. The similarity is oftenestimated based on a distance measure $d(,)$ and a positive radius parameter σ along a manifold

$$\mathbf{D}_{MR}(\mathbf{I}_q, \mathbf{I}_c) = \exp\left\{-\frac{d(\mathbf{I}_q, \mathbf{I}_c)}{\sigma}\right\}, \qquad (4.7)$$

where L1 distance is usually selected for $d(,)$.

In a more general situation, an image $\mathbf{I}$ is represented by a set of vectors and weights. Each vector (also referred to as *distribution*) corresponds to a specific region or modality, and the weight indicates the significance of associating this vector to the others. The earth mover's distance (EMD) represents a soft matching scheme for features in the form of a set of vectors [391]. The EMD "lifts" the distance from individual features to full distributions. The EMD distance is given by

$$\mathbf{D}_{EMD}(\mathbf{I}_q, \mathbf{I}_c) = \frac{\sum_{i=1}^{M^0} \sum_{j=1}^{M^1} s_{ij} d(f_q(i), f_c(j))}{\sum_{i=1}^{M^0} \sum_{j=1}^{M^1} s_{ij}}, \qquad (4.8)$$

where $d(,)$ is the ground distance between two vectors that can be defined in diverse ways depending on the system, s_{ij} minimizes the value of Eq. (4.8) subject to the following constraints:

$$s_{ij} \geq 0, 1 \leq i \leq M^0, 1 \leq j \leq M^1$$

$$\sum_{j=1}^{M^0} s_{ij} \leq \omega_i^0, 1 \leq i \leq M^0$$

$$\sum_{i=1}^{M^1} s_{ij} \leq \omega_j^0, 1 \leq j \leq M^1 \qquad (4.9)$$

$$\sum_{i=1}^{M^0}\sum_{j=1}^{M^1} s_{ij} = \min\left(\sum_{i=1}^{M^0} \omega_i^0, \sum_{j=1}^{M^1} \omega_j^1\right).$$

When ω_i^0 and ω_j^1 are probabilities, EMD is equivalent to the Mallows distance [87]. Another matching-based distance is the integrated region matching (IRM) distance [87]. The IRM distance uses the most similar highest priority (MSHP) principle to match different modalities or regions. The weights s_{ij} are subject to the same constraints as in the Mallows distance, except that $d(,)$ is not computed by minimization. Another way to perform the adjustment of weights ω_i in image similarity is relevance feedback, which captures the user's precise needs through iterative feedback and query refinement. The goal of relevance feedback is to find the appropriate weights to model the user's information need [392]. The weights are classified into *intra-* and *inter-* weights. The intra-weights represent the different contributions of the components within a single vector (i.e., region or modality), whereas the inter-weights represent the contributions of different vectors. Intuitively, the intra-weights are decided based on the variance of the same vector components in the relevant feedback examples, whereas the inter-weights are directly updated according to user feedback in terms of the similarity based on each vector. For the comparison among these distance metrics, refer to [87] for more details.

In the context of an image being represented by a set of salient points and their corresponding local descriptors, image similarity is computed based on the Euclidean distance between each pair of salient points [237]. An alternative method is representing each image into a bag of code words that are obtained through the unsupervised learning of the local appearance [120]. A large vocabulary of code words is built by clustering a large amount of local features, and then the distribution of these code words is obtained by counting all the points or patches within an image. Since the image is described by a set of distributions, histogram intersection and EMD, defined in Eq. (4.2) and Eq. (4.8) can be employed to compute the similarity.

4.4 Concept-Based Search Ranking

For visual search by QBE, the visual features are used to find visual documents in the database that are most similar to the query image. A drawback, however, is that these low-level visual features are often too restricted to describe visual documents on a conceptual or semantic level, which constitutes the so-called *semantic gap* problem.

To alleviate such a problem, visual search with a set of high-level concept detectors has attracted increasing attention in recent years [201,222,230,234,265,325,363]. The basic idea of concept-based methods is to utilize the results from concept detection to aid search, thereby leveraging human annotation on a finite concept lexicon to help answer infinite search queries. As a fundamental point, the rich set of predefined concepts and their corresponding training and testing samples available in the community have made it possible to explore the semantic description of a query in a large concept space. For example, 101 concepts are defined in MediaMill [324], 374 in LSCOM-Light [380], 834 in LSCOM [262], 17,624 in ImageNet [96], and so on. Except for the concept detectors, the key factor of the concept-based search is how to recognize related concepts and search with the recognized concepts.

4.4.1 Query-Concept Mapping

Intuitively, if queries can be automatically mapped to related concepts, search performance will benefit significantly. For example, the "face" concept can benefit people-related queries, and the "sky" concept can also be high-weighted for outdoor-related queries. Motivated by these observations, the problem of recognizing related concepts, also called "query-concept mapping," has been the focus of many researchers. For example, Kennedy *et al.* [201] mine the top-ranked and bottom-ranked search results to discover related concepts by measuring mutual information. The basic idea is that if a concept has high mutual information with the top-ranked results and low mutual information with the bottom-ranked results, it will be considered as a related concept. Avoiding the ambiguity problem, Li and Liu *et al.* leverage a few query examples to find related concepts [222,230]; specifically, Li *et al.* [222] use the tf-idf-like scheme, and Liu *et al.* [230] explore mutual information measurement. Both methods are motivated by the information-theoretic point of view, that is, the more query examples bear more information of a concept, the more the concept will be related to the corresponding query.

However, these methods leverage only the visual information extracted from either the top-ranked results or the query examples. The other types of information, such as text, are entirely neglected. To solve this problem, Mei *et al.* use WordNet to compute the lexical similarity between the textual query and the descriptions for each concept detector [255]. Wang *et al.* linearly combine the text and visual information extracted from the text query and visual examples, respectively [363].

Nevertheless, most practical text queries are very short, often represented by one or two words or phrases, from which it is difficult to obtain robust concept-relatedness information. In addition, the problem of ambiguity also cannot be avoided, such as when the query "jaguar" may be related to both an "animal" and a "car," but the two concepts have little relation to each other.

To address this problem, Liu *et al.* first fed the text query to a commercial visual Web search engine and collected the visual documents along with the associated text; to avoid the ambiguity problem, query examples were utilized to filter the Web results, and the cleaner "Web examples" could then be obtained. By combining the filtered visual Web examples and associated text, the following two methods are explored to detect the related concepts [232]:

- Using pretrained concept detectors over Web examples.

The detectors are trained by SVM over three visual features: color moments on a 5-by-5 grid, an edge distribution histogram, and wavelet textures. The confidence scores of the three SVM models over each visual document are then averaged to generate the final concept detection confidence. The details of the features and concept detection can be found in [255], in which a set of concept detectors are built mainly based on the low-level visual features and SVM for "high-level feature detection task."

- Mining the surrounding text of Web examples.

The standard stemming and stopword removal [255] are first performed as a pre-process; then J terms with the highest frequency are selected to form a keyword set K and match the concepts in the lexicon. Here Google Distance (GD) [72] is adopted to measure two textual words:

$$GD(\omega_i, \omega_j) = \frac{\max(\log f(\omega_i), \log f(\omega_j)) - \log f(\omega_i, \omega_j)}{\log G - \min(\log f(\omega_i), \log f(\omega_j))}, \qquad (4.10)$$

where $f(\omega_i)$ and $f(\omega_j)$ are the numbers of images containing words ω_i and ω_j, respectively, and $f(\omega_i, \omega_j)$ is the number of images containing both ω_i and ω_j. These numbers can be obtained by performing a search of textual words on the Google image search engine [141]. G is the total number of images indexed in the Google search engine. The operation *log* is used to avoid an extremely large value. We can see that GD is a measure of semantic interrelatedness derived from the number of hits returned by the Google search engine for a given set of keywords. Keywords with the same or similar meanings in a natural language sense tend to be "close" in the units of GD, whereas the words with dissimilar meanings tend to be separated far away from each other. If the two search terms never occur together on the same Web page but do occur separately, the GD between them is infinite. If both terms always occur together, their GD is zero.

By combining these two methods, the relatedness of the j concept to a given query, i.e., y_j, is given by:

$$y_j = \lambda \frac{\sum_{k=1}^{K} Cf(e_k, c_j)}{K} + (1 - \lambda) \frac{\sum_{i=1}^{J} GD(\omega_i, c_j)}{J}, \qquad (4.11)$$

where $Cf(e_k, c_j)$ is the confidence score of the concept c_j of the Web example e_k obtained from the pretrained concept detectors. λ is a parameter to tune the contribution of concept detectors and surrounding text. Empirically, a relatively lower λ would be more suitable for the concept detector with limited performance.

4.4.2 Search with Related Concepts

Researchers have proven that when the number of semantic concepts is relatively large, even if the accuracy of the concept detectors is low, semantic concepts can still significantly improve the accuracy of the search results [232,325].

The straightforward way is to represent the query (with the query examples) as well as visual documents as multiple related concepts and perform the search with text-based technologies. For example, Li *et al.* have shown that when provided with a visual query example, searching through concept space is a good supplemental procedure in the text and low-level feature spaces [222,235]. They first built a concept space (with 311 concepts) over the whole dataset, where each document was associated with multiple relevant concepts (called *visual terms*). Given a query, they employed concept detectors over the query example to obtain the presence of concepts, and then they adopted c-tf-idf, a tf-idf like scheme to measure the usefulness of the concepts to the query. The c-tf-idf is used in a traditional text-based search pipeline, e.g., a vector model or a language model, to measure the relevance between the given query and a document. These concept-based search results are finally combined with those from other modalities (e.g., text and visual) in a linear way. Liu *et al.* propose a multi-graph-based query independent learning for video search by using a set of attributional features and relational features based on the LSCOM-Lite lexicon (composed of 39 concepts) [234,235]. The attributional features are generated using detection scores from concept detectors, whereas relational features indicate the relationship between query and video shots by viewing videos shots as visual documents and the concepts as visual terms, such as "visual TFIDF," "visual BM25," and "visual query term distribution." By using these concept-based features, they propose a query-independent learning framework for video search. Under this framework, various machine learning technologies can be explored for visual search.

Mei *et al.* first obtained confidence scores from those concept detectors and treated them as the weights for the corresponding concepts (i.e., hidden text), further used them in a text alike search (e.g., inverted index based on term and document frequency) or as a feature vector in a concept space for searching via QBE [255]. Ngo *et al.* present a concept-driven multimodality fusion approach in their automatic video search system [266]. They first generated a set of concepts for a given query. To obtain the optimal weight for combining the search results based on each concept, they conducted a simulated search evaluation, in which a concept is treated as a simulated query associated with concepts and 10 randomly chosen positive visual samples. Then, the unimodal search performance for the concept and its related visual samples against a training dataset were manually labeled. With the simulated search evaluation, given a testing query, they estimated the concept-based fusion weights by jointly considering query-concept relatedness and the simulated search performance of all concepts.

4.5 Visual Search Reranking

Due to the great success of text search, most popular image and video search engines, such as Google [141], Yahoo! [377], and Bing [32], build on text search techniques by using text associated with visual content, such as the title, description, user-provided tags, and surrounding text of the visual content. However, this kind of visual search approach has proven unsatisfying, since it often entirely ignores the visual content as a ranking signal [57,87,164,296].

To address this issue, search reranking has received increasing attention in recent years [164,165,201,230,264,284,304,343,346,379]. It is defined as reordering visual documents based on multimodal cues to improve search performance. The documents might be images or video shots. The research on visual search reranking has proceeded along four paradigms from the perspective of the knowledge exploited: (1) *self-reranking*, which mainly focuses on detecting relevant patterns (recurrent or dominant patterns) from the initial search results without any external knowledge; (2) *example-based reranking*, in which the query examples are provided by users so that the relevant patterns can be discovered from these examples; (3) *crowd reranking*, which mines relevant patterns from the crowdsourcing knowledge available on the Web, e.g., the multiple image/video search engines or sites or user-contributed online encyclopedias like Wikipedia [368]; and (4) *interactive reranking*, which involves user interaction to guide the reranking process. Figure 4.2 illustrates the four paradigms for visual search reranking.

4.5.1 First Paradigm: Self-Reranking

The topmost flowchart of Figure 4.2 shows the first paradigm, self-reranking. In this paradigm, the reranking objective is to discover recurrent patterns from the initial ranked list that can provide relevant clues for reranking. Although quite "noisy" due to the unsatisfying text-only search performance, the initial search results, especially the top-ranked documents, can be regarded as the main resource for mining some relevant clues, since the analysis on clickthrough data from a very large search engine log shows that users are usually interested in the top-ranked portion of a set of search results [337].

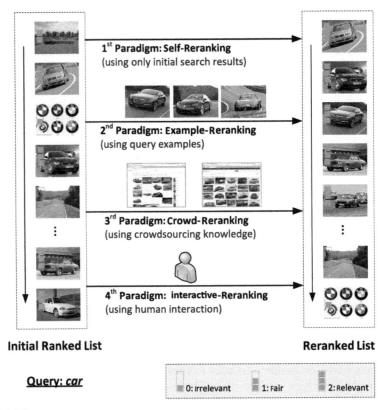

Initial Ranked List

Reranked List

Query: *car*

0: Irrelevant   1: Fair   2: Relevant

FIGURE 4.2

The four paradigms for visual search reranking.

Generally, the key problem in self-reranking is finding a way to mine the relevant patterns from the noisy initial ranked list and to treat these documents for reranking. In many cases, we can assume that the top-ranked documents are the few relevant (called *pseudo relevant*) documents that can be viewed as "positive." Those pseudo-relevant samples can be further used in any learning method to classify the remaining documents into relevant or irrelevant classes, be used as query examples to compute the distance to the remaining documents, or be the feedback to the system for query term re-weighting or reformulation. For example, Hsu *et al.* formulate the reranking process as a random walk over a context graph, where video stories are nodes and the edges between them are weighted by multimodal similarities [164]. Zisserman *et al.* first performed the visual clustering on initial returned images by probabilistic latent semantic analysis (pLSA), learning the visual object category, and then reranking the images according to the distance to the learned categories [284].

Most existing self-reranking methods mainly exploit the visual cues from initial search results. In addition to the commonly employed visual information, other

Search results for query "jaguar."

FIGURE 4.3

Examples of top 30 ranked results from a commercial Web image search engine.

modalities associated with the documents, such as text (e.g., caption, keywords, and surrounding text), audio (e.g., speech and music in video shots), and linkage in the Web pages are also worth taking into account for judging the relevance. To address this issue, co-reranking and circular reranking have recently been proposed to leverage multimodal cues via mutual reinforcement [384,385]. Different from existing techniques, the reranking procedure encourages interaction among modalities to seek consensus that is useful for reranking.

Although self-reranking relies little on external knowledge, it cannot deal with the ambiguity problem that is derived from the text queries. Taking the query "jaguar" as an example, the search system cannot determine what the user is really searching for, whether it is an animal or a car. As illustrated in Figure 4.3, results with different meanings but all related to "jaguar" can be found in the top-ranked results of "jaguar." To address this problem, other paradigms leverage some auxiliary knowledge, aiming to better understand the query.

4.5.2 Second Paradigm: Example-Based Reranking

The second paradigm, example-based reranking, leverages a few query examples to mine the relevant information. The search performance can be improved due to relevant information derived from these query examples.

There are many ways to use these query examples. The most common way is QBE-like approaches, which aim to find and rank documents higher that are visually similar to the query examples [348]. Another popular way is to use these query examples to mine relevant semantics, often represented by a set of high-level concepts. The motivation is similar to the concept-based search. If the documents have correlated semantics with query examples, they will be ranked higher than the others.

For example, a search query like "Find shots of bridge" could be handled by searching against the transcript to find occurrences of "bridge," but also by giving positive weight to the shots that are positive for the concepts of "bridge," "water," and "river" (since "bridge," "water," and "river" are highly correlated concepts) and negative for "indoor." The key problems here are how to select relevant concepts from a predefined lexicon with hundreds of concepts and how to leverage these concept detectors for reranking. The first problem is often called *query-concept mapping*, which is explained in Section 4.4.1. For the second problem, Kennedy *et al.* leveraged a large pool of 374 concept detectors for unsupervised search reranking [201]. Each document in the database was represented by a vector of concept confidence scores by running the 374 concept detectors. They form a feature vector for each document consisting of the related concept confidence scores and train a SVM model based on the pseudo positive and negative samples from the initial search results. The SVM testing results are finally combined with the initial ranking scores on average to rerank the documents. Liu *et al.* [232] formulated reranking as an optimization problem in which a ranked list is globally optimal only if any arbitrary two documents in the list are correctly ranked in terms of relevance. To find the optimal ranked list, they convert the individual documents to document pairs, each represented as an ordinal relation. Then they detect the optimal document pairs that can maximally preserve the initial rank order while simultaneously keeping consistency with the auxiliary knowledge represented by the mined concept relatedness.

4.5.3 Third Paradigm: Crowd Reranking

Considering that the approaches in the second paradigm often suffer from the limitation of lack of query examples, the third paradigm, crowd reranking, aims to leverage crowdsourcing knowledge collected from multiple search engines [228]. This idea was inspired by the following two observations: (1) Different search engines have different search results, since they might have different data sources and metadata for indexing, as well as different search and filtering methods for ranking. Using search results from different engines can inform and complement the relevant visual information in a single engine. Thus, reranking performance can be significantly improved due to the richer knowledge involved. (2) Although a single search engine cannot always have enough cues for reranking, it is reasonable to assume that across the search results from multiple engines there exist common visual patterns relevant to a given query. Therefore, the basis of crowd reranking is then to find the representative visual patterns as well as their relations in multiple search results.

First, a textual query is fed into multiple search engines to obtain lists of initial search results. Then the representative visual words are constructed based on the local image patches from these search results. Two visual patterns are explicitly detected from the visual words through a graph propagation process: *salient* and *concurrent patterns*. The former pattern indicates the importance of each visual word; the latter expresses the interdependence among those visual words. Intuitively, a visual word with a strong salient pattern for a given query indicates that other concurring words (i.e., with strong concurrent patterns) would be prioritized. The reranking is then formalized as an optimization problem on the basis of the mined visual patterns and the initial ranked list. The objective is to maximize the consistence $Cons(\mathbf{r}, \mathcal{K})$ between the learned knowledge (i.e., visual patterns) $\mathcal{K}$ and the reranked list $\mathbf{r}$ as well as minimizing the disagreement $Dist(\mathbf{r_0}, \mathbf{r})$ between the initial ranked list $\mathbf{r_0}$ and the reranked list $\mathbf{r}$ as follows:

$$\mathbf{r}^* = \arg \min_{\mathbf{r}} \{Dist(\mathbf{r}_0, \mathbf{r}) - \lambda Cons(\mathbf{r}, \mathcal{K})\}, \tag{4.12}$$

where λ tunes the contribution of the learned knowledge $\mathcal{K}$ to the reranked list. The distance function could be formalized as either pointwise or pairwise distance, whereas the consistence is defined as the cosine similarity between a document and the mined visual patterns.

4.5.4 Fourth Paradigm: Interactive Reranking

Although automatic reranking methods have improved over the initial search results, visual search systems with a human user in the loop have consistently outperformed fully automatic search systems. This has been validated every year through a search performance evaluation in the TRECVID video search evaluation forum [350], since human beings can provide more concise information to guide the ranking procedure.

In the interactive reranking procedure, a user is required to either issue additional queries or annotate a part of the initial results, whether they are relevant or not. Such a setting is very similar to the traditional *relevance feedback*, where users are required to annotate a subset of initial search results, whether each of them is relevant or not at each iteration [4,347,392,412]. The works in [27,101,166,192,347] leverage relevance feedback to identify the relevant clusters for improving browsing efficiency. They first employ clustering techniques such as Bregman bubble clustering (BBC) [101,166] and latent Dirichlet allocation (LDA) [27] to cluster the top image search results, and then they ask users to label the relevance of those clusters. The images within the clusters are then ranked according to their similarities to the cluster centers. Cui *et al.* developed a real-time search reranking system [80,81], which enables users to first indicate a query image from the initial search results and then classify the query image into one of several predefined categories. The feature weights for grouping together a visual similarity within each category are learned by minimizing a rank loss for all query images in a training set through RankBoost.

The MediaMill system introduces the concept of video threads to visualize the reranked video search results [324]. A *thread* is a linked sequence of shots in specific order types, including query result thread, visual thread, semantic thread, top-rank thread, textual thread, and time thread. The system further supports two models for displaying threads: CrossBrowser and RotorBrowser. The former is limited to show only two fixed threads (the query result and time threads), whereas the latter shows all possible relevant threads for each retrieved shot to users. Users can browse along any thread that catches their interest.

Different from conventional sketch- or shape-based systems, which retrieve images with similar sketch or shape [53,113,383], the search-by-color-map system enables users to indicate how their preferred colors are spatially distributed in the desired image by scribbling a few color strokes or dragging an image and highlighting a few regions of interest in an intuitive way [364]. The concept-based interactive visual search system leverages human interaction to reformulate a new query, leading to a better search performance based on the spatial layout of concepts [376,397]. Given a textual query, CuZero, developed by Columbia University, is able to automatically discover relevant visual concepts in real time and allows users to navigate seamlessly in the concept space at will [397]. The search results are then reranked according to the arbitrary permutations of multiple concepts given by users.

4.6 Learning and Search Ranking

4.6.1 Ranking by Classification

Most current approaches to visual search ranking and reranking take *classification performance* as the optimization objective, in which the ranking and reranking is formulated as a binary classification problem to determine whether or not a visual document is relevant and then increase the ranking order of the relevant documents.

According to whether unlabeled data are utilized in the training stage or not, these methods can be classified into *inductive* and *transductive* ones. The goal of an *inductive* method is to create a classifier that separates the relevant and irrelevant images and generalizes well on unseen examples. For instance, Tong *et al.* [328] first computed a large number of highly selective features then used boosting to learn a classification function in this feature space. Similar in spirit, the relevance feedback method proposed in [403] trains a SVM model from labeled examples, hoping to obtain a small generalization error by maximizing the margin between the two classes of images. To speed up the convergence to the target concept, active learning methods are also utilized to select the most informative images that will be presented to and marked by the user. For example, the support vector machine active learning algorithm (SVM$_{active}$) proposed by Tong *et al.* [328] selects the points near the SVM boundary so as to maximally shrink the size of the version space. Another active learning scheme, the maximizing expected generalization algorithm (MEGA) [216], judiciously selects samples in each round and uses positive examples to learn the target concept while using negative examples to bound the uncertain region. One major problem with inductive methods is the insufficiency of labeled examples, which might bring great degradation to the performance of the trained classifier.

On the other hand, *transductive* methods aim to accurately predict the relevance of unlabeled images that are attainable during the training stage. For example, the discriminant-EM (DEM) algorithm proposed by Wu *et al.* [373] makes use of unlabeled data to construct a generative model, which will be used to measure relevance between the query and database images. However, as pointed out in [373], if the components of data distribution are mixed up, which is often the case in CBIR, the performance of DEM will be compromised. Despite the immaturity of transductive methods, we see their great potential, since they provide a way to solve the small sample size problem by utilizing unlabeled data to make up for the insufficiency of labeled data. He *et al.* [151] propose a transductive learning framework called *manifold-ranking-based image retrieval* (MRBIR), which is initially inspired by a manifold-ranking algorithm [408,409]. In MRBIR, relevance between the query and database images is evaluated by exploring the relationship of all the data points in the feature space, which addresses the limitation of present similarity metrics based on pair-wise distance. However, manifold ranking has its own drawbacks in handling large-scale data sets: it has cost in both graph construction and ranking computation stages, which significantly limits its applicability to very large datasets. Xu *et al.* [375] extend the original manifold ranking algorithm and propose a new framework named *efficient manifold ranking* (EMR). Specifically, an anchor graph instead of the traditional k-nearest neighbor graph is built on the dataset, and a new form of adjacency matrix is utilized to speed up the ranking computation.

A similar idea to transductive learning has been implemented for visual search reranking [164,169,181,182,225].

4.6.2 Classification vs. Ranking

Although some systems of ranking by classification have obtained a high search performance, it is known that an optimal classification performance cannot guarantee an optimal search performance [393]. In this section, we present the relationship between *classification* and *ranking* models.

Suppose that we have a hypothesis space with the two hypothesis functions, h_1 and h_2. The two hypotheses predict a ranking for a query over a document corpus. x is the indicator of document relevance ($h_i(q) = 1$: relevant, 0: irrelevant) to the query q. Using the example shown in Tables 4.1 and 4.2, we can demonstrate that models that optimize for *classification* performance are not directly concerned with *ranking*, which is often measured by average precision (AP) [350].

When we learn the models that optimize for the classification performance (such as "accuracy"), the objective is to find a threshold such that documents scoring higher than the threshold can be classified as relevant and documents scoring lower as

Table 4.1   Classification and reranking.

Order		1	2	3	4	5	6	7	8	9	10
x	$h_1(q)$	0	0	1	1	1	1	1	1	0	0
	$h_2(q)$	1	1	1	0	0	0	1	1	1	0

Table 4.2   Performance comparison between classification and ranking.

Hypothesis	Optimal Accuracy	AP	Number of Pairs Correctly Ranked
$h_1(q)$	**0.80**	0.59	12
$h_2(q)$	0.70	**0.81**	**15**

irrelevant. Specifically, with $h_1(q)$, a threshold between the documents 8 and 9 gives two errors (documents 1–2 incorrectly classified as relevant), yielding an accuracy of 0.80. Similarly, with $h_2(q)$, a threshold between documents 3 and 4 gives three errors (i.e., documents 7–9 are incorrectly classified as relevant), yielding an accuracy of 0.70. Therefore, a learning method that optimizes for classification performance would choose h_1, since it results in a higher level of accuracy. However, this will lead to a suboptimal ranking measured by the AP scores and the number of pairs correctly ranked. In other words, conventional approaches to ranking by classification fail to provide a global optimal ranking list.

4.6.3 Learning to Rank

To address the issues of *ranking by classification*, *learning to rank* has attracted much attention in recent years in computer vision and visual search field. The main task is to learn the ranking model from the ranking orders of the documents. The objective is to automatically create a ranking model by using labeled training data and machine learning techniques. It is mostly studied in the setting of supervised learning, which typically includes a *learning* stage followed by a *ranking* stage [48,54]. In the learning stage, a ranking function is built using the training samples with relevance degrees or ranking orders, whereas in the ranking stage, the documents are ranked according to the relevance obtained by the ranking function. When applied to visual search, the ranking order represents the relevance degree of the visual documents (i.e., images or video shots) with respect to the given query.

Generally, existing methods for learning to rank fall into three dimensions: *pointwise*, *pairwise*, and *listwise* learning. For a given query and a set of retrieved documents, *pointwise learning* tries to directly estimate the relevance label for each query-document pair. For example, Prank [77] aimed to find a rank-prediction rule that assigns each sample a rank that is as close as possible to the sample's true rank. Although one may show that these approaches are consistent for a variety of performance measures [76], they ignore relative information within collections of documents.

Pairwise learning, as proposed by [48,156,185], takes the relative nature of the scores into account by comparing pairs of documents. For example, ranking SVM is such a method that reduces ranking to classification on document pairs. Pairwise learning approaches ensure that we obtain the correct order of documents, even in the case when we may not be able to obtain a good estimate of the ratings directly [76]. Content-aware ranking is proposed to simultaneously leverage the textual and visual information in the ranking learning process [136]. It is formulated based on large margin structured output learning by modeling the visual information into a regularization term. The direct optimization of the learning problem is nearly infeasible, since the number of constraints is huge. The efficient cutting plane algorithm is adopted to learn the model by iteratively adding the most violated constraints.

Finally, *listwise learning*, as proposed by [54,341,374], treats the ranking in its totality. In learning, it takes ranked lists as instances and trains a ranking function through the minimization of a listwise loss function defined on the predicted list and the ground truth list [374]. Each of those dimensions focuses on a different aspect of the dataset while largely ignoring others. Recently, Moon *et al.* proposed a new learning-to-rank algorithm, IntervalRank, by using isotonic regression to balance the tradeoff between the three dimensions [259].

It is observed that most of these methods for learning to rank are based on the assumption that a large collection of "labeled" data (training samples) is available in learning stage. However, the labeled data are usually too expensive to obtain, since users are reluctant to provide enough query examples (which can be regarded as "labeled" data) while searching. To alleviate the problem of lacking labeled data, it is desired to leverage the vast amount of "unlabeled" data (i.e., all the documents to be searched). For this purpose, a graph-based semisupervised learning-to-rank method (GLRank) was proposed for visual search [229]. Specifically, the query examples are first combined with the randomly selected samples to form the labeled pairs and then form the unlabeled pairs with all the samples to be searched. Second, a relation graph is constructed in which sample pairs, instead of the individual samples, are used as vertices. Each vertex represents the relevance relation of a pair in a semantic space, which is defined by the vector of confidence scores of concept detectors [222,235,342]. Then the relevance relationships are propagated from the labeled pairs to the unlabeled pairs. When all the unlabeled pairs receive the propagated relevance relation, a round-robin criterion is explored to obtain the final ranking list. Clearly, the GLRank belongs to pairwise learning.

In recent years, some approaches to *learning to rerank* have been proposed. For instance, Liu *et al.* claim that the best ranked list cannot be obtained until any two arbitrary documents from the list are correctly ranked in terms of relevance [233]. They first cluster the initial search results. Then they propose to incrementally discover the so-called "pseudo-preference pairs" from the initial search results by considering both the cluster typicality and the local typicality within the cluster. Here, typicality (i.e., the visual representativeness of a visual document with respect to a query) is a higher-level definition than relevance. For example, an image with "boat" may be relevant to the query "find the images with boat" but may not be typical, since the boat object is quite small in the image. The ranking support vector machine (RSVM) is then employed to perform pairwise classification [156]. The documents are finally reranked by predicting the probabilities of the RSVM. In [233], the optimal pairs are identified purely based on the low-level visual features from the initial search results. Later, the authors observed that leveraging concept detectors to associate a set of relevant high-level concepts to each document will improve discovery of optimal pairs [232]. Kang *et al.* [197] proposed exploring multiple pairwise relationships between documents in a learning setting to rerank search results. In particular, a set of pairwise features was utilized to capture various kinds of pairwise relationships, and two machine learned reranking methods were designed to effectively combine these features with a base ranking function: a pairwise comparison method and a pairwise function decomposition method. Jain *et al.* [172] hypothesized that images clicked in response to a query are most relevant to the query, thus reranking the initial search results so as to promote images that are likely to be clicked to the top of the ranked list. The reranking algorithm employs Gaussian process regression to predict the normalized click count for each image and combines it with the initial ranking score.

4.7 Conclusions and Future Challenges

In this chapter we presented an overview of visual search ranking, including three main dimensions: text-based, query example-based, and concept-based search ranking. The related technologies and representative works in each dimension were also introduced. To address the issues of text-based visual search approaches, visual search reranking has received increasing attention in recent years, resulting in introduction of paradigms and techniques on visual search reranking. In addition, as a promising paradigm, learning-based visual search ranking has attracted considerable attention in the literature; we discussed the relationships between learning and ranking problems. Although significant progress in visual search ranking has been made during the past few decades, many emerging topics deserve further investigation and research. We summarize the future challenges here:

- Personalized visual search ranking. Generally speaking, the primary goal of a search system is to understand the user's needs. Rich personal clues mined from search logs and community-based behaviors or mobile devices can be considered to better understand user preference and guide the ranking process. Keeping users in the search loop is another way to perform the human-centered search.
- Efficient visualization tools for visual search ranking. An efficient and user-friendly interaction tool is the key to achieving an efficient search, since it is convenient for users to express their search intent, and visual data are particularly suited for interaction because a user can quickly grasp the vivid visual information and thus judge the relevance at a quick glance.
- Context-aware visual search ranking. When a user is conducting a search task, she actually provides rich context to the search system, e.g., past behaviors in the same session, the browsed Web pages if a search is triggered from browsing behavior, geographic location and time of the user, social network if the user remains signed in, and so on. All these contexts provide valuable cues for contextual search.
- Ranking aided by the crowdsourcing. Crowdsourcing is a popular concept in the so-called Web 2.0 era, indicative of the trend of enabling open community as content creators or knowledge providers. Specifically, crowdsourcing may include the heterogeneous relationship between various entities in a social network, search results from multiple visual search engines available on the Internet, well-organized online knowledge sites such as Wikipedia [368] and Mediapedia [253], and user profiles on mobile devices. All these contexts provide valuable cues for contextual search. Crowdsourcing-aided reranking brings a new challenge to the computer vision community.

Mobile Search Ranking

INTRODUCTION

The wide availability of Internet access on mobile devices, such as phones and personal media players, has allowed users to search and access Web information on the go. According to a recent report from comScore,[1] as of July 2011, there were over 234 million mobile users in the United States, with nearly 50 percent searching on their mobile devices. The availability of continuous fine-grained location information on these devices has enabled mobile local search, which employs user location as a key factor to search for local entities, and has overtaken a significant part of the query volume. Sohn *et al.*'s study [326] found that 38% of mobile information needs are local. This is also evident in recent reports by BIA/Kelsey[2] showing that 30% of all search volume will be local in nature by 2015 as well as in the rising popularity of location-based search applications on mobile devices such as Bing Local, Google Local, Yahoo! Local, and Yelp. A screenshot of Bing Local is shown in Figure 5.1.

The service quality of any mobile local search engine is mainly determined by its ranking function, which formally specifies how to retrieve and rank local entities in response to a user's query. Even though it is similar to general Web search in that they both boil down to a similar problem of relevance/click prediction and result ranking, there are fundamental differences as well as challenges in developing effective ranking functions for mobile local search.

First, the ranking signals in mobile local search are quite different from general Web search. On one hand, Web search handles a wide range of Web objects, particularly Web pages, whereas mobile local search focuses mostly on ranking local entities and businesses (e.g., restaurants). Therefore, special domain knowledge about the ranking objects in mobile local search could be exploited to improve ranking accuracy. For instance, businesses may receive *ratings* and *reviews* from their customers thanks to the Web 2.0 services, which have been shown to be useful signals for ranking businesses [26,402]. On the other hand, local search users generally prefer businesses that are physically close to them; this is particularly critical for mobile users who are on the go and their range of reach might be limited. For example, a user would be more

---

[1] www.comscore.com.
[2] www.biakelsey.com.

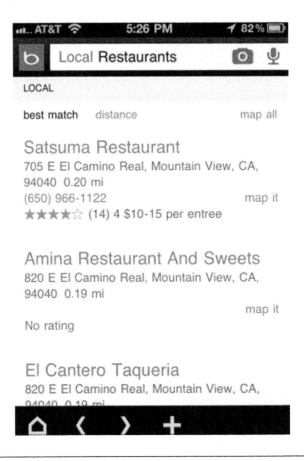

FIGURE 5.1

Sample search result page of Bing Mobile Local.

likely to visit a restaurant within 1 kilometer than another one within 2 kilometers to get breakfast if the two restaurants are similarly good in other aspects. The *distance* between the result business and the user's location has been recognized as an important ranking signal in mobile local searches [132,26,248]. In fact, the customer rating score, the number of reviews, and the distance are all shown explicitly to users in the search result user interface of mobile local search, as shown in Figure 5.1, and therefore play an important role in influencing the user's click decision. Properly studying and modeling how this information affects user click behavior is arguably the key to improving ranking accuracy.

In spite of the recognition of these new ranking signals, early studies have mostly treated them as a black box to extract very basic features (e.g., raw rating scores and distance values) without going inside the signals to study how exactly they affect the relevance or click rate of a business. For example, it is unclear how a business's click rate changes with its rating score. Does a lower rating score necessarily lead to a lower click rate? In the aforementioned restaurant example, a 1 kilometer difference in distances may lead to significantly different click rates of two restaurants, but would the same 1 kilometer distance difference also cause similar click rate differences for another two restaurants that are further away from the user's location, say, 10 and 11 kilometers instead of 1 and 2 kilometers away?

It is critical to understand the underlying behaviors and heuristics of a ranking signal, which would guide us to design more effective ranking features; this has been demonstrated extensively in the development of retrieval functions for general Web search [290,317,119,78,247]. For example, the term *frequency signal*, which assigns a higher score to a document if it contains more occurrences of the query term, should be normalized to prevent the contribution of repeated occurrences from growing too large due to the burstiness phenomenon [290,119], and the term *frequency signal* should also be normalized by document length, since long documents tend to use the same terms repeatedly [290,317,119]. All effective retrieval models in Web searches have implemented these heuristics [119], and previous work has also shown that a retrieval function tends to work poorly if any desirable retrieval heuristic is violated [119,247].

Inspired by the successes and lessons from the development of retrieval models, Lv *et al.* [246] attempted to explore the ranking heuristics in mobile local search and tried to understand how exactly a ranking signal in mobile local search is related to the click rate or relevance of a business. They followed a data-driven methodology to study the behavior of these ranking signals in mobile local search using a large-scale query log; their findings reveal interesting heuristics that can be used to guide the exploitation of different signals. For example, users often take the *mean* value of a signal (e.g., rating) from the business result list as a "pivot" score and tend to demonstrate different click behaviors on businesses with lower and higher signal values than the pivot. The click rate of a business generally is *sublinearly* decreasing with its distance to the user, and so on. Inspired by the understanding of these heuristics, they further proposed different transformation methods to generate more effective ranking features.

The rest of this chapter is organized as follows: We first overview the special ranking signals in mobile local search in Section 5.1. Section 5.2 presents and discusses a recent data analysis that explores the ranking heuristics behind these special signals to develop more effective ranking features. We summarize current achievements in acquiring ranking signals and heuristics as well as discuss several interesting future research directions in Section 6.6.

5.1 Ranking Signals

There have been several large-scale studies on mobile search query log analysis for deciphering mobile search query patterns [193,194,71,387,69]. The goal of these studies is to provide quantitative statistics on various aspects of mobile search that can help gain better insight on mobile users' information needs, but few of these efforts have contributed concrete ranking signals. More recently, the exploration of ranking signals has attracted many efforts [10,209,26,248], which have recognized that the ranking signals in mobile local search are quite different from general Web search. We summarize these special ranking signals in this section.

5.1.1 Distance

Local search users generally prefer businesses that are physically close to them; this issue is particularly critical for mobile users who are on the go and with a limited range of reach. For example, a user would be more likely to visit a restaurant nearby than another restaurant far away to get breakfast if the two restaurants are similarly good in other respects. The distance between the result business and the user's location has been recognized as an important ranking signal in mobile local search [132,209,26,248,246].

In the case of the measurement of distance, it is easy to compute the geographic distance between a user and a local entity or business once their locations are known. People have further noticed that the absolute distance value itself, however, sometimes does not really reflect the effort required for a user to travel to the business. For example, how sensitive a user is to the geographic distance depends on the type of business that is being ranked (e.g., users may be willing to drive 20 minutes for a furniture store but not for a coffee shop) [209,26], the search time (e.g., users may be willing to travel a longer distance for a dinner than for a lunch) [209], the traffic status and attractiveness of a location (e.g., users tend to travel a longer distance in Texas than in New York) [26,248], etc.

Although an effective ranking signal, Teevan *et al.* [344] report that users care about how close a business is to their current location only in a portion, 40%, of mobile local searches. Instead, mobile local searchers are often in transit (68%) and want information related to their destination location (27%), en route to their destination (12%), or near their destination (12%) [344]. Therefore, finding a way to automatically identify these different cases and predict the destination location would be an interesting future direction in mobile local search.

5.1.2 Customer Reviews and Ratings

Mobile local search focuses mostly on ranking local businesses (e.g., restaurants). Therefore, special domain knowledge about the ranking objects in mobile local searches could be exploited to improve ranking accuracy. For instance, businesses may receive ratings and reviews from their customers thanks to the Web 2.0 services. Intuitively, the customer rating score and the number of reviews of a business would significantly affect users' click behaviors in mobile local search, since users are acclimated to consulting other people's ratings and opinions about an entity to help make their own decisions [273]. Recent work has already shown that this information can be useful signals for ranking businesses [26,248,246].

Nevertheless, customer reviews and ratings are not unique ranking signals in mobile local searches; they have also been exploited in some other search tasks.

For example, in opinion retrieval [273], the goal of the task is to locate documents (primarily blog posts) that have opinionated content; Ganesan and Zhai [133] studied the use of the content of customer reviews to represent an entity (e.g., business) in entity ranking; Zhang *et al.* [402] proposed different methods to aggregate the counts of thumb-ups and thumb-downs for rating prediction, etc. But the roles of customer ratings and reviews are clearly different in mobile local searches.

However, many businesses, especially new businesses, might not have any customer ratings or reviews. For instance, we analyzed a sample of 5 million businesses that were shown or clicked by real users on a commercially available search engine and found that over 4 million of these businesses did not receive any reviews. Given this level of data sparseness, the process of properly extracting and effectively using these signals for ranking becomes challenging.

5.1.3 Personal Preference

Compared to general Web search, mobile local search is more "actionable" [248,344] in the sense that mobile users often take an action (such as visiting a restaurant) as soon as they finish a local search session. However, on the other hand, mobile local queries (e.g., the most popular query is "restaurants" in our analysis) are often general and not well specified [71,344,30],[3] which could match many businesses from different categories, not all of which are interesting to the user. Therefore, understanding the user's personal preference is particularly important in successfully answering a mobile local query. For instance, knowing that a mobile user searching for restaurants prefers Chinese food, we can rank more Chinese restaurants on the top to avoid bothering the user with other types of restaurants.

However, conversely to Web search, it is nontrivial to build user profiles for capturing personal preference for different businesses in mobile local search. On one hand, the text associated with each business is often very sparse, so it would be hard to build content-based user profiles as proposed previously [312,339]. On the other hand, due to the local nature, a user tends to click only nearby businesses, so it is hard to find users who live far away from each other but share similar business click patterns, making it difficult to apply the collaborative filtering approaches (e.g., [331,107]) or statistical topic modeling approaches (e.g., [161,33,251]) for user profiling.

Due to these challenges, to the best of our knowledge, few efforts have exploited personalization for mobile local search except Lv *et al.*'s work [246], which we discuss in more detail in Section 5.2.

5.1.4 Search Context: Location, Time, and Social Factors

We need to balance multiple ranking signals to develop an effective ranking function. However, because of mobile local search's actionable nature, the role of the user's search context, such as location, time, and social activities, is particularly important

---

[3] Although there are also navigational queries aiming at finding a specific business such as "Pizza Hut," they are easily identified and processed and thus not considered in our work.

in influencing the way these signals are balanced. For instance, a mobile user in Manhattan on a Friday evening around 5:00 p.m. most probably is willing to travel only a short distance to visit a business because of the heavy traffic. However, a mobile user in Texas might be willing to drive a longer distance because of the ease of access to the highway. In contrast, the context of a desktop user who does similar searches from the comfort of his house right before he goes to sleep on a Monday night might be irrelevant, given that the search session might be for some future plan in the next week.

5.1.4.1 *Location*

Location is one of the most important context factors in mobile local search, since users at different locations tend to make different decisions, either due to geographic properties of their regions or demographics of the area they live in. For example, a recent data analysis [248] shows that only 10% of the mobile local queries in the state of Texas result in clicking a business within 1 km of the user location, whereas this percentage doubles (20%) when we consider the state of New York.

Lymberopoulos *et al.* [248] have attempted to study mobile local search. They augmented the feature space with a set of new location-aware features, such as the average traveling distance and the standard deviation of traveling distance within the ZIP code, and then they put forward a machine learning algorithm to build ranking models. More specifically, they evaluated three approaches: (1) training a single model to automatically leverage these features, which implicitly takes location context into account; (2) training a model for each specific location and choosing the corresponding ranking model based on the location of the query; and (3) combining these two models adaptively based on some additional statistics of the location. Their experiments show that the three approaches all work generally more effectively than location-independent ranking, in particular the third one, though building a different ranking model for each location might not scale well in real applications.

Location is important in mobile local search, not only because people are often mobile while searching but also because they are searching for places with a geographic location. Therefore, besides the current location of the searchers, mobile local ranking is also often sensitive to the destination location, i.e., the location of businesses [344,26]. One interesting observation is the phenomenon of distance asymmetry [26]. For example, it is common for users from Redmond, Washington, to drive to Seattle for dinner, but the converse does not hold. Berberich *et al.* [26] has presented an approach to indirectly incorporate distance asymmetry into the ranking function by modeling the destination location's attractiveness in terms of its popularity and its distance to other businesses.

5.1.4.2 *Time*

Time plays a particularly important role in the decision process of mobile local users [209,344]. On one hand, people's behavior and the activities they want to engage in vary depending on whether it is a weekday or a weekend or if it is evening or morning.

For example, Church and Smyth [70] found that 8% of mobile queries mentioned time explicitly; Teevan *et al.* [344] reported that 14% of mobile local searches were at least partly triggered by the time (e.g., breakfast time or dinner time). On the other hand, users usually will take an action immediately following their searches. For example, Teevan *et al.* [344] observed that 89% of mobile local searchers plan to visit the business on the same day as the search, including 44% who plan to visit as soon as possible and 29% as part of their current trip. Consequently, people's preference in mobile local search would be influenced by the time. For example, Lane *et al.*'s data analysis [209] shows that when searching restaurants, people prefer fast-food places, informal restaurants, and local coffee shops during weekday mornings, but the preference for these businesses reduces significantly during weekends and weekday evenings, with the highest drop happening during weekend evenings.

Although time has been shown to be an effective ranking signal in [209], its performance appears to be inconclusive in two recent studies [248,246]. Thus it would be interesting to further explore how to effectively extract and model the time signal in mobile local search.

5.1.4.3 *Social Factors*

Social factors appear to be surprisingly important for mobile local search [82,344,286]. In Teevan *et al.*'s survey [344], a large majority (63%) of respondents said their most recent mobile search was discussed with someone else, suggesting that mobile local searches often tend to have been triggered by social means, such as a conversation or group need. After finishing searches, mobile users often like to share results by simply speaking aloud or sometimes showing their mobile phone screen to others, as reported by [286].

To the best of our knowledge, such kinds of social factors have not been studied before in the ranking problem of mobile local search. It would be a promising direction to explore and understand the ranking issues when mobile meets social.

5.2 Ranking Heuristics

In spite of recognizing these new ranking signals, early studies have mostly treated them as a black box to extract very basic features (e.g., raw rating scores and distance values) without going inside the signals to study how exactly they affect the relevance or click rate for a business. Although some statistics of these signals are also often used as complementary features, such as the average distance and the standard deviation of distance in the current location [248], these studies rely purely on machine learning techniques to combine all features without going inside the signals.

On the other hand, in mobile local search, customer rating scores, numbers of reviews, and distance values are not only the key back-end ranking signals, they are also important information displayed explicitly in the search result user interface (UI), as shown in Figure 5.1. Although the "personal preference" signal and the context factors (e.g., location, time, and social factors) are not explicitly shown to users,

users certainly know their own preference and search context. That being said, all these ranking signals are directly observable by users, and users' click behaviors presumably would be heavily dependent on these signals. Therefore, understanding how exactly a user's decision relates to these signals would potentially lead to better ways of modeling these signals and thus to improving mobile local searches.

In this section, we present and discuss a recent data analysis of the behavior of some of these ranking signals, including customer rating scores, numbers of reviews, distance, and user preference, in mobile local search using a large-scale query log [246], which reveals interesting heuristics that can be used to guide the exploitation of these signals. We first give an overview of the dataset and the experimental settings used in [246] to discover these heuristics.

5.2.1 Dataset and Experimental Setting

Lv *et al.* [246] used clickthrough information to approximate the relevance judgments, realizing the challenges in acquiring relevance judgments in mobile local search. Although each individual user click may not be very reliable, the aggregation of a great number of user clicks from a large-scale query log could still provide a powerful indicator of relevance. Thus, it is very likely that features that help improve click prediction will be useful in ranking as well.

Therefore, the problem setting was, given a query, to predict whether a candidate business would be clicked, and then rank the candidate businesses based on the click prediction. In the experiments, the query was sampled from the search log, whereas the candidate businesses were all businesses that were shown to the user for that query. To learn and evaluate a click prediction model, the query log was split into four parts. The first nine months of data were kept out as the "history" data and were used purely for estimating the popularity of a business and the user's personal preference. Queries were sampled from the next three, one, and one months of data, respectively, for training, validating, and testing the click prediction models.

Three preprocessing steps have been applied to make these four datasets more practical and representative: (1) Queries that did not receive any clicks or received clicks for every candidate business were excluded, since these queries will not influence the average ranking performance in the experiments. (2) Queries that match a business name exactly, e.g., "Starbucks," were identified and filtered out; solving such kinds of queries is a relatively easy task, since users usually have clearer information needs (e.g., visiting a nearby Starbucks) compared to other more general queries, e.g., "Coffee." In doing this, we can place an emphasis on difficult queries in our study. (3) They empirically removed queries (from all the four datasets) by "users" who issued more than 1,000 queries in total in the training, validation, and test datasets, because such "users" are more likely to be robots. Finally, 60,475, 18,491, and 23,152 queries were obtained as the training, validation, and test queries; the average number of clicks and the average number of candidate businesses for each query were 1.34 and 17, respectively.

Since multiple signals need to be leveraged for click prediction, this work seeks help from machine learning. They adopted MART [372], a learning tool based on *multiple additive regression trees*, to provide a common learning framework on top of which one can compare the performance of different ranking features. MART is based on the stochastic gradient boosting approach described in [131,129], which performs gradient descent optimization in the functional space. In the experiments of [246] on click prediction, the log likelihood was used as the loss function, steepest descent (gradient descent) was used as the optimization technique, and binary decision trees were used as the fitting function.

A training instance for each query-business pair was constructed, which consists of a set of features (e.g., distance, rating, etc.) and a click label that indicates whether the user clicked the business (1 for click and 0 otherwise). The training and validation data were fed into MART to build a binary classification model, which was used to estimate the probability of clicks in the test data.

Note that the choice of machine learning algorithms is not critical in this data analysis study: Machine learning is only taken as a black-box tool to evaluate the proposed heuristics and features, so any other appropriate learning algorithm, such as more advanced learning-to-rank algorithms [226], could also be used instead of MART. MART was chosen mainly because it can potentially handle a nonlinear combination of features, and it is widely adopted in current commercially available search and advertisement ranking engines.

The main goal of the experiments was to explore and evaluate effective ranking heuristics for boosting the special ranking signals in mobile local searches. The baseline feature set contained six representative features that were selected based on previous research studies [132,209,248]. These features were: (1) the distance between the query and the business locations, (2) the popularity measure of the business as defined by the number of clicks in the history search logs, (3) the click rate of the business in the history data as defined by the number of clicks divided by the number of impressions and defined as 0 if it did not occur in the history data, (4) the customer rating score of the business in a range of [0, 10], (5) the number of customer reviews of the business, and (6) a time code that represents both the timeframe within a day (one out of five timeframes) that the query was submitted and the day of the week on which the query was submitted (weekend or weekday). Since only top-ranked businesses from a commercial mobile local search engine were re-ranked in the experiments, and those businesses that did not match the query keywords at all were already eliminated, they thus do not involve any textual matching feature and focus only on the special signals of mobile local search.

The retrieval performance in terms of mean average precision (MAP) and the precision at different recall levels were compared. Because the experiments only involved reranking a set of top-ranked businesses in response to a query, the recall score would be the same for any ranking model. In other words, MAP will be influenced only by the positions of the relevant results. So, in this study, MAP can be a good measure to capture the ranking accuracy of top-ranked results. Besides, the importance of each

Table 5.1 Relative feature importance in baseline.

Distance	1	Rating	0.3794
#Clicks	0.7193	#Reviews	0.3462
ClickRate	0.9976	Timeframe	0.1752

feature in constructing the MART model was also compared, following the relative importance measure proposed in [131].

5.2.2 Customer Rating

Intuitively, the customer rating score of a business would significantly affect users' click behaviors in mobile local searches, since users are accustomed to consulting other people's ratings and opinions about an entity to help make their own decisions [273]. To verify this intuition, a model is trained using the baseline features described in the previous section. The relative importance of the different features is shown in Table 5.1, indicating that conversely to our intuition, the importance of the rating score as a feature is relatively low in our baseline system.

5.2.2.1 *Likelihood of Clicks/Relevance*

To examine this observation, this work [246] analyzes the likelihood of relevance (i.e., click rate) for businesses of all rating scores and plots these likelihoods against the rating score to obtain a *click pattern*. Intuitively, the likelihoods should increase monotonically with the rating score.

To estimate these likelihoods, all the businesses in the training data are sorted in order of increasing rating score and divided into several equally sized (i.e., 1,000) "bins," yielding 1,032 different bins. Then the mean rating score in each bin is selected to represent the bin on the graphs used in later analysis. We can then compute the probability of a randomly selected business from the i-th bin that is clicked, which is the ratio of the number of clicked businesses from the i-th bin, and the bin size. In terms of conditional probability, given a business b, this ratio of the i-th bin can be represented by $p(b$ is clicked $|b \in Bin_i)$.

Figure 5.2(a) shows how the probabilities obtained from this analysis relate to the mean rating score in a bin. Surprisingly, there seems to be no clear relationship between the likelihood of a click and the rating score.

This antiintuitive observation could be caused by the potentially incomparable rating scores across different queries; result businesses retrieved by some queries may have higher rating scores than those retrieved by some other queries. To verify this possibility, the popular zero-one score normalization method is adopted. This method linearly normalizes the rating scores of every query to a range of [0, 1]. Such a normalization strategy has been widely used for feature normalization in many learning-to-rank tasks, e.g., [59]. After that, we do a similar analysis of the probabilities of a click, but against the normalized rating score. The results are shown

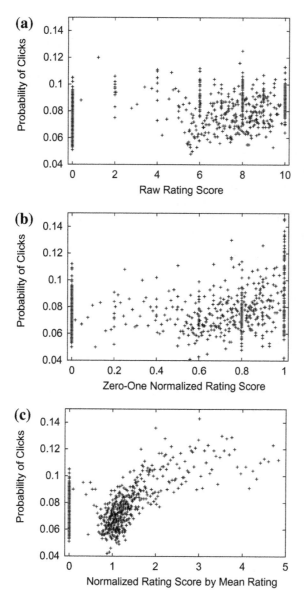

FIGURE 5.2

Probability of clicks for businesses from a bin, plotted against the mean rating score of this bin.

in Figure 5.2(b). Unfortunately, there is still no clear relationship, suggesting that the ineffectiveness of the rating score as a feature is not purely caused by the incomparable score range.

5.2.2.2 *The "Mean" Normalization Scheme*

To diagnose the problem, we further look into the distribution of rating scores of businesses that get clicked. Since the distribution of rating scores is intuitively related to the type or category of businesses, we do this analysis in a category-aware way. Specifically, we compare the rating score of a clicked business with the mean rating score of all businesses from the same category. In doing this, we hope to understand whether the clicked businesses are among the highly rated businesses in a category. The comparison results are illustrated in Figure 5.3, in which we show 10% of randomly selected *clicked* businesses from the training data.

Interestingly, we can see that the rating scores of most of the clicked businesses are above their corresponding categories. For example, when the category mean rating score is 4, few businesses with a rating score lower than 4 get clicked. This shows that the rating score is indeed useful and is directly related to users' click behaviors. However, how does a user know the mean rating score of a category so as to click businesses above this score?

In reality, we expect that users do not really know the mean score of a category. However, users may be able to approximately estimate this mean score through looking over the retrieved business list; the retrieved businesses for a query often belong to the same category and thus could be used as a sample set of businesses from that category, the mean rating score of which can be viewed as approximately the mean category rating. If this assumption is true, it may suggest that users often take the mean rating score from the business result list as a "pivot" score and tend to click businesses with higher scores than this pivot. This intuitively makes sense: A user's click decision, although influenced by the rating score, is not entirely based on it, but if the rating of a business is above the user's expectation (i.e., the pivot), which the

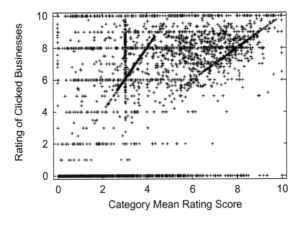

FIGURE 5.3

Rating of clicked businesses, plotted against the mean rating score of the corresponding business category.

user learns from the result list in an ad hoc way, the business would be more likely to be clicked.

Inspired by this analysis, Lv *et al.* proposed to normalize rating scores using the mean rating score of the retrieved businesses. A straightforward approach is to divide the original rating score using this mean value, which not only makes the rating scores more comparable across queries but also aligns them at the corresponding mean rating scores of each query. The probabilities of clicks against the normalized rating scores are then plotted; see Figure 5.2(c). It is clear that the probability of a click increases monotonically with the normalized rating when the normalized rating is larger than 1 (i.e., the mean point), whereas the probability tends to be random when the normalized rating is lower than 1. This is an empirical verification of the fact that users tend to take the mean rating score from the observed results as a "pivot" score and a clear demonstration of different click behaviors on businesses with lower and higher scores than the pivot score.

To examine whether the proposed simple mean normalization scheme can really improve ranking accuracy, the normalized rating score was used to replace the original rating score to learn a new model, labeled *MeanNorm*, and its performance is compared with the baseline model. In addition, the widely used zero-one strategy for rating normalization is also taken as another baseline run, which is labeled *ZeroOneNorm*. The comparison results are reported in Table 5.2 and show that the mean normalization scheme works best, achieving significant improvement over both baseline runs. At the same time, the zero-one normalization does not improve the accuracy of the baseline model. This suggests that we can improve ranking performance by pointing out the mean rating value.

Another approach to explicitly normalizing the rating of a business with the mean rating of all result businesses would be to encode the mean rating of result businesses as an additional feature and let the training algorithm itself decide how to do the normalization. To evaluate this approach, a new model, labeled *AutoNorm-Q*, was trained by adding the mean rating score of businesses from the same single *query*

Table 5.2 Comparison of methods for modeling rating scores. Norm+Pred combines methods tagged using ∗. $b/z/m/c/q/r$ indicates the significance over Baseline, ZeroOneNorm, MeanNorm, AutoNorm-C, AutoNorm-Q, and Rating-Pred, respectively, at the 0.001 level using the Wilcoxon nondirectional test.

Methods	MAP	P@0.3	P@0.5	P@0.8
Baseline	.419	.441	.434	.403
ZeroOneNorm	.419	.442	.434	.403
MeanNorm*	$.425^{bz}$	$.448^{bz}$	$.440^{bz}$	$.409^{bz}$
AutoNorm-C	$.422^{b}$	$.445^{b}$	$.437^{b}$	$.406^{b}$
AutoNorm-Q*	$.431^{mc}$	$.454^{mc}$	$.446^{mc}$	$.415^{mc}$
RatingPred*	$.428^{b}$	$.451^{b}$	$.443^{b}$	$.413^{b}$
Norm+Pred	$.438^{qr}$	$.461^{qr}$	$.453^{qr}$	$.421^{qr}$

into the baseline feature set. They also trained another model, labeled *AutoNorm-C*, in which the mean rating score of businesses from the same *category* was added into the baseline. We present the performance of these two runs in Table 5.2. The results demonstrate that AutoNorm-Q works much better than AutoNorm-C, confirming that users select the "pivot" from the businesses shown to them. AutoNorm-Q improves over the baseline by approximately 3%. Moreover, AutoNorm-Q improves over Mean-Norm, suggesting that the mean normalization scheme can be boosted by optimizing the way of exploiting the mean in a supervised manner.

5.2.2.3 *Cluster-Based Smoothing of Ratings*

It is often the case that a business does not receive any customer rating. In the presence of missing rating scores, a default value of 0 is often used, which, however, may be inaccurate because: (1) a business that does not receive any customer rating does not necessarily mean that it should be rated low; and (2) it could be unfair to use the same default rating score for all businesses. Even if a business receives a rating score, it may still be inaccurate if the rating is only contributed by a very small number of customers. Therefore, more accurate prediction/smoothing of ratings could potentially improve ranking accuracy, and Lv *et al.* [246] also proposed a cluster-based method to predict or smooth rating values.

The basic idea is based on the cluster hypothesis [254] and averages rating scores $r(x)$ from all businesses x in the same cluster C to smooth the rating $r(b)$ of business b so as to obtain an updated rating $r'(b)$. The intuition is that businesses in the same cluster should receive similar ratings, and the rating stability of a cluster would benefit an individual business. Formally,

$$r'(b) = f\left(r(b), \frac{1}{|C|} \sum_{x \in C, b \in C} r(x)\right), \tag{5.1}$$

where f is a function to control rating update. The key component is thus the business cluster. Two types of clusters are used in [246]: business category and business chain. The former allows us to use the rating of all businesses in a given category to estimate the rating of an unrated business in that category (e.g., use all businesses in the "Coffee & Tea" category to estimate the rating score of a Starbucks business). Because a business may belong to multiple categories, it would intuitively help to predict the primary categories of businesses [196]. The latter approach allows us to estimate the rating score of a business by exploiting the rating score of other businesses belonging to the same chain (e.g., use different Starbucks coffeehouses' rating scores to estimate the rating score of an unrated Starbucks coffeehouse).

There are two challenges with this approach: how to choose function f and how to leverage the evidence from two types of clusters. Inspired by the effective performance of automatic feature normalization in the previous section, the same learning algorithm can be used to optimize these two factors in a supervised way. Specifically, both a category mean rating and a business-chain mean rating are provided as two separate features to the learning algorithm. In addition, two description variables for these two new features, i.e., the size of the category and the size of the business chain, are also introduced to the learning algorithm.

This method is labeled *RatingPred*, and the experiment results are presented in Table 5.2. We can see that RatingPred improves significantly over the baseline, suggesting that the proposed cluster-based smoothing can indeed improve rating values. Furthermore, RatingPred can be combined with the proposed feature normalization methods, leading to a new run labeled *Norm+Pred*. It is observed from Table 5.2 that Norm+Pred outperforms either single method alone, suggesting that smoothing ratings and normalizing ratings are complementary to each other. Norm+Pred improves over the baseline by more than 4.5%.

5.2.3 Number of Reviews

The number of reviews represents another signal from the opinionated content, which can intuitively reflect the popularity of a business. However, it shows that the importance of this signal is also low in the baseline model, as presented in Table 5.1. Similarly to the rating score analysis, Lv *et al.* [246] reveal that this is because users often take the mean number of reviews from their observed businesses as a pivot and demonstrate different click patterns on businesses with lower and higher number of reviews than the pivot. However, the learning algorithm fails to capture this important information. To better exploit the strengths of this signal, we also need to feed this pivot number (i.e., mean number of reviews) to the learning algorithm. That is, we should either manually normalize the number of reviews using the pivot or introduce the pivot as an additional feature for automatic normalization.

The experimental results presented in Table 5.3 show that the ranking performance can be significantly improved by the "mean" normalization scheme. Different notations in the table are defined similarly to their counterparts in Table 5.2 but applied to normalize review count. Specifically, the simple mean normalization method (i.e., MeanNorm) performs significantly better than the widely used score normalization

Table 5.3 Comparison of methods for modeling review counts. Norm+Pred combines methods tagged using ∗. The description of notations $b/z/m/c/q/r$ are the same as Table 5.2.

Methods	MAP	P@0.3	P@0.5	P@0.8
Baseline	.419	.441	.434	.403
ZeroOneNorm	.421	.444	.436	.405
MeanNorm*	.425^{bz}	.448^{bz}	.441^{bz}	.409^{bz}
AutoNorm-C	.423^{b}	.445^{b}	.438^{b}	.407^{b}
AutoNorm-Q*	.431^{mc}	.454^{mc}	.446^{mc}	.414^{mc}
ReviewsPred*	.429^{b}	.451^{b}	.443^{b}	.413^{b}
Norm+Pred	.438^{qr}	.461^{qr}	.453^{qr}	.421^{qr}

method (i.e., ZeroOneNorm), which does not leverage the mean value; furthermore automatic normalization (i.e., AutoNorm-Q) works more effectively than manual normalization (i.e., MeanNorm).

In addition, similar to the rating score, the ranking performance can be improved by smoothing the number of reviews based on the cluster hypothesis to make it more accurate (this run is labeled *ReviewsPred*). The mean normalization scheme and the cluster-based smoothing can be leveraged together (i.e., Norm+Pred) to further improve performance, achieving 4.5% improvement in MAP.

5.2.4 **Distance**

Local search differs from other search tasks, mainly because its ranking signals feature geographical distance. In fact, distance has also been shown to be one of the most important features in Table 5.1.

To understand how distance affects users' click patterns, Lv *et al.* [246] also plot in Figure 5.4(a) the likelihood of clicks for a business against its distance from the user. Interestingly, there is indeed a monotonically decreasing trend of the likelihood with respect to distance; this may explain why distance appears to be the most important feature in Table 5.1. Furthermore, it is observed that the likelihood is decreasing sublinearly with distance; the likelihood decreases with distance, but the decreasing speed drops as distance becomes large. This intuitively makes sense: A restaurant within 1 mile of a user would have clear advantages over another similar restaurant within 2 miles, but two restaurants within 9 miles and 10 miles of the user may not have much difference. That is, the relevance of a business is more sensitive to its distance when the distance value is smaller.

With the analysis [41], it is easy to show there is approximately a logarithm transformation. To illustrate it, Lv *et al.* [246] plotted the likelihood of clicks with respect to the logarithm transformation of distance, as shown in Figure 5.4(b). Linear scaling in distance would overly penalize businesses that are relatively far away from the user, while the logarithm transformation generally improves modeling distance.

Similar to ratings and review counts, distance is also observable to users. One interesting question is whether there is also a pivot click phenomenon. To answer this question, the distance of clicked businesses against the mean traveling distance to businesses in the same category was also plotted, as shown in Figure 5.5. Indeed, the plot shows that users tend to click businesses closer than the category mean distance, suggesting that the mean normalization scheme could also be applicable in the case of the distance feature. Yet the pivot phenomenon of distance is not as clear as that of ratings and review counts. One possible reason is that users can generally understand distance better than ratings and review counts because distance is a concrete concept, whereas ratings and review counts appear to be more abstract and subjective; as a result, users tend to rely more on the statistics of the observed business list to make sense of ratings and review counts, but absolute distance itself may have already made much sense. This is also consistent with the previous observation that there is a clear

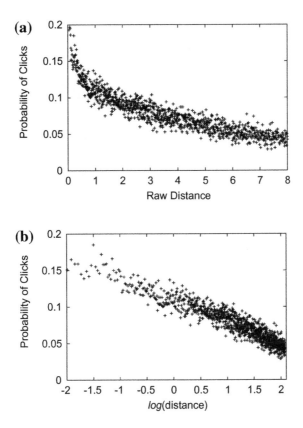

FIGURE 5.4

Probability of click for businesses from a bin, plotted against the mean distance and *log*(distance) scores of this bin.

relationship between raw distance values and the probability of clicks, as shown in Figure 5.4(a).

To verify this analysis, empirical experiment results are reported in Table 5.4. The simple mean normalization method is first applied to divide distance by the mean distance value of all observed businesses for the same query. This run is labeled *MeanNorm*. We can see it significantly improves over the baseline system, which suggests that feature normalization still helps, even though absolute distance values are already largely comparable. Next MeanNorm is compared with MeanNorm+, in which the simple mean normalization method is applied to *log*(distance). Apparently, MeanNorm+ works more effectively, confirming the previous analysis that the logarithm transformation is useful for better modeling distance. In addition, another run ZeroOneNorm+ is also created, which differs from MeanNorm+ in that the zero-one normalization is used. It is observed that ZeroOneNorm+ works significantly worse

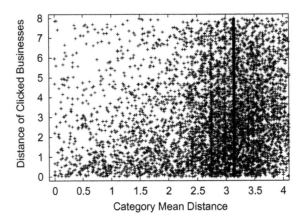

FIGURE 5.5

Distance of clicked businesses, plotted against the mean (traveling) distance of the corresponding business category.

Table 5.4 Comparison of methods for modeling distance. Methods with an indicator "+" apply logarithm transformation. $b/z/m/a$ indicates the significance over Baseline, ZeroOneNorm+, MeanNorm, and AutoNorm, respectively, at the 0.05 level using the Wilcoxon nondirectional test.

Methods	MAP	P@0.3	P@0.5	P@0.8
Baseline	.419	.441	.434	.403
MeanNorm	$.429^b$	$.451^b$	$.443^b$	$.414^b$
ZeroOneNorm+	$.428^b$	$.451^b$	$.443^b$	$.413^b$
MeanNorm+	$.435^{mz}$	$.457^{mz}$	$.449^{mz}$	$.420^{mz}$
AutoNorm	$.434^m$	$.456^m$	$.449^m$	$.419^m$
AutoNorm+	$.435^{ma}$	$.457^{ma}$	$.450^{ma}$	$.420^{ma}$

than MeanNorm+, confirming another previous analysis that the "mean" normalization scheme works well for distance and suggesting that users would also like to click businesses with a distance smaller than the pivot (i.e., mean distance in the result list).

Finally, the two automatic mean normalization runs, namely AutoNorm and Auto Norm+, are also evaluated, where the mean values of distance and log(distance) in the search results are added as additional features into the feature space during the training process to let the learning algorithm automatically normalize the distance and the log(distance) features, respectively. First, AutoNorm+ outperforms AutoNorm, though the improvement is small; this suggests that sublinear transformation of distance is beneficial, yet its advantage tends to be weakened as we use automatic feature normalization, because MART can potentially handle nonlinear combination automatically. Second, by comparing AutoNorm(+) with MeanNorm(+), we can see that automatic normalization can work better than or comparable to the simple mean normalization. Overall, both automatic normalization and manual normalization can improve over baseline by approximate 4% with the proposed new features.

5.2.5 **Personal Preference**

The goal here is to build user profiles so that we can compute the user preference of a business so as to rank businesses in a user-adaptive way. However, it is nontrivial to build content-based user profiles [312,339] in mobile local search, since the text associated with each business is often very sparse. Thus, we choose to use the collaborative filtering approach [161,251,33], based on the history click data, to estimate the likelihood that a user u likes business b, formally the conditional probability $P(b|u)$. Yet there is another challenging problem: Due to the local nature of the task, a user tends to only click nearby businesses, so the co-occurrences are also of local nature and thus very sparse. For example, it is very hard to find users who live far away from each other but share similar business click patterns. To solve this problem, Lv *et al.* [246] exploited the domain knowledge of businesses and instead estimated the likelihood that a user u likes business category c, i.e., $P(c|u)$: Because a business category can cover businesses from different locations, co-occurrences of categories and users can happen across locations. As a byproduct, the number of categories, which is about 3,000, is only about 1/5000 of the number of businesses, significantly reducing the dimension. Lv *et al.*'s experiments show that building profiles for 1 million users can be done in several hours on a single machine.

Although the category information of a business that the user has clicked can be obtained directly from the history data due to the data sparseness problem of many users, Lv *et al.* [246] followed the idea of statistical topic modeling to estimate $P(c|u)$ in a more smoothing way. First, hidden variables Z are introduced with states z for every user-category pair. The possible set of states z is assumed to be finite and of size k, where k is empirically set to 100 in this work. Then the problem can be mapped to the standard topic modeling problem: The original document-term matrix is replaced by a user-category matrix, and the original co-occurrence relationship is replaced by a click. In Lv *et al.*'s work, they adopted PLSA [161] and LDA [33]. Since these two models performed similarly effectively in their experiments, only the results based on PLSA were reported.

Considering observations in the form of clicks (c, u) of categories and users, PLSA models the probability of each click (i.e., a user u clicks a business of category c) as a mixture of conditionally independent multinomial distributions:

$$P(c, u) = \sum_z P(z)P(u|z)P(c|z) = P(u) \sum_z P(z|u)P(c|z) \qquad (5.2)$$

Since the problem is to estimate user preference, the conditional model is used:

$$P(c|u) = \sum_z P(z|u)P(c|z) \qquad (5.3)$$

The model can be estimated using the (EM) algorithm to obtain parameters $P(z|u)$ and $P(c|z)$. Now a user profile $P(c|u)$ has been constructed. Then, given any business b, since b may belong to multiple categories, the conditional probabilities of these corresponding categories are averaged as the user preference of a business, i.e., $P(b|u)$.

Some users may have more history clicks, and the profiles of these users would intuitively be more reliable than those of some other users who make fewer clicks. To make the model more intelligent so as to be able to automatically learn how much personalization we should apply for each user, Lv *et al.* encoded both the user preference, i.e., $P(b|u)$, and the number of history clicks of the user into the learning algorithm. No other normalization was used, and this run is labeled NoNorm. It is compared with the baseline and shows that, though NoNorm outperforms the baseline significantly, the improvement is indeed minor.

To examine the reason, following Section 5.2.2.1, the probability of clicks for businesses against the user preference is also plotted, as shown in Figure 5.6(a). We can see that the probability of clicks generally does not vary a lot when the user preference changes; this may be one possible reason NoNorm does not work very well. Then the zero-one normalization is applied to generate another plot in Figure 5.6(b). It shows that the zero-one normalization essentially stretches the plot along the x-axis. There also appears to be an increasing trend only when the user preference is very small. Next, the mean normalization method is applied in Figure 5.6(c). It shows clearly that when the user preference is below the mean value (i.e., $x = 1$) of the current search results, the probability of clicks increases monotonically with user preference and the increasing speed decreases as the user preference approaches its mean value. However, after the user preference reaches the mean value, the probability of click even has a tendency to decrease slightly. Again, this observation shows that users choose the mean value as a pivot score and have different click behaviors on the two sides of the pivot. Furthermore, it is interesting to see that the probability of clicks is maximized when the user preference is around the mean value: Too low preference may mean that the business is not interesting to the user (i.e., irrelevant business), whereas too high preference may indicate that the business could be too similar to what the user clicked before (i.e., redundant business). The pivot observation seems to demonstrate that a user's decision may be like an exploration-exploitation tradeoff: Exploit what the user knows, but meanwhile explore what the user does not know.

Inspired by this analysis, Lv *et al.* developed a manual mean normalization run (MeanNorm) and an automatic mean normalization run (AutoNorm) for feature normalization. According to the results shown in Table 5.5, AutoNorm improves over both the baseline and MeanNorm significantly, whereas MeanNorm does not perform very well. This could be because of the sublinear increasing curve of the mean normalization method, as shown in Figure 5.6(c); similar to the previous observations of distance normalization, automatic normalization using MART can potentially handle nonlinear combination well, whereas manual normalization cannot. To verify this intuition, a logarithm transformation based on the Box-Cox transformation analysis [41] is first applied onto user preference, and then the two normalization methods are

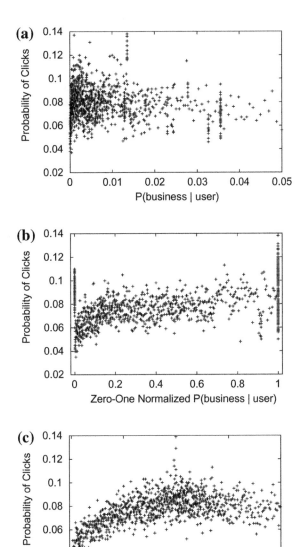

FIGURE 5.6

Probability of click for businesses from a bin plotted against the mean user preference of this bin.

Table 5.5 Comparison of methods for modeling user preference. Methods with an indicator "+" apply logarithm transformation. $b/n/m$ indicates the significance over Baseline, NoNorm, and MeanNorm, respectively, at the 0.01 level using the Wilcoxon nondirectional test.

Personalization	MAP	P@0.3	P@0.5	P@0.8
Baseline	.419	.441	.434	.403
NoNorm	$.420^b$	$.442^b$	$.434^b$	$.404^b$
MeanNorm	$.420^b$	$.442^b$	$.434^b$	$.404^b$
MeanNorm+	$.428^{nm}$	$.450^{nm}$	$.442^{nm}$	$.411^{nm}$
AutoNorm	$.427^{nm}$	$.450^{nm}$	$.442^{bm}$	$.411^{bm}$
AutoNorm+	$.428^{nm}$	$.450^{nm}$	$.443^{nm}$	$.412^{nm}$

added on top of the transformed feature, leading to two new runs MeanNorm+ and AutoNorm+. Table 5.5 shows that these two runs perform similarly well and the best among all methods, verifying our hypothesis and showing the necessity of sublinear transformation. Overall, by normalizing the personalization features, over 2% MAP improvements can be obtained.

5.2.6 Sensitivity Analysis

The most effective modeling methods for all four signals are then combined into a final model, including Norm+Pred from Table 5.2 for modeling rating, Norm+Pred from Table 5.3 for modeling review count, AutoNorm+ and MeanNorm+ from Table 5.4 for modeling distance, and AutoNorm+ and MeanNorm+ from Table 5.5 for modeling user preference. The final model is labeled All and shown in Table 5.6. Table 5.7 lists the 23 features in the All model as well as where each feature comes from. We can see that the All model outperforms the baseline by more than 7%, suggesting that

Table 5.6 Sensitivity analysis. These data show that combining the proposed new features (i.e., All) can improve the Baseline over 7%.

Methods	MAP	P@0.3	P@0.5	P@0.8
Baseline	.419	.441	.434	.403
All	.449	.472	.464	.433
All-Rating	.448	.471	.463	.432
All-Reviews	.449	.472	.464	.433
All-Distance	.441	.464	.456	.425
All-Personalization	.448	.471	.463	.431
All-Rating-Reviews	.442	.464	.456	.426
All-Rating-Reviews Personalization	.436	.458	.450	.420

Table 5.7 Relative feature importance in the final model.

	Features	Imp.	Contributor
1	MeanNorm_Log_Distance	1	Distance
2	ClickRate	0.5859	Baseline
3	#Clicks	0.5152	Baseline
4	#Reviews_Mean	0.3692	Reviews
5	Log_UserPref_Mean	0.3646	Personalization
6	Rating_Mean	0.3453	Rating
7	MeanNorm_#Review	0.3137	Reviews
8	—BusinessChain—	0.3132	Rating & Reviews
9	Log_MeanNorm_UserPref	0.2897	Personalization
10	MeanNorm_Rating	0.2242	Rating
11	—Category—	0.2229	Rating & Reviews
12	Log_Distance_Mean	0.1814	Distance
13	#CategoryReviews	0.1731	Reviews
14	CategoryRating	0.1665	Rating
15	User_#Clicks	0.1651	Personalization
16	Log_Distance	0.1434	Distance
17	#BusinessChainReviews	0.1394	Reviews
18	Distance	0.1122	Baseline
19	BusinessChainRating	0.1100	Rating
20	Rating	0.1071	Baseline
21	Log_UserPref	0.1057	Personalization
22	#Reviews	0.0686	Baseline
23	TimeFrame	0.0660	Baseline

understanding the behaviors and heuristics behind ranking signals can indeed lead to better modeling methods and thus improve ranking accuracy.

It has been shown that the selected modeling methods (now as components in the final All model) perform very well in modeling each individual signal. To examine how sensitive these methods are when they are combined, Lv *et al.* removed some new modeling method(s) at a time while keeping all other modeling methods and the baseline features. For example, All-Rating in Table 5.6 was constructed by excluding from the All model the proposed novel features in the Norm+Pred method for rating modeling, while the features occurring in other models, including all baseline features, are kept. From Table 5.6, we can see that when Distance is removed, the performance drops the most, suggesting that Distance is very sensitive in the final model and its effect cannot be replaced. However, when Rating, Reviews, or Personalization are excluded, the performance decreases only slightly or even does not change. It suggests that the effect of these signals may have a large overlap; as a result, although they perform well as individual signals, their performance could not add together.

To go a step further, Lv *et al.* removed Rating and Reviews at the same time and found that its performance degrades much more than that of All-Rating and All-Reviews. This observation confirms that ratings and review counts are highly redundant to each other. After removing Rating and Reviews, we also remove Personalization in the last row of Table 5.6. We can see that the performance degradation is much larger than when we remove Personalization from the All model, suggesting that the personalization features also tend to be redundant to Rating and Reviews, probably due to the general consistency between global preference and individual preference.

Finally, feature-level analysis is also done to examine the relative importance of each feature, as shown in Table 5.7. Apparently distance, with the proposed normalization method, appears to be the most important feature. The two popularity measures from the baseline are the second and the third most important features. These observations show that distance and popularity dominate the ranking signals of mobile local search. However, other signals have also contributed many useful features. For example, the top six features cover all feature contributors.

Two particularly interesting observations are that (1) three mean values are ranked very highly, and (2) 8 out of the top 12 features are directly related to the mean normalization scheme, suggesting that the proposed "mean" normalization scheme indeed helps model signals in mobile local search. Due to the effectiveness of the proposed new features, many features from the baseline have been pushed to the bottom of Table 5.7.

5.3 Summary and Future Directions

It has been recognized that the ranking signals in mobile local searches, such as distance, customer ratings, and reviews, are quite different from general Web searches. We summarize the current understanding of these signals in existing studies. For example, how sensitive distance depends on the type of business that is being ranked (e.g., users may be willing to drive 20 minutes for a furniture store but not for a coffee shop), the search time (e.g., users may be willing to travel a longer distance for a dinner than for a lunch), the traffic status and attractiveness of a location (e.g., users tend to travel a longer distance in Texas than in New York), and so on. Next we present and deeply discuss several heuristics that can guide the development of effective ranking features. For example, a common ranking heuristic for many ranking signals is that users often take the mean value of a signal from the business result list as a pivot score and tend to demonstrate different click behaviors on businesses with lower and higher signal values than the pivot; we can thus encode the pivot information into feature normalization or into model training, which has been shown to significantly improve modeling these signals.

Mobile local search is an emerging search task, and there are many interesting research problems that are underexplored. Here we discuss a few of them.

5.3.1 Evaluation of Mobile Local Search

The process of acquiring relevance judgments to evaluate mobile local search is a challenging problem. First, the Cranfield-style evaluation that has been used in the evaluation of many traditional information retrieval and search tasks [302] would not work here, since the relevance judgments in mobile local search are particularly dependent on the search context, e.g., location of the user [209,248]. Second, asking users to make explicit relevance judgments can be very costly because it is necessary to cover a diverse set of queries in different contexts. Third, although Joachims *et al.* have developed methods for extracting relative relevance judgments from user clickthrough data in general Web searches [190], it is unclear whether these methods also work for mobile local search where the position bias of clickthrough and the interpretation of clickthrough could be different from general Web search. For example, Ghose *et al.* [140] have shown that search results that appear at top positions are more likely to be clicked in mobile searches than in Web searches.

In addition, a recent work [286] reports that mobile searches are often not to satisfy a specific information need but rather to kill time (e.g., waiting for the bus) or to satisfy curiosity. In such "casual" search scenarios, finding the relevant answer to a given query and ranking that answer as high as possible may not be the main goals [370]. This suggests that the measure of success of a casual search process should intuitively also be based on how users enjoy the search process, posing another challenge in the evaluation of mobile local search. These challenges make the evaluation of mobile local search still an open problem.

5.3.2 User Modeling and Personalized Search

Mobile local search is more "actionable" in the sense that mobile users often take an action (e.g., visiting a restaurant) as soon as they finish a local search session. Therefore, understanding the user's personal preference is particularly important in terms of successfully answering a mobile local query. However, mobile local search logs are often seriously sparse because clickthrough is geographically distributed across locations, as we discussed in Section 5.2. On the other hand, users often bring their mobile devices wherever they visit, so mobile devices are capable of knowing more about a user than traditional PCs. This provides opportunities to go beyond search logs and build better user models for mobile local search based on rich user activities, but meanwhile it raises an interesting challenge: how to best utilize and integrate all the available information to build an optimal user model?

Entity Ranking

6.1 An Overview of Entity Ranking

The goal of current Web search engines is to help users retrieve relevant documents on the Web—more precisely, those documents that match the intent of the user's query. During Web searches, some users are looking for specific information; others may plan to access rich media content (images, videos, etc.) or explore a specific topic. In the latter scenario, users do not have a fixed or predetermined information need but are using the search engine to discover information related to a particular object of interest. Therefore, in this scenario, we say that the user is in a browse mode.

To provide satisfying experience for users in browse mode, a machine learning-based ranking framework can be applied to rank related entities. Such ranking framework orders related entities according to two dimensions: a lateral dimension and a faceted dimension. In the lateral dimension, related entities are of the same nature as the queried entity. For example, if the queried entity is "Hyderabad," "Bangalore" is a good related entity in the lateral dimension. For another example, if the queried entity is "Angelina Jolie," "Brad Pitt" is a good related entity in this dimension. In the faceted dimension, related entities are usually not of the same type as the queried entity and refer to a specific aspect of the queried entity (e.g., Hyderabad and India, or Brad Pitt and Fight Club). Entity ranking is a recent paradigm [95,64,358] that focuses on retrieving and ranking related entities from different (structured) sources. Entity ranking can occur in various forms and scenarios as proposed in [267,152]. Entities typically have a canonical name, a main type, alternate names, and several subtypes. They are related to each other through labeled relationships, such as *IsLocatedIn*, *CastsIn*, etc. For example, "Bangalore" *IsLocatedIn* "India," and "Brad_Pitt" *CastsIn* "Fight_Club." This kind of information can be represented as an entity-relationship graph, which shows many similarities to the graphs underlying social networks [180].

The amount of structured data sources such as DBPedia[1] and Freebase[2] on the Web are increasing [283]. The availability of such large collections of structured data enables a realm of possibilities beyond the basic textual Web search. Popular Web search engines are already providing a rich experience, mining structured data, query logs, and Web documents to provide rich information in the search results (e.g.,

---

[1] http://dbpedia.org.
[2] www.freebase.com.

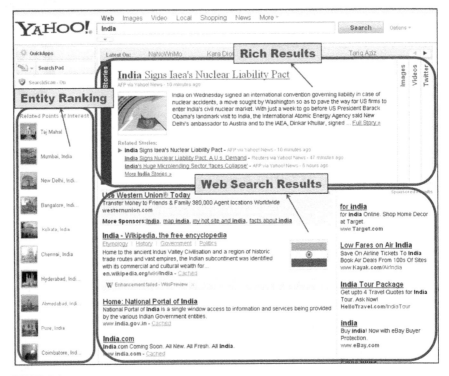

FIGURE 6.1

Screenshot of entity ranking results embedded into the left-side rail of the search results page.

movie plot, genre, cast, reviews, and show times at the user location) or direct answers to the users' question-like queries (e.g., "date of birth Brad Pitt") while displaying related news articles, images, videos, and tweets for queries about popular people, organizations, media works, and locations whenever possible.

To enhance this experience, it is critical to provide well-qualified related entities. A snapshot of the overall enhanced experience appears in Figure 6.1. Related entities, which are points of interest for the query "India" in this example, are shown as suggestions on the left-side rail of the search results page. The types of related entities to show depend on the category of the query entity. For example, for movie queries, the goal is to show both lateral information in terms of related movies and faceted information in terms of cast information. The challenge that we propose to address in this work is to select the appropriate set of related entities, depending on the queried entity and its type, and to rank them in order of relevance.

It is natural to cast the problem of entity ranking as a supervised machine learning problem [48,407] with the goal of predicting the relevance of the related entity to the query entity. Although the previous work in this area [354,356,418] focuses on optimizing the clickthrough rate (CTR) of the related entities alone, this chapter presents an approach to jointly learn the relevance among the entities using both the user click data and the editorially assigned relevance grades. In contrast to Web search, the entity search results are grouped by categories of related entities, which complicates the ranking problem. We address how to incorporate the categories of related entities into the loss function and show how to leverage relationships between related entities with different categories ("intercategory" relationships) to improve relevance.

This chapter presents an extensive analysis of Web-scale object ranking, based on machine learned ranking models using ensembles of pairwise preference models. The proposed system for entity ranking uses structured knowledge bases, entity-relationship graphs, and user data to derive useful features to facilitate semantic search with entities directly within the learning-to-rank framework. This chapter also describes a suite of novel features in the context of entity ranking and presents a detailed feature space analysis, followed by further discussions on how entity ranking is different from regular Web search in terms of presentation bias and the interaction of categories of query entities and result facets. Some experiments will be provided based on validation on a large-scale graph containing millions of entities and hundreds of millions of relationships. The results show that the proposed ranking solution clearly improves on the simple user behavior-based ranking model.

The rest of this chapter is organized as follows: Section 6.2 provides background details about the terminology that we use as well as the knowledge base and the Web search experience where entity ranking is used. Section 6.3 introduces the extensive features that we utilize based on both various data sources and the entity-relationship graph itself. Section 6.4 presents details about the pairwise comparison model that produces highly robust pairwise preferences and describes how to incorporate category information in the loss function. Moreover, Section 6.5 reports the experimental results obtained on a large collection of structured knowledge sources. Finally, Section 6.6 concludes this chapter with some insights into future work.

6.2 Background Knowledge

In this section, we describe the terminology that we use throughout the rest of the chapter, give an overview of the system used for building the knowledge base that supports the whole experience, and describe the Web search experience where this entity ranking is utilized.

6.2.1 Terminology

This subsection first introduces the terminology used in this chapter. The application of entity ranking, as presented in this chapter, is to support users in Web search by providing related entity information, which allows them to explore a topic of their interest. Given a *user query (q)* entered in the search box and a large knowledge base of known entities with binary directed relationships between them, we detect entities present in the query. We refer to such an entity as the *query entity (qe)*. A *facet (f)* is defined as the directed relationship between two entities, starting from the query

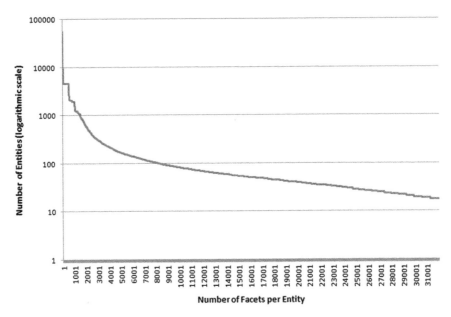

FIGURE 6.2

Distribution of the number of facets per entity. The number of entities is in logarithmic scale. Although some entities have large numbers of facets (typically these are location entities that are connected to many other points of interest), some entities have fewer related facets.

entity to a *facet entity (fe)*. For popular entities, we typically have several hundreds of facets in our knowledge base, as well as a few dozen facets for the infamous entities. Figure 6.2 shows the distribution of the facets per entity in our knowledge base.

For each entity, the following information is maintained. The *reference* is used internally to identify and manage the entity. The *canonical name* is shown to the user when the entity ranking experience is triggered in the search engine results page. The *type* indicates the semantic class of the entity, that is, whether the entity is a person, a location, a media work, etc. The *subtypes* provide a more fine-grained typology for the entity. An entity can have several subtypes. For example, a person in a film knowledge base can be both an actor and a producer. In addition, an entity can have one or more *variants* (e.g., alternate names, birth names, aliases) that capture colloquial references to this entity. We assume that problems related to de-duplication of known entities with identical canonical names and types are resolved within the knowledge base, as is the handling of other disambiguation problems. For ease of reference when computing a ranking, we assume that an entity can be uniquely identified through its *normalized* canonical name and type.

For each facet, the following information is maintained: the reference to the query entity, the reference to the facet entity, and the relationship type as well as how frequently we observe that relationship in the sources feeding our knowledge base.

Table 6.1 Example entity.

reference	ID::286186
canonical name	India
variant	India; Bharat
type	location
subtype	country

Table 6.2 Example facet.

query entity	ID::286186 (i.e., India)
facet entity	ID::2295414 (i.e., city of Hyderabad, India)
type	has_point_of_interest

Typically, multiple facets can be defined between an *entity-facet pair* ($f\langle qe, fe\rangle$), reflecting the different roles that can occur between any two entities.

To illustrate this concept with an example, consider the location *India*. Table 6.1 shows the typical data that we would have on file for this particular location. In any of our ranking sources, both the canonical name and its variants are used as references for this entity. India is a *location* of subtype *country*.

Table 6.2 shows the information stored for a facet, which simply contains a reference to both entities and the type of the relationship.

6.2.2 Knowledge Base

As mentioned, the type of experience described in this chapter relies on a knowledge base of entities and the relationships between them. The construction of the first version of that knowledge base is described in [356]. This section describes the new knowledge base and its building process.

The system we have designed and implemented for building this knowledge base is called Yalinda. Yalinda extracts various form of knowledge, including entities, their attributes (i.e., reference, canonical name, variants, type, subtypes, other attributes) and the relationships between them (i.e., labeled directed binary relationships). Yalinda extracts this knowledge from structured sources. This extraction is done automatically and frequently, using data scraping and data feed processing techniques. The extracted knowledge is normalized and serialized into semantic graphs, one per input source and domain, providing unified views that are convenient for consumption. Yalinda is implemented as a framework consisting of general modules that provide the common features and pluggable modules with special features such as wrappers for specific data. It follows a three-step process: the data acquisition step, the knowledge extraction step, and the knowledge serialization step, as described in a moment.

Regarding input source selection, a typology of potential sources has been defined, and potential sources have been reviewed and analyzed regarding practical knowledge extraction. To maximize the tradeoff among precision, coverage, and cost, the focus has been set on extracting knowledge from large high-quality structured sources. Selected sources include both internal specialized sources, such as Yahoo! properties (e.g., Y! Movies, Y! Sport, Y! TV, Y! Music, Y! GeoPlanet, etc.), and broad-coverage reference sources such as online collaborative encyclopedias (e.g., Wikipedia, Freebase). Depending on the source, the knowledge base is updated daily, weekly, or quarterly.

In the data acquisition step, new data are retrieved from remote locations and made available locally in a standard processable way to ease extraction. Main challenges include dealing with various protocols, APIs, encodings, and formats. Sometimes input data must also be retrieved and combined from several sources to form a convenient input dataset. Resulting data and metadata are stored locally as structured data feeds. In the knowledge extraction step, entities, attributes, and relationships are extracted from the data feeds and normalized. Entities and associated facts are extracted using wrappers specific to a schema or format. Entities and their attributes are normalized according to their semantics using rules, focusing on the main attributes and the attributes that can be used as pivot for building relationships. Challenges depend on the source processed. In the knowledge serialization step, extracted knowledge is refined and serialized into entity-relationship graphs. The main challenge is to identify and model the meaningful relationships and to materialize them using specific attribute values as pivots.

Overall, the resulting knowledge base includes millions of entity instances (100+ fine-grain types) and hundreds of millions of relationship instances (300 fine-grain relationship types, including both first- and second-order relations). The domains currently covered include Automotive, Book, Finance, Movie, TV, Music, Notability, Periodical, Product, Sport, etc. For popular entities we typically have in our knowledge base on the order of several hundred relationships and a few relationships for the infamous entities. Figure 6.2 shows the distribution of the facets per entity in our knowledge base.

6.2.3 Web Search Experience

The research presented in this chapter is powering the faceted search experience in Web searches. Figure 6.1 depicts a screen shot of the experience, where the user has searched for "India." The Web search results page is organized into three columns; the left column is used to present entity ranking results whenever the query contains entity terms, the middle column contains the traditional Web search results along with their snippets that show a summary of the match between the Web page and the query, and the right column is used to display relevant ads if the query contains commercial intention. In addition to the three-column layout, rich results are embedded in the middle column above the traditional Web search results whenever the corresponding structured data are available, depending on the type of query.

Though our ranking strategy blends the facets and entities of different types, when shown to the user the facets are grouped by their type to enhance user comprehension.

In addition, we show a mini-thumbnail for each facet to aid users and capture their attention. Both aspects are variable across different queries and will affect user engagement. When training and evaluating the ranking strategies presented here, we deploy clickthrough behavior as well as editorial assessments. The latter allows us to eliminate any bias in the evaluation with respect to these two variables.

6.3 Feature Space Analysis

Previous studies have introduced a probabilistic feature framework that allows us to quickly derive a pool of features from various rankings sources, such as Web search query logs, Flickr, and Twitter, as shown in Figure 6.3. Section 6.3.1 gives a brief overview of these features. In addition, in Section 6.3.2 we experiment with a new set of features, based on the analysis of the entity graph that forms our knowledge base.

6.3.1 Probabilistic Feature Framework

van Zwol *et al.* [355] introduced a framework to uniformly compute a set of features from various ranking sources. In this chapter, we discuss how to use this framework to compute the features over Web search query logs, tags used to annotate photos in Flickr, and entity pairs detected in tweets from Twitter users. For each source, we can compute both term-based and session-based statistics.

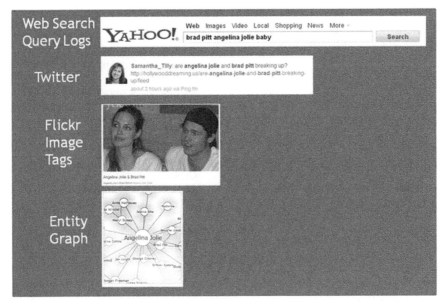

FIGURE 6.3

Feature sources for entity ranking.

The features can be classified into four groups:

- Atomic features that work on one of the entities in the facet (qe, fe)—for example, the entity probability or its entropy
- Symmetric features such as the point-wise mutual information and joint probability
- Asymmetric features such as the conditional probability and KL-divergence
- Combinations of features such as $P_u(f|e) * P(f)$ that combine the conditional (user) probability of a facet f given entity e and the probability of the facet; according to Skowron and Araki [319], this allows the learning algorithm to make a more informed decision if the combined feature is more descriptive
- Table 6.3 lists a set of example features we can extract.

The corpus of Web documents is a valuable source to compute the similarity among related entities. All the probabilistic features we have described can be computed within the context of Web pages. In fact, a simple approximation of these corpus-based features can be computed by retrieving the number of documents that contain the entity alone, the facet alone, and both the entity and facet together. These co-citation features for the entity and the facet are computed from the Web search results as total hits and deep hits.

Table 6.3 Features.

Feature	Description
$P(qe)$	Entity probability
$P(fe)$	Facet entity probability
$E(qe)$	Entity entropy
$E(fe)$	Facet entity entropy
$KL(qe)$	KL-divergence of entity vs. collection
$KL(fe)$	KL-divergence of facet vs. collection
$P(qe, fe)$	Joint probability
$P_u(qe, fe)$	Joint user probability
$SI(qe, fe)$	Pointwise mutual information
$CS(qe, fe)$	Cosine similarity
$P(qe|fe)$	Conditional probability
$P_u(qe|fe)$	Conditional user probability
$P(fe|qe)$	Reverse conditional probability
$P_u(fe|qe)$	Reverse conditional user probability
$P_u(qe|fe) * P(fe)$	Combined feature 1
$P_u(ee|qf)/P(fe)$	Combined feature 2
$P_u(fe|qe) * P(fe)$	Combined feature 3
$P_u(fe|qe) * E(fe)$	Combined feature 4
$P_u(qe, fe) * P(fe)$	Combined feature 5
$P_u(qe, fe)/P(fe)$	Combined feature 6
$P_u(qe, fe) * E(fe)$	Combined feature 7
$P_u(qe, fe)/E(fe)$	Combined feature 8

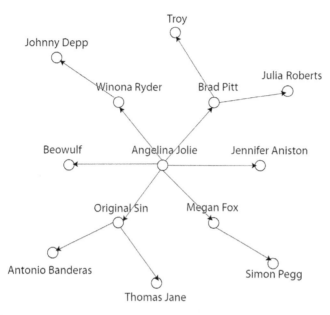

Troy

Johnny Depp

Julia Roberts

Winona Ryder   Brad Pitt

Beowulf   Angelina Jolie   Jennifer Aniston

Original Sin   Megan Fox

Antonio Banderas   Simon Pegg

Thomas Jane

FIGURE 6.4

Entity graph: An example.

6.3.2 Graph-Based Entity Popularity Feature

An entity-facet pair $f\langle qe, fe\rangle$ illustrates the relation between a query entity and a facet entity. We can deduce a whole entity network over all the entities if we connect all the pairs. The network can be built by simply connecting the facet of one pair to the entity of another pair if the two are of the same surface form.

Figure 6.4 shows a subnet of the network, centered around "Angelina Jolie." Three labeled nodes represent three entities, "Angelina Jolie," "Brad Pitt," and "Troy." A direct connection between "Angelina Jolie" and "Brad Pitt" denotes an entity-facet pair $f\langle qe, fe\rangle$. But the entity "Angelina Jolie" and "Troy" is related through "Brad Pitt."

The entity network is very similar to a social network. Each node in the social network refers to a user, whereas this node equals an entity in the entity network. We can extract many features from the entity network that are useful in the context of entity ranking. Some obvious features include the shortest distance between two entities, the number of paths between two nodes, and the number of shared connections. The concept of shared connections is inspired from the idea of mutual friends in social networks [180]. The intuition is that if two entities have many shared nodes or connections in the entity graph, they are more related to each other. We utilize normalized shared connections at various depths as features in our framework.

In addition to these graph-based features, we incorporated another feature based on the entity popularity on the entity network. The intuition is that more popular entities

Table 6.4   Entity popularity feature values of top entities.

entity	$\tilde{\pi}_i$
law and order	−8.24
er	−8.43
strong medicine	−9.27
bill kurtis	−9.32
las vegas	−9.81
michael mckean	−9.81

are more likely to be "eye sparking" and more often clicked by users. Mathematically, we represent this graph as a $m \times m$ adjacency matrix, $\mathbf{W}$, where $W_{ij} = 1$ if entity i connects to entity j. In practice, we normalize $\mathbf{W}$ so that $\sum_j W_{ij} = 1$. Given this matrix and an eigen system, $\mathbf{W}\pi = \lambda\pi$, the eigenvector, π, associated with the largest eigenvalue, λ, provides a natural measure of the centrality of the user [38]. The analog in Web search is the PageRank of a document [44]. This eigenvector, π, can be computed using power iteration,

$$\pi_{t+1} = (\lambda\mathbf{W} + (1 - \lambda)\mathbf{U})\pi_t \qquad (6.1)$$

where $\mathbf{U}$ is a matrix whose entries are all $\frac{1}{m}$. The interpolation of $\mathbf{W}$ with $\mathbf{U}$ ensures that the stationary solution, π, exists. The interpolation parameter, λ, is set to 0.85. We perform 15 iterations (i.e., $\tilde{\pi} = \pi_{15}$).

We computed $\tilde{\pi}$ for 4 million entities. Table 6.4 lists the top six entities associated with the highest values of $\tilde{\pi}_i$.

6.4 Machine-Learned Ranking for Entities

Machine learning has been used extensively for many ranking tasks [48]. In this book, we follow the gradient-boosted decision tree framework applied to pairwise preferences [407], which has been successful for some ranking problems. In the entity ranking problem, there are three main challenges:

- There is small amount of editorial data, which is a common situation in developing a ranking function for a new domain.
- User clicks are sparse and very noisy. Since entity search results are shown along with Web search results, clicks are considerably fewer compared to Web search. Also, the thumbnails for entities add a strong bias, which leads to very noisy clicks.
- Entity search results are grouped by categories of facets, which complicates the ranking problem. This also requires a new problem definition for learning a ranking function.

To overcome the problem of sparse editorial data, we propose to augment the training data using the clickthrough data (in Section 6.4.3). However, without a proper mechanism to deal with sparse and noisy clicks, the augmented training data would not produce a robust ranking function. Hence, we propose a method of combining multiple click models to tackle the problem of sparse and noisy clicks (in Section 6.4.2). To deal with categories of facets, a new loss function can be proposed, since it utilizes the category information (in Section 6.4.3).

6.4.1 Problem Definition

In contrast to Web search, the entity search results are grouped by categories of facets. For example, for a movie actor entity, a group of person facets is first shown in a group, and a group of movie facets follow. The order of these groups is predetermined by user behavior (Section 6.5.2) based on the category of the query entity.

In the Web search ranking problem, a set of n documents $\mathcal{D}$ is given as input and a permutation τ of $\{1, \ldots, n\}$ is returned as output. In our entity ranking problem, $\mathcal{D}$ is split into a set of groups by categories of results: $\mathcal{D} = \mathcal{D}_1 \cup \cdots \cup \mathcal{D}_m$, where $\mathcal{D}_i$ contains results with category i. Our goal is to generate a permutation or ranking τ_i for each category i.

A straightforward approach would be to train a ranking function for each category separately using only the subset of training data for the category. However, there are two problems:

1. The training data for each category may be too small to train a robust ranking function (even the entire available training data are small).
2. We may lose some useful relationships between facets with different categories. For example, assuming that $f \in \mathcal{D}_1$ and $f', f'' \in \mathcal{D}_2$, if we have "intercategory" relationships in our training data that $f' > f$ and $f > f''$, these may be leveraged to provide an "intracategory" constraint $f' > f''$.

In this way, "intercategory" relationships may help "intracategory" ranking. Thus, we propose to generate a single ranking τ for the whole $\mathcal{D}$ to leverage these "inter-category" relationships. The ranking τ_i for each category i is then derived from τ by simply ordering $\mathcal{D}_i$ according to τ.

6.4.2 Pairwise Comparison Model

In generating pairwise preferences as additional training data using click models [58,110], the high accuracy of the pairwise preferences is necessary to learn a robust ranking function. However, in our entity ranking problem, a common way of generating the pairwise preferences [58,110] may not work due to sparseness and noisiness of user clicks.

In this section, we introduce an approach, called the *pairwise comparison model* (PCM), that learns robust pairwise preferences for entity pairs based on *pairwise* click features.

Some click models [58,110] have been used to enrich the training data for the boosting algorithm [407] in two steps:

1. They compute a relevance score for each (query, URL) pair.

2. The pairwise preference between two URLs is decided by the relevance scores of the two URLs: a facet f_i is preferred to a facet f_j if $r(\mathbf{x}_i) > r(\mathbf{x}_j)$ where r is a click model and $\mathbf{x}_i$ is a feature vector for f_i.

The second step raises some questions. First, this method relies on a single-click model r to generate pairwise preferences. If the accuracy of the click model is not sufficiently high (due to noisiness of clicks in our data), the generated preference data may not improve a ranking function when it is added to the editorial data. Thus, it raises the question of whether we may leverage multiple click models, which can possibly complement each other to get more reliable preferences. Second, in this method, the pairwise preferences are indirectly derived from "pointwise" scores ($r(\mathbf{x}_i)$ and $r(\mathbf{x}_j)$). This motivates us to design a model that directly predicts a preference between two facets.

The *pairwise comparison model* (PCM) takes a "pairwise" feature vector as input and predicts a preference. Given two facets f_i and f_j, we extract a pairwise feature vector $\mathbf{w}_{ij}$. Then the pairwise comparison model h is applied to $\mathbf{w}_{ij}$ to obtain the preference between f_i and f_j : f_i is preferred to f_j if $h(\mathbf{w}_{ij}) > 0$. The key insight is that we use the responses of multiple click models as features ($\mathbf{w}_{ij}$) and train a model (h) using them. We first describe how we extract a pairwise feature vector $\mathbf{w}_{ij}$ for two facets. Then, we show how we train the pairwise comparison model.

Some pairwise features can be derived from two facets. For each (entity, facet i, facet j) tuple, we have the following pairwise features:

- SkipAbove$_{ij}$: ncc_{ij}/cnc_{ij} for the click sessions in which the facet i is ranked higher than the facet j, where ncc_{ij} is the number of sessions in which facet i was not clicked but facet j was clicked, and cnc_{ij} is the number of sessions in which facet i was clicked but facet j was not clicked.
- SkipNext$_{ij}$: cnc_{ij}/ncc_{ij} for the click sessions in which facet i is ranked one position higher than facet j.

In addition, we have some features derived from each facet. For each (entity, facet) pair, we have the following pointwise features:

- CTR.
- skipCTR : $\#clicks/(\#clicks + \#skips)$, where $\#clicks$ denotes the number of sessions where a facet f was clicked, and $\#skips$ denotes the number of sessions where f is not clicked but some other facets ranked below f are clicked. skipCTR is a reasonable approximation of the DBN model score [58].
- Cumulated relevance (Cumrel) [111], a state-of-the-art click model that estimates the relevance of a document based on user behavior.

Although these features are pointwise ones, the concatenation or ratio of two pointwise features can be considered a pairwise feature. We define the feature vector for each (entity, facet i, facet j) as follows:

$$\mathbf{w}_{ij} = (SkipAbove_{ij}, SkipAbove_{ji}, SkipNext_{ij}, SkipNext_{ji},$$
$$CTR_i, CTR_j, skipCTR_i, skipCTR_j, Cumrel_i, Cumrel_j,$$
$$CTR_i/CTR_j, skipCTR_i/skipCTR_j, Cumrel_i/Cumrel_j). \quad (6.2)$$

Given all these pairwise features, we have the following training data for each training entity e:

$$\mathcal{T}_e = \{(\mathbf{w}_{ij}, l_i - l_j) | i, j \in \{1, \dots, N\}, i \neq j\}, \tag{6.3}$$

where l_i is a numerical label given by human editors to facet i out of a finite set of labels L (e.g., $L = \{4, 3, 2, 1, 0\}$) and N is the number of facets to be ranked for e. We choose $N = 10$ to get enough click information among the facets and restrict the size of the training data.

We apply the gradient-boosting algorithm [129] on our training data $\{\mathcal{T}_e | e$ is a training entity$\}$ to obtain a function $h(\mathbf{w}_{ij})$, which predicts the relative relevance of two facets f_i and f_j.

6.4.3 Training Ranking Function

In this section, we propose how to incorporate facet categories in the loss function to learn a ranking function. We start with a simple loss function that ignores facets categories and then show a new loss function incorporating facet categories.

The boosting algorithm [407] uses pairwise preferences as input to learn a ranking function. We have two sets of pairwise preferences:

- $\mathcal{P}_E = \{(f_i, f_j) | l_i > l_j\}$, where l_i is a numerical label given by human editors to a facet f_i (the larger, the more relevant)
- $\mathcal{P}_C = \{(f_i, f_j) | h(\mathbf{w}_{ij}) > \lambda\}$, where h is the pairwise comparison model described in Section 6.4.2 and λ is a threshold to obtain reliable preferences

For each (*entity, facet*) pair, we extract a feature vector $\mathbf{x}$ containing all the features described in Section 6.3. The boosting algorithm optimizes the following loss function:

$$\frac{1 - \delta}{|\mathcal{P}_E|} \sum_{(\mathbf{x}_i, \mathbf{x}_j) \in \mathcal{P}_E} \max(0, 1 - (f(\mathbf{x}_i) - f(\mathbf{x}_j)))^2$$

$$+ \frac{\delta}{|\mathcal{P}_C|} \sum_{(\mathbf{x}_i, \mathbf{x}_j) \in \mathcal{P}_C} \max(0, 1 - (f(\mathbf{x}_i) - f(\mathbf{x}_j)))^2 \tag{6.4}$$

where δ is a parameter that controls the balance between the two sets.

Note that this loss function ignores facet categories. We now introduce a new loss function that considers facet categories. First we define some notation. $\mathcal{P}_E$ and $\mathcal{P}_C$ can be split into two sets:

$$\mathcal{P}_E = \mathcal{P}_E^{inter} \cup \mathcal{P}_E^{intra} \tag{6.5}$$

$$\mathcal{P}_C = \mathcal{P}_C^{inter} \cup \mathcal{P}_C^{intra} \tag{6.6}$$

where

$$\mathcal{P}_E^{inter} = \{(f_i, f_j) | (f_i, f_j) \in \mathcal{P}_E, \text{ category of } f_i \neq \text{ category of } f_j\} \tag{6.7}$$

$$\mathcal{P}_E^{intra} = \{(f_i, f_j)|(f_i, f_j) \in \mathcal{P}_E, \text{ category of } f_i = \text{ category of } f_j\} \qquad (6.8)$$

$$\mathcal{P}_C^{inter} = \{(f_i, f_j)|(f_i, f_j) \in \mathcal{P}_C, \text{ category of } f_i \neq \text{ category of } f_j\} \qquad (6.9)$$

$$\mathcal{P}_C^{intra} = \{(f_i, f_j)|(f_i, f_j) \in \mathcal{P}_C, \text{ category of } f_i = \text{ category of } f_j\}. \qquad (6.10)$$

The new loss function is

$$\frac{\alpha(1-\delta)}{|\mathcal{P}_E|} \sum_{(\mathbf{x}_i,\mathbf{x}_j)\in\mathcal{P}_E^{inter}} \max(0, 1 - (f(\mathbf{x}_i) - f(\mathbf{x}_j)))^2$$

$$+\frac{1-\delta}{|\mathcal{P}_E|} \sum_{(\mathbf{x}_i,\mathbf{x}_j)\in\mathcal{P}_E^{intra}} \max(0, 1 - (f(\mathbf{x}_i) - f(\mathbf{x}_j)))^2$$

$$+\frac{\alpha\delta}{|\mathcal{P}_C|} \sum_{(\mathbf{x}_i,\mathbf{x}_j)\in\mathcal{P}_C^{inter}} \max(0, 1 - (f(\mathbf{x}_i) - f(\mathbf{x}_j)))^2$$

$$+\frac{\delta}{|\mathcal{P}_C|} \sum_{(\mathbf{x}_i,\mathbf{x}_j)\in\mathcal{P}_C^{intra}} \max(0, 1 - (f(\mathbf{x}_i) - f(\mathbf{x}_j)))^2. \qquad (6.11)$$

In this new loss function, we introduce a parameter α that controls the weight for "inter"-category pairs of facets. If $\alpha = 1$, the new loss function is equivalent to (6.4). If $\alpha = 0$, we are considering different groups of facets as though they are from different queries. α between 0 and 1 may help intercategory ranking, which is empirically shown in Section 6.5.

6.5 **Experiments**

In this section we present experimental results to validate our approach. Two types of experiments are conducted to validate our algorithms. The first set of experiments are to evaluate the performance of our approach on editorially judged entity pairs; the second set of experiments uses the user behavior data on the search results page to compute the efficacy of our approach.

6.5.1 **Experimental Setup**

We use the query log from the Yahoo! Search Engine to sample entity queries that match from our dictionary of entity names. For each of these entities, we extract the related entities from their connections in the entity graph. For all of these related entities, a five-point relevance grade is obtained that indicates the match between the query entity and the facet entity. A feature vector is computed for each of these relationships. The dataset for our experiments consists of the pair of entities that are related, the relevance grade that indicates the match between the entities and the feature vector.

Our dataset consists of 6,000 query entities and overall 33,000 entity-facet pairs, including both training and test data. These entity-facet pairs were given a five-point editorial grade that indicates the relevance of the facet entity to the query entity. The inter-editor agreement among the editors for this study was close to 78%. Since the relevance of the facet to the query is sometimes objective, this is understandable, and thus we propose methodologies to combine the editorial data with the user preference data obtained from clickthrough logs. In our training data, we combine two sets $\mathcal{P}_E$ and $\mathcal{P}_C$: $\mathcal{P}_E$; the set of pairwise preferences generated by the previous editorial data contains 93,000 (entity, facet i, facet j) tuples. $\mathcal{P}_C$, the set of pairwise preferences generated by the pairwise comparison model consists of 189,000 (entity, facet i, facet j) tuples.

Our baseline is a simple linear combination of the conditional probabilities, as explained in Section 6.3.1, across different feature sources, such as Web search query terms, Web search query logs, Flickr, and Twitter. We chose this baseline because it is a good representation of a simplistic user preference model that is derived from user behavior data. The conditional probability is also normalized for the number of users to make sure that each user is counted only once.

The evaluation is based on the discounted cumulative gain (DCG) [177] and the pairwise accuracy. The DCG is computed as follows:

$$\text{DCG-K} = \sum_{i=1}^{K} \frac{g(i)}{log(1+i)}, \qquad (6.12)$$

where $g(i)$ is the gain associated with the rating of result at rank i and K is the maximum depth result to consider. In this chapter, we use gains of $10, 7, 3, 0.5$, and 0, respectively, corresponding to the five ratings or relevance grades.

The pairwise accuracy is the ratio of correct pairs

$$\frac{\{(f_i, f_j)|\tau(f_i) < \tau(f_j), h(\mathbf{w}_{ij}) > \lambda\}}{\{(f_i, f_j)|\tau(f_i) < \tau(f_j)\}}, \qquad (6.13)$$

where $\tau(f_i)$ is the position of f_i in the search results and h is the pairwise comparison model.

A metric is computed for each query, and the average values over all the queries in our test data are reported.

6.5.2 User Data-Based Evaluation

6.5.2.1 CTR Analysis of Web Search and Entity Ranking

Before we present the results of our proposed methodologies, we show the differences in presentation and user behavior between traditional Web search results and entity ranking results to help explain the difference in the presentation bias between the two presentations. As shown in Figure 6.1, the Web search results page is organized into three columns, where the left column is used to present entity ranking results whenever the query contains entity terms, the middle column contains the traditional Web search results along with their snippets that show a summary of the match between the Web page and the query, and the right column is used to display relevant ads if the query

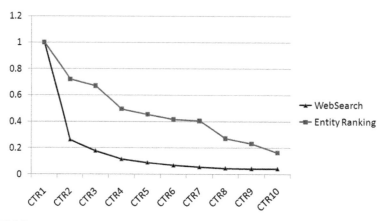

FIGURE 6.5

Comparison of positionwise CTR between traditional Web search results and entity ranking. All the CTRx in both presented results have been normalized so that CTR at position #1 is 1.

contains commercial intention. In addition to the three-column layout, rich results are embedded in the middle column above the traditional Web search results whenever the corresponding structured data are available, depending on the type of query. Figure 6.5 shows the positionwise CTR for both traditional Web search results and entity ranking results. All the CTRx in both presented results have been normalized so that CTR at position #1 is 1. We can see that Web search has a sharp decline at position #2 and slowly decays monotonically for the lower positions. The entity ranking results also experience a similar monotonic decay, but the decline is not that steep. In fact, there is a short plateau region between position #3 and position #7. This indicates that users are more in exploratory mode when interacting with the entity ranking results and browse through various facet entities. The clicks on the entity ranking results also depend on the quality of the thumbnails shown for the entities. Choosing the right thumbnails for the candidate entities is important to mitigate the presentation bias, but solving this problem is beyond the scope of this work.

6.5.2.2 *Category Interaction Analysis of Entities*

For some categories of query entities, such as movie actors and sports athletes, the facet entities could be of different categories. For example, movie entities will have movie actors and related movies as results, and they belong to two different categories. There are several ways of presenting the category information of the facet entities in the entity ranking results section. We chose to group the related entities of the same category and decide the order of the categories depending on the type of the query entity. However, it is not trivial to determine the order of categories given a query entity. To understand how the categories of the query entities and facet entities interact, we experimented with a small portion of the Web search traffic where we randomized the order of various categories of the facet entities. Table 6.5 shows the

Table 6.5 CTR on category of the query entity vs. facet entity. Each row represents the category of the query entity and the column represents the category of the facet entity; each cell represents aggregate CTR at the intersection. The CTR values are normalized for each row such that the category with the highest CTR in each row is given 1.0. The missing entries indicate that the data for the intersection of those particular categories are not available.

Query/Facet	Person	Movie	TV Show	Movie Actor	Music Artist	Sports Team	Sports Athlete
Person	0.98%	0.43%	0.34%	**1.0%**	0.63%	–	0.72%
Movie	**1.0%**	0.92%	–	0.85%	0.37%	–	0.53%
Movie Actor	**1.0%**	0.57%	0.52%	0.96%	0.66%	–	0.61%
Music Artist	0.63%	0.52%	0.59%	0.56%	**1.0%**	–	0.56%
TV Show	**1.0%**	–	–	0.27%	–	–	–
Music Album	0.93%	–	–	–	**1.0%**	–	0.81%
Sports Team	0.66%	–	–	–	0.95%	0.74%	**1.0%**
Sports Athlete	0.91%	–	–	0.73%	0.31%	0.73%	**1.0%**

CTR for various categories of query entities on the categories of the facet entities. The CTR values have been normalized to the maximum values in each row. For example, the first row shows normalized CTR for entities of the type "Person" across various categories such as "Person," "Movie," "TV Show," etc., i.e., the normalized CTR on movies for "Person" queries is 0.43%. Similarly, the normalized CTR for various combinations of categories of the entities is shown in the table. From this experiment, it is evident that the person entities typically have higher CTR compared to other entities such as movies, TV shows, and sports teams. To understand this interaction of the categories among various facet entities, we conducted other experiments to evaluate the effect of including the category information of the facets into the loss function, as described in the following sections.

6.5.2.3 *Evaluation of Pairwise Comparison Model*

Each click model/feature in the pairwise comparison model can be used to predict the preference between two facets. Given a click model c, we predict that f_i is preferred to f_j if $c(f_i) - c(f_j) > \tau$. The accuracy of the prediction can be measured by editorial labels given to f_i and f_j. Hence, this is a binary classification problem. With a different τ, we can plot a precision-recall graph. Figure 6.6 shows the precision recall for each click model and the PCM. It is clear that a single model is not robust; for small recall, precision is not high. Even a state-of-the-art click model such as the cumulated relevance model (Cumrel) shows the same trend. This implies that the user clicks in entity rankings are highly noisy, which we suspect is affected by the presentation bias due to thumbnail images. However, the pairwise comparison model combining these models outperforms all the single models and seems much more robust to noisy clicks.

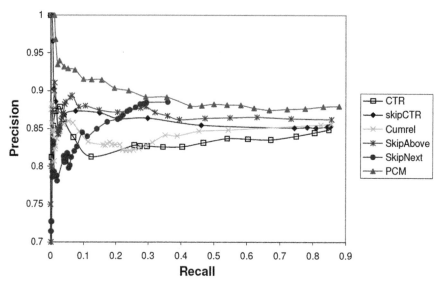

FIGURE 6.6
Precision vs. recall of several click models and the pairwise comparison model (PCM). The tradeoff between precision and recall is obtained by different thresholds used for a pairwise preference prediction.

6.5.3 Editorial Evaluation

6.5.3.1 Evaluation of Category Based Loss Function

Table 6.6 shows the DCG gains with various intercategory weights α over the baseline, which is a linear combination of the conditional probabilities across various feature data sources. If $\alpha = 1$, facet categories are ignored in the training of a ranking function. If $\alpha = 0$, pairs of facets with different categories are not used. The result shows that

Table 6.6 Relevance improvements with various intercategory weights over the baseline. The smaller α, the more the intracategory relationships between facets are emphasized. DCG is computed for each group of facets with the same category.

Intercategory Weight	DCG-1 Gain	DCG-5 Gain	DCG-10 Gain	Pairwise Accuracy Gain
$\alpha = 0.0$	2.50%	1.97%	0.88%	20.68%
$\alpha = 0.2$	2.58%	1.95%	0.88%	20.87%
$\alpha = 0.4$	2.52%	1.98%	0.86%	20.90%
$\alpha = 0.6$	2.41%	1.97%	0.86%	20.90%
$\alpha = 0.8$	2.45%	1.94%	0.87%	20.82%
$\alpha = 1.0$	2.14%	1.96%	0.84%	20.82%

Table 6.7 DCG gain of various sets of features over the baseline.

Feature Sources	DCG-1 Gain	DCG-5 Gain	DCG-10 Gain
Query terms only	−1.18%	0.31%	−0.15%
Query session only	−3.83%	−1.12%	−0.86%
Flickr only	2.30%	1.09%	0.43%
All user data features	5.38%	3.35%	1.53%
All features	8.01%	4.98%	2.25%

the relevance is improved by using $\alpha < 1$. Also, α between 0 and 1 provides the best relevance, which implies that the intercategory relationships between facets help the intracategory ranking (ranking within each group of facets with the same category).

6.5.3.2 *Evaluation of Various Types of Features*

Table 6.7 shows the DCG gains with various types of features over the baseline, which is a linear combination of the conditional probabilities across various feature data sources. The table shows that the query log features by themselves are not better than the baseline, but when they are combined with the other feature sources such as Flickr, the overall gain is more than the gain from individual sources. Of all the individual data sources, Flickr seems to be most valuable because it is natural that if two entities, mostly celebrities, appear together in a photo, it is likely that these two celebrities are related. While the user data features provide a DCG-10 gain of 1.53%, all features including the graph features such as popularity features and corpus based features provide an overall DCG-10 gain of 2.25%.

6.6 **Conclusions**

This chapter presented a system for ranking related entities in the context of the Web search. We presented an extensive analysis of features for Web-scale entity ranking. We also proposed novel techniques for entity ranking based on machine-learned ranking models using an ensemble of pairwise preference models. We showed how to work with categories in the context of entity ranking by introducing inter- and intracategory weighting. We showed the results on one of the large knowledge bases containing millions of entities and hundreds of millions of relationships. The experiments reveal that our proposed ranking solution clearly improves simple user behavior-based ranking and several baselines. The future directions for this work include investigating the affect of time-sensitive recency-based features on related entity ranking for the buzzy entities. Another line of future work is to extend this framework to rank and recommend related entities for a given Web page, given the content and the context around the page.

Multi-Aspect Relevance Ranking

INTRODUCTION

Along with the popularity of search engines, end users' information needs continue being refined. One of the emerging trends is vertical search intents. For example, a user might want to find a restaurant near her current location; another user might want to follow the recent development of a breaking news event such as an earthquake in Japan. Some recent studies show that at least 20% of Web queries have some local intent [357]. As a result, vertical searches start attracting more and more attention. For example, many search engines provide specialized vertical searches such as local search [1,3] and real-time search [55]. Furthermore, vertical search results are often slotted into general Web search results [15,16] to provide more diversified search results. Thus, designing effective ranking functions for vertical searches has become important to improve users' search experience.

A natural way to build a vertical search is to apply the existing ranking techniques on a vertical. In the TREC conference [2], several specialized tracks such as blog and chemical tracks have been introduced to build a testbed to study retrieval tasks on these special text collections. The main focus of these tracks is on content-based relevance, and most participants extend the traditional IR techniques to consider a few task-specific ranking signals. Recently, learning-to-rank approaches [187,47,407] have been studied extensively and shown to be effective to combine many useful signals into a ranking function. To adapt such a technique on a vertical, an intuitive approach is to construct a training dataset by collecting a set of queries and documents that belong to the vertical and asking human editors to give a single relevance label between a query and a document. A ranking function thus can be learned for the vertical.

However, as we observed that in many verticals, the meaning of relevance is domain-specific and usually consists of multiple well-defined aspects. For example, in, and are both important: A stale result that matches a query perfectly is no longer interesting to end users. In local search, as shown in Figure 7.1, to find a "restaurant" in "Sunnyvale CA," a satisfactory search result should not only be about a dining place (matching aspect), it should also require the place to be close to the search location (distance aspect) and with good user reviews (reputation aspect). Usually, there is no result that is the best in all these aspects. Ranking the results based on a single aspect such as matching is not optimal. A desired ranked list of results needs to trade off these different aspects appropriately. In such a vertical, blindly applying the conventional

FIGURE 7.1

An example of local search result.

learning-to-rank approaches by ignoring these vertical-specific domain knowledge approaches may not be cost-effective to collect training data, for the following reasons: (1) Since there are several pertinent aspects in a vertical, human editors naturally need to consider and trade off the relevance from different aspects before making the overall relevance judgement. Thus, assessing aspect relevance is a necessary step. (2) Trading off multiple aspects is not trivial, since such a tradeoff can vary for different queries or in different contexts. For example, in local search, the reputation aspect can be more important for "restaurants" queries, but the distance aspect can be more important for "banking centers" queries. (3) For different verticals, different aspects are involved, and the tradeoff among aspects is vertical-dependent. Collecting training data with overall relevance for a new vertical needs human editors to learn how to appropriately trade off different aspects.

In this chapter, we propose a novel formulation to leverage the vertical-specific knowledge in a cost-effective way. Instead of asking editors to provide the overall relevance directly, our key idea is to collect aspect relevance labels and *learn* the trade-off among them in a *quantitative* way. Specifically, in our formulation, the relevance between a query and a document is judged only with respect to individual aspects. Intuitively, the aspect relevance is more finely specified. Thus it is less dependent on other contexts and can be presumably judged by editors with less effort. To learn a ranking function using our multi-aspect relevance formulation, we study two types of learning-based approaches to trade off these aspect relevancies: a label aggregation approach and a model aggregation approach.

- In the label aggregation approach, we first learn an aggregation function that predicts the overall relevance given the aspect relevance labels. After we get the overall relevance labels, conventional learning-to-rank algorithms can be applied to obtain a ranking function.

- In the model aggregation approach, we first train several aspect-specific ranking models based on the aspect relevance labels. The model aggregation function is then learned to combine the output of these aspect ranking models to generate the final overall relevance output.

Compared with the first approach, the second one has the advantage that we can use different ranking models for different aspects. Since there are only a few aspects in a vertical, a minimal amount of data is needed to learn either the label aggregation function or the model aggregation function. Furthermore, in our aggregation approaches, a *mapping function* that converts editorial labels (such as "exact match," "plausible match," and "no match") to numerical values for each aspect is necessary. Such a function can be defined heuristically, but we show that we can automatically learn such a function based on training data. Thus our proposed methods are completely free from heuristics.

A main advantage of our learning-based approaches is that they are vertical-independent and can be easily applied to different vertical searches. Specifically in this chapter, we focus on learning a generic ranking function for each of the two types of queries in local search: business name queries (e.g., "walmart") and category queries (e.g., "restaurant"). We use a training dataset with relative preferences to learn the aggregation functions and study several variants on a large dataset of local search. The experimental results show that our proposed methods for multi-aspect relevance formulation are quite promising. The two types of aggregation methods perform more effectively than a set of baseline methods including a conventional learning to rank method.

The rest of the chapter is organized as follows: In Section 7.1, we introduce related work. We define our problem in Section 7.2 and describe our methods to aggregate aspect relevancies in Section 7.3. We present our experimental results in Section 7.4 and conclude our chapter in Section 7.5.

7.1 **Related Work**

Modeling relevance is the central topic in the information retrieval community, and most of the past work focuses on overall relevance. In particular, almost all the evaluation methodology is based on overall relevance. For example, in the TREC conference [2], benchmark datasets are labeled by human editors with overall relevance. The relevance labels can be either binary or graded [178]. In the past, many models were proposed to capture overall relevance [301,293,281,401,47]. Most of the existing work treats overall relevance as a unit and has not studied it in a finer granularity.

Vertical searches have become popular recently. For example, in the TREC conference, there are multiple tracks, some of which, such as blog track and legal track, focus on articles from specific domains. Specific characteristics have been explored for vertical search ranking mechanisms. Most participants in the TREC conference designed task-specific ranking features. For example, Elsas *et al.* [114] went beyond single blog articles and studied how to rank blog feeds. Das Sarma *et al.* [86] advocated a comparison-based ranking scheme to rank items in Twitter-like forums. Yi *et al.* [388] tried to discover implicit geographic local search intents of queries automatically. Lu *et al.* [239] proposed to use the geographic information to personalize Web search results. On top of different verticals, past works such as [15,16] studied how to select appropriate verticals by predicting the vertical intents of different queries based on multiple sources of evidence. Our work focuses on the learning-to-rank approaches of individual verticals, and our multi-aspect relevance formulation is novel for vertical searches.

Our work is related to multifaceted search [386, 404]. The goal of multi-faceted search is to use facet metadata of a domain to help users narrow their search results along different dimensions. In a recent TREC blog track [249], a special track of "faceted blog distillation" is initiated, and the task of this track is to find results relevant to a single facet of a query in the blog collection. This task is tied in with the multifaceted search in that it is intended to study how to rank blog articles after a user has selected a facet (e.g., "opinionated" or "factual") to refine the original query. Although facets are usually categorical and intended to help explore search results, our definition of aspects is closely related to the notion of relevance and intended to capture partial relevance.

We note that our model aggregation technique is closely related to rank aggregation, which includes score-based and rank-based methods such as [231,111] and model interpolation [134]. We are not contributing any new techniques to this body of work. Rather, we show that supervised score-based aggregation techniques can be used in our multiaspect relevance formulation. Our work is also different from multi-label learning [139], the primary focus of which is to explore the label correlation to improve learning accuracy.

Multi-objective optimization has been applied to both recommendation [294, 5, 6] and general search problems [336]. For example, in [5] and [6], both "click shaping" and its personalized version are proposed for online news article recommendation to consider both article clicks and downstream utility such as time spent. These pieces of work are in the recommendation setting, whereas our focus is on vertical searches. In [336], the focus is to optimize multiple objectives in the learning-to-rank framework for Web search. It considers multiple label sources and design optimization procedures based on the LambdaMART method. In their work, the priority of different label sources and the combination weights are predefined; thus it is not easy to handle a large number of label sources. In our work, the combination weights between different aspects are learned automatically and our formulation is more scalable with respect to the number of aspects. Furthermore, in our method, we will compare with a rule-based baseline method that is similar to their *graded measure* in the sense that we predefine the aspect priority and use the labels with lower priority to break the ties of labels with higher priority.

7.2 Problem Formulation

In this section, we formally define our problem. We first describe a conventional learning-to-rank approach for vertical searches and then propose our relevance formulation.

7.2.1 Learning to Rank for Vertical Searches

Although vertical searches involve multiple aspects such as matching, reputation, and distance, we can still apply conventional learning-to-rank methods. Given a query q, let $\mathcal{D}_q = \{(\mathbf{x}_1, z_1), \ldots, (\mathbf{x}_n, z_n)\}$ be the training data of n documents, where $\mathbf{x}_i \in \mathbb{R}^d$ is the feature vector and z_i is the overall relevance label of the i-th document. In a ranking problem, $\mathcal{D}_q$ is given as input and a permutation τ of $\{1, \ldots, n\}$ is returned as output. $\mathbf{x}_i$ is ranked higher than $\mathbf{x}_j$ if $\tau(\mathbf{x}_i) < \tau(\mathbf{x}_j)$ and this means $\mathbf{x}_i$ is more relevant to q than $\mathbf{x}_j$. Typically, a *ranking function* $f : \mathbb{R}^d \rightarrow \mathbb{R}$ is trained and applied to $\mathcal{D}_q$. A permutation or ranking τ is generated by ordering the $f(\mathbf{x}_i)$ in the descending order.

The overall relevance label z_i is a discrete label given by human editors. In this work, we follow a common five-grade labeling scheme: {Perfect, Excellent, Good, Fair, Bad}. To reduce disagreement among editors, it is a common practice that an *editorial guideline* is drawn up. Any editorial guideline is essentially a set of rules that specify a condition for each grade of the overall relevance label.

In this section, we use a local vertical search as an example to describe an editorial guideline. A unique characteristic of local search is that the query intents are to find some locations such as restaurants, hotels, or business centers. This also implies that users intend to use some services provided by the local businesses. Therefore, a user would prefer a location that is close and at the same time whose reputation for services is good. For example, to find a restaurant in local search, a satisfactory search result is not only about a dining place (matching aspect), but it also requires the place to be close to the search location (distance aspect) and with good user reviews (reputation aspect). Overall, we have found that three aspects, i.e., matching, distance, and reputation, are the common and most important aspects for local information needs.

Figure 7.2 shows an example of an editorial guideline for local searches. We have several questions that are intended to capture the desired properties of a local search. Questions 1, 2, and 3 are meant to capture the matching, distance, and reputation aspects, respectively. Each question has a graded judgment that will be labeled by editors. Finally, an aggregation guideline specifies a rule for each grade of the overall relevance label. An aggregation guideline is important since it defines the learning targets. It is necessary for most conventional learning-to-rank tasks, especially those that involve multiple aspects of relevance. Without a good aggregation guideline, the training data will have too much noise to train a good ranking function due to disagreement among editors regarding the overall relevance.

```
Given a query and a list of documents, answer the the following
questions for each document.

Question 1 : How does this document match the query?
[ ] Exact match
[ ] Plausible match
[ ] No match

Question 2 : What is the relative distance between the document location
and the query location?
[ ] Same location
[ ] Reasonable location
[ ] Too far

Question 3 : How is the rating from different raters?
[ ] Excellent rating
[ ] Good rating
[ ] Bad rating
```

Question 4: Overall Relevance

Matching	Distance	Reputation	Overall
Exact	Same	Excellent	Perfect
Exact	Same	Good	Excellent
Exact	Same	Bad	Good
Exact or Plausible	Same or Reasonable	-	Fair
No	-	-	Bad

FIGURE 7.2

An example of an editorial guideline for local search. Note that the overall relevance question is *NOT* needed in our aggregation methods. The overall relevance is used only for the conventional method.

For example, given the query "Bank of America, Los Angeles, CA 90018," the result "Bank of America, 2907 Crenshaw Blvd, Los Angeles, CA" has a distance of about 1.01 miles, and the average rating from two people is 3 out of 5. In this case, the labels for these questions are Exact match, Same location, and Good rating. The overall relevance is assigned as Excellent, considering all these aspects.

Such a rule-based approach is similar to [336] in the sense that we predefine the aspect priority and use the labels with lower priority to break the ties of labels with higher priority. The drawbacks of the conventional rule-based approach are: (1) defining the right rules needs deep domain knowledge and thus is nontrivial; (2) the rules are very coarse and cannot capture the true preferences in a finer granularity; and (3) this method will not scale, since the complexity of defining rules can grow exponentially as the number of aspects increases, though it is feasible for the three aspects in our work.

7.2.2　Multi-Aspect Relevance Formulation

In the conventional learning setting, the intermediate questions regarding aspects are only used to help editors reach the final overall relevance and are usually discarded when training a ranking function. Ways to leverage these aspect relevance labels effectively are not well explored. In this section, we propose a new learning-to-rank framework for multi-aspect relevance to tackle the drawbacks of the conventional rule-based overall relevance scheme.

First, we define the following concepts:

Definition 1 (Aspect relevance).　Given a query q, a document d, and the k-th aspect, the corresponding *aspect relevance* is the relevance between q and d with respect to this aspect. An aspect relevance label $\hat{l} \in L_k = \{l_{k,1} \prec, \ldots, \prec l_{k,n_k}\}$ is used to represent the degree of the relevance where $\prec$ ($\succ$) means the left label is less (more) relevant than the right label.

For example, in the editorial guideline shown in Figure 7.2, each intermediate question is to assess a single aspect relevance label. An aspect relevance label is independent of other aspect relevance labels.

Definition 2 (Multi-aspect relevance).　Given a vertical that has m pertinent aspects, the *multi-aspect relevance* between a query and a document is a m-dimensional vector with each entry corresponding to an aspect relevance label between the query and the document.

Each entry in a multi-aspect relevance vector corresponds to an aspect relevance label. This label can be mapped to a numerical value by a mapping function as defined here:

Definition 3 (Mapping function).　A *mapping function* of the k-th aspect $\phi_k : L_k \rightarrow \mathbb{R}$ maps an aspect relevance label to a numerical value. For example, ϕ_1(matching= Plausible match) = 0.5. A mapping function is consistent if $\phi_k(l_{k,i}) > \phi_k(l_{k,j})$ for $l_{k,i} \succ l_{k,j}$. We use Φ as the general notation of the m aspect mapping functions.

A mapping function can be manually defined or learned. In the following, for ease of exposition, we use notation $\mathbf{y}$ to represent a multi-aspect relevance vector of either labels or values unless clarified in the context.

7.2.3　Label Aggregation

Given our definitions, the basic idea is to train a function that can *quantitatively* aggregate the multi-aspect relevance values into an overall relevance value.

Definition 4 (Label aggregation function).　A *label aggregation function* $h : \mathbb{R}^m \rightarrow \mathbb{R}$ is a function that maps a multi-aspect relevance vector $\mathbf{y}$ to an absolute overall relevance value z, i.e., $h(\mathbf{y}) = z$.

To learn an aggregation function h, we need training data with overall relevance signals, either *absolute* relevance labels or *relative* preferences. In this chapter, we focus on the relative preferences and use $\mathcal{P} = \{(\mathbf{x}_i, \mathbf{x}_j) | \mathbf{x}_i \succ \mathbf{x}_j\}$ to represent the data, where $\mathbf{x}_i \succ \mathbf{x}_j$ denotes that $\mathbf{x}_i$ is preferred to $\mathbf{x}_j$. Since there are only a few aspects in a vertical, training the aggregation function needs a minimal amount of data. After learning an aggregation function, we can then apply it to the large amount of multi-aspect relevance labels and thus generate a large amount of training data with overall relevance.

In summary, we have a large dataset with ranking features $\mathbf{x}$ and the corresponding multi-aspect relevance vectors $\mathbf{y} : \mathcal{F} = \{(\mathbf{x}, \mathbf{y})\}$ and a small set of relative preference data $\mathcal{P}$. Since there is one-to-one correspondence between $\mathbf{x}$ and $\mathbf{y}$ in our data, we use either $(\mathbf{x}_i, \mathbf{x}_j) \in \mathcal{P}$ or $(\mathbf{y}_i, \mathbf{y}_j) \in \mathcal{P}$. We have the following steps:

- Learn an aggregation function $h(\mathbf{y})$ (and a mapping function Φ if not manually defined) using $\mathcal{P}$.
- Apply $h(\mathbf{y})$ on $\mathcal{F}$ and generate dataset $\hat{\mathcal{F}} = \{(\mathbf{x}, h(\mathbf{y}))\}$.
- Train a ranking function f_h using $\hat{\mathcal{F}}$ based on a conventional learning-to-rank method.

7.2.4 Model Aggregation

The label aggregation method converts the problem of learning from multi-aspect relevance into a conventional learning-to-rank problem. All the rank features related to different aspects are treated uniformly in this method. The idea of model aggregation is to train an individual ranking model for each aspect. The function is to aggregate the output of aspect ranking functions to generate the overall relevance scores.

Definition 5 (Aspect ranking function). An *aspect ranking function* $f_a : \mathbb{R}^k \to \mathbb{R}$ is a function that maps a feature vector $\mathbf{x}$ to an aspect relevance score.

Definition 6 (Model aggregation function). A *model aggregation function* $h : \mathbb{R}^m \to \mathbb{R}$ is a function that aggregates the estimated aspect relevance scores into the final overall relevance scores.

In summary, we have the following steps for model aggregation:

1. For each aspect a_i, learn an aspect ranking function f_{a_i} based on the aspect relevance labels and the mapping function.
2. For each $\mathbf{x}$ in $\mathcal{P}$, generate an m-dimensional vector $\mathbf{f}(\mathbf{x}) = [f_{a_1}(\mathbf{x}), \ldots, f_{a_m}(\mathbf{x})]$.
3. Train the aggregation function h based on the feature vector $\mathbf{f}(\mathbf{x})$ and the training pairs in $\mathcal{P}$.

For this method, the final ranking score is computed as $h(\mathbf{f}(\mathbf{x}))$. Then the central question is how to learn these aggregation functions (and the mapping function Φ). We explore different formulations in the next section.

7.3 Learning Aggregation Functions

In this section, we propose various methods to learn based on the pairwise preferences.

7.3.1 Learning Label Aggregation

We propose two different approaches: a linear aggregation approach, and a joint learning approach.

7.3.1.1 *A Linear Aggregation Method*

In this section, we explore a linear model for aggregation by assuming that we have a predefined mapping function. A simple mapping function for an aspect label set L_k can be constructed as

$$\phi_k(l_{k,s}) = \frac{s-1}{n_k - 1} \text{ for } s = 1, \dots, n_k,$$

In our local search, such a fixed mapping function is given in Table 7.1. We have an unknown parameter vector $\mathbf{w}$, and the linear function takes the form $h(\mathbf{y}) = \mathbf{w}^T \mathbf{y}$. We use the following loss function on the pairwise training data:

$$\mathcal{L} = \frac{1}{2} \sum_{(\mathbf{y}_i, \mathbf{y}_j) \in \mathcal{P}} \left(\max(0, 1 - \mathbf{w}^T \mathbf{y}_i + \mathbf{w}^T \mathbf{y}_j) \right)^2$$

Furthermore, to ensure the monotonicity, we have to constrain $\mathbf{w}$ to be non-negative element-wise:

$$\mathbf{w} \succeq 0.$$

We solve the optimization problem using a simple gradient descent approach in a similar way as the joint learning model in the next section.

Table 7.1   The aspect relevance mapping function for local search.

Aspect	Label	Score
Matching	Exact Match	$y_1 = 1.0$
	Plausible Match	$y_1 = 0.5$
	No Match	$y_1 = 0$
Distance	Same Location	$y_2 = 1.0$
	Reasonable Location	$y_2 = 0.5$
	Too Far	$y_2 = 0$
Reputation	Excellent Rating	$y_3 = 1.0$
	Good Rating	$y_3 = 0.5$
	Bad Rating	$y_3 = 0$

7.3.1.2 *A Joint Learning Method*

This method assumes that we have a predefined mapping function and learn the aggregation function directly on the numeric values of aspect relevance. But such a mapping is in an ad-hoc fashion. In this section we propose a joint learning model that learns the mapping function and the aggregation weight simultaneously. Without loss of generality, for each aspect we assign 0 to its lowest relevance label and 1 to its highest one, i.e., $\phi_k(l_{k,1}) = 0$ and $\phi_k(l_{k,n_k}) = 1$ for $k = 1, \ldots, m$. Our joint learning method will automatically determine the numeric values for the middle labels.

Formally, our goal is to learn the values of all the labels in $L_1, \ldots, L_m$ and weights $\mathbf{w}$ to minimize the following loss function:

$$
\mathcal{L} = \frac{1}{2} \sum_{(\mathbf{y}_i, \mathbf{y}_j) \in \mathcal{P}} \left(\max(0, 1 - \mathbf{w}^T \Phi(\mathbf{y}_i) + \mathbf{w}^T \Phi(\mathbf{y}_j)) \right)^2
$$

Here we use $\mathbf{y}$ to specifically denote an aspect *label* vector. We have the following differences compared with the linear method: (1) $\Phi(\mathbf{y}_i) = [\phi_1(y_{i,1}), \ldots, \phi_m(y_{i,m})]^T$, the vector after applying the mapping function. It is also unknown and needs to be optimized. (2) We have the following additional consistency constraint which ensures that a better label gets a higher mapped score:

$$
0 = \phi_k(l_{k,1}) \leq \phi_k(l_{k,2}) \ldots \leq \phi_k(l_{k,n_k}) = 1 \text{ for } k = 1, \ldots, m.
$$

It is easy to verify that the spaces with the constraints are convex. However, such a problem is not easy to optimize due to the quadratic terms in the objective function. Since the dimensionality of the problem is not high, we thus propose a gradient descent approach with projection to optimize the objective function. Let $\mathcal{A}_{k,s} = \{(\mathbf{y}_i, \mathbf{y}_j) \in \mathcal{P} | y_{i,k} = l_{k,s}, y_{j,k} \neq l_{k,s}\}$ and $\mathcal{B}_{k,s} = \{(\mathbf{y}_i, \mathbf{y}_j) \in \mathcal{P} | y_{i,k} \neq l_{k,s}, y_{j,k} = l_{k,s}\}$. The gradient for each variable with respect to the objective function is:

$$
\frac{\partial \mathcal{L}}{\partial w_k} = \sum_{(\mathbf{y}_i, \mathbf{y}_j) \in \mathcal{P}} \max(0, 1 - \mathbf{w}^T \Phi(\mathbf{y}_i) + \mathbf{w}^T \Phi(\mathbf{y}_j))
$$
$$
\cdot (-\phi_k(y_{i,k}) + \phi_k(y_{j,k}))
$$
$$
\frac{\partial \mathcal{L}}{\partial \phi_k(l_{k,s})} = \sum_{(\mathbf{y}_i, \mathbf{y}_j) \in \mathcal{A}_{k,s}} \max(0, 1 - \mathbf{w}^T \Phi(\mathbf{y}_i) + \mathbf{w}^T \Phi(\mathbf{y}_j))(-w_k)
$$
$$
+ \sum_{(\mathbf{y}_i, \mathbf{y}_j) \in \mathcal{B}_{k,s}} \max(0, 1 - \mathbf{w}^T \Phi(\mathbf{y}_i) + \mathbf{w}^T \Phi(\mathbf{y}_j)) \cdot w_k
$$

We use t to denote the iteration in the gradient descent. After iteration t, we project the estimated parameters to the convex space defined by the constraints. We use the norm-2 distance for the projection

$$\min_{\mathbf{w}, \phi_k(l_{k,s})} ||\mathbf{w} - \mathbf{w}^{(t)}||^2 + \sum_{k,s} |\phi_k(l_{k,s}) - \phi_k(l_{k,s})^{(t)}|^2$$

$$\text{s.t. } 0 = \phi_k(l_{k,1}) \leq \phi_k(l_{k,2}) \ldots \leq \phi_k(l_{k,n_k}) = 1$$

$$\mathbf{w} \succeq 0,$$

The projection can be efficiently solved, since it is a standard quadratic programming problem [303].

7.3.2 Learning Model Aggregation

In this section, we propose another method for our multi-aspect relevance formulation, the model aggregation method, which is formulated in Section 7.2.4. In this method, we first learn an aspect ranking function f_{a_i} for each aspect a_i and use a supervised linear model as our aggregation function:

$$h(\mathbf{f}(\mathbf{x})) = \mathbf{w}^T \mathbf{f}(\mathbf{x}).$$

To learn an aspect ranking function f_{a_i} using a method such as GBRank [407], we need to assign numerical values to aspect labels, i.e., the mapping function. We have proposed to automatically learn the mapping function in the joint learning method in the previous section; thus we use the obtained mapping function Φ to convert the aspect labels.

To learn the parameter $\mathbf{w}$, we use the following loss function:

$$\mathcal{L} = \frac{1}{2} \sum_{(\mathbf{x}_i, \mathbf{x}_j) \in \mathcal{P}} (\max(0, 1 - \mathbf{w}^T \mathbf{f}(\mathbf{x}_i) + \mathbf{w}^T \mathbf{f}(\mathbf{x}_j)))^2$$

where $\mathbf{f}(\mathbf{x}) = [f_{a_1}(\mathbf{x}), \ldots, f_{a_m}(\mathbf{x})]$. This model is very similar to the linear model in the label aggregation methods. The difference is that we replace the labels by the output of aspect ranking functions.

Compared to the label aggregation methods, there are two benefits of the model aggregation method. First, we can use a different type of model for each aspect ranking function. This is desired in the sense that different aspects are not necessarily homogeneous. For example, the matching aspect can be complex and thus needs a ranking function with high model complexity, but a simple regression model may be good enough for the distance aspect. In particular, we use a model GBRank [407] for the matching aspect, which shows excellent performance in learning such a function. On the other hand, we use two linear regression models for distance and reputation aspect, respectively. Hence, the combination of various types of models for different aspects gives great flexibility to the final ranking function.

Also, in the model aggregation method, we can exploit preference data inferred from other sources, such as user clicks, to learn the aggregation function. Unlike the label aggregation methods, each document in $\mathcal{P}$ does not need aspect relevance labels $\mathbf{y}$, and we only need $\mathbf{f}(\mathbf{x})$, the output of aspect ranking functions, to learn the aggregation function. This provides flexibility to quickly adapt the aggregation function to different contexts. For example, this makes it possible to provide personalized search rankings: We may collect preference data $\mathcal{P}$ for a user u and use it to learn a user-specific aggregated function $\mathbf{w}_u^T \mathbf{f}(\mathbf{x})$. Note that we do not need to learn aspect ranking functions for each user, since each aspect ranking should be common among users, but the tradeoff among aspects depends on personal preference. Similarly, we can provide customized search rankings for different search applications. For example, in mobile search, the distance aspect may be more important than in desktop search. We can easily build a separate ranking function for mobile search using the preference data obtained from user clicks in mobile search.

7.4 **Experiments**

In this section, we present experimental results to validate our approaches. The main objective of our experiments is to study the effectiveness of our multi-aspect relevance formulation and the proposed aggregation methods in local search ranking. We report both offline results and online bucket-test results in this section.

7.4.1 **Datasets**

The datasets we use are from a commercial local search engine, where a document is called a *business listing* or *listing* for short. We follow the editorial guideline similar to the guideline in Figure 7.2 to obtain the training data with *only* multi-aspect relevance. Specifically, each query in our data has an associated location (e.g., "Target Sunnyvale CA"). For each (query, listing) pair, we have three aspects: matching, distance, and reputation, as discussed in Section 7.2.1, and we ask editors to provide the three aspect relevance labels. Note that we do not ask editors to provide the overall relevance labels to reduce the labelling cost. Table 7.2 shows the statistics of this dataset. In particular, we have two types of queries: category queries and business name queries. A category query such as "Chinese restaurant Los Angeles, CA 90018" is similar to informational queries and can be broadly matched by any Chinese restaurant, whereas a business name query such as "Bank of America, Los Angeles, CA 90018" is more like a navigational query and can only be matched by the corresponding bank centers. Intuitively, the relative importance of each aspect for these two types of queries can be potentially different.

Table 7.2   Statistics of multi-aspect relevance data.

		#query	#listing
Category queries	Training	4211	70701
	Test	1055	17675
	Total	5266	88376
Business name queries	Training	6966	76343
	Test	1739	18550
	Total	8705	94893

(a)

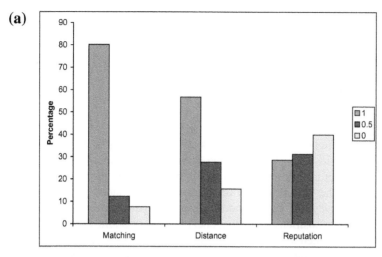

(b)

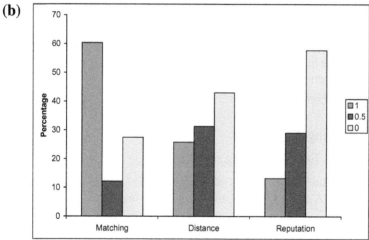

FIGURE 7.3

Distribution of aspect relevance labels. The 1, 0.5, and 0 correspond to the aspect labels in Table 7.1. (a) Category queries; (b) business name queries.

In Figure 7.3, we show the distribution of the labels for different types of queries and different aspects. We can see clear differences between them. The differences of the statistics regarding matching and distance aspects are due to the different densities of businesses for the two query categories: There are more matching businesses for category queries than for business name queries (e.g., typically there are more restaurants than Target stores in a city). The high percentage of the "Bad Rating" label for the reputation aspect for business name queries is due to two reasons: (1) when there is no user review, it is considered a "Bad Rating" in our guideline, and (2)

Table 7.3 Statistics of overall relative preference datasets obtained through side-by-side comparison.

	#Training $\mathcal{P}_{train}$	#Test $\mathcal{P}_{test}$
Category queries	549	493
Name queries	445	457

about 50% of the business name queries are *chain* queries, such as "Walmart," and users typically do not bother reviewing chain stores. Indeed, we will show that the reputation aspect is not particularly important for business name queries.

We obtain the overall relative preference using the side-by-side comparison as follows: Given any query, we randomly sample a pair of documents and put them side by side. The positions of the two documents are randomly shuffled to avoid any kind of bias. We then ask the editors to judge which one is better than another. The obtained overall training signals are thus relative preferences. Previous studies have shown that relative preferences are more reliable than absolute judgements in many scenarios [189,24]. This idea is very critical when the training data are small. However, it is expensive to obtain a large amount of such data. Fortunately, our experiment results show that only a small amount of such data is needed to obtain highly accurate aggregation functions. Table 7.3 summarizes the statistics of this dataset. We split these data into training ($\mathcal{P}_{train}$) and test ($\mathcal{P}_{test}$) to evaluate our aggregation functions.

7.4.2 Ranking Algorithms

We compare the following ranking algorithms:

- **Rule**: A traditional one overall relevance label scheme described in Section 7.2.1.
- **Ed-overall**: A ranking function trained directly using editorial pairwise preference data $\mathcal{P}_{train}$.
- **Click**: A ranking function trained using pairwise preference data induced from the click model [186].
- **Linear**: The linear aggregation function described in Section 7.3.1.1.
- **Joint**: The joint learning model described in Section 7.3.1.2.
- **ModAgg**: The model aggregation method described in Section 7.3.2.

Rule, Ed-overall, and Click serve as baselines. Rule, a traditional one-overall relevance label scheme described in Section 7.2.1, is similar to the *graded measure* used in [336] in the sense that the secondary labels are used to break the tie of the primary labels. Ed-overall and Click are other baselines to show the benefit of our multi-aspect relevance. Both are learned using the GBRank models [407]. The click data are easy to obtain but they are noisy. We have 1,441,975 and 58,782 click-based training (query, listing) pairs for category and name queries, respectively. In all our label aggregation methods, the final ranking functions are learned using the GBRank models [407].

7.4.3 **Offline Experimental Results**

We report our offline experiment results based on the datasets with editorial labels.

7.4.3.1 *Evaluation Metrics*

To evaluate aggregation functions, we consider two types of pair accuracy with respect to the test dataset $\mathcal{P}_{test}$. (1) Label aggregation accuracy: How accurate is an aggregation function to aggregate the multi-aspect relevance to generate the overall relevance? This accuracy is only applied to label aggregation methods. (2) Ranking accuracy: How effective is a ranking function trained using either label or model aggregation methods?

Let h be a label aggregation function and f be a final ranking function trained using either label aggregation or model aggregation methods. The label aggregation accuracy of h is:

$$\frac{|\{(\mathbf{y}_i, \mathbf{y}_j)|h(\mathbf{y}_i) > h(\mathbf{y}_j), (\mathbf{y}_i, \mathbf{y}_j) \in \mathcal{P}_{test}\}|}{|\mathcal{P}_{test}|} \qquad (7.1)$$

and the ranking accuracy of f is:

$$\frac{|\{(\mathbf{y}_i, \mathbf{y}_j)|f(\mathbf{x}_i) > f(\mathbf{x}_j), (\mathbf{y}_i, \mathbf{y}_j) \in \mathcal{P}_{test}\}|}{|\mathcal{P}_{test}|}. \qquad (7.2)$$

Note that an NDCG-like metric seems to be possible to compare the ranking accuracy of different aggregation methods, since a label aggregation function can generate absolute overall relevance values. However, different label aggregation methods can generate different overall values for the same (query, listing) pair. Thus we do not have a common ground on which to compare them. Hence, we use the pair accuracy as a more isolated and unbiased metric for evaluation.

7.4.3.2 *Results on Label Aggregation Accuracy*

Table 7.4 shows the comparison of various aggregation functions based on the label aggregation accuracy, which is defined in Eq. (7.1). In this experiment, we use only the data in Table 7.3. We learn the aggregation functions for each type of query separately. Table 7.4 shows the results of category queries and business name queries, respectively. From this table, we make the following observations. (1) The Rule method performs much worse than all the learning-based methods in both types of queries.

Table 7.4 Evaluation of aggregation functions on label aggregation accuracy. Linear and Joint are significantly better than Rule (p-value < 0.01).

	Category Queries	Business Name Queries
Rule	0.640	0.650
Linear	**0.825**	**0.926**
Joint	**0.825**	**0.932**

For example, for category queries, the rule-based method has about 64% accuracy, and all other methods have 82.5% accuracy. This shows that the rules are too coarse to capture the desired tradeoff. (2) They perform equally well on both category and business name queries. The pair accuracy is 83% on category queries and 93% on business name queries. This demonstrates high consistency between the aggregated overall relevance and the true one. (3) Comparing the two types of queries, we can see higher accuracy for business name queries than category queries. This is expected, since the relevance for category queries is naturally more complex than for business name queries.

7.4.3.3 Results on Ranking Accuracy

Table 7.5 shows the comparison of the ranking accuracy for both label and model aggregation methods. For a label aggregation method, we first use the training data in Table 7.3 to learn the label aggregation function and then apply it to obtain the overall relevance for the set of training queries in Table 7.2. We then test the ranking function using $\mathcal{P}_{test}$. The pair ranking accuracy is defined in Eq. (7.2). For the model aggregation method, we use the training data with aspect relevance label data in Table 7.2 to learn the aspect ranking functions and then use the training data in Table 7.3 to learn the model aggregation function. We then apply the obtained aspect ranking functions and model aggregation function together on the test data. In this table, we make the following observations: (1) For category queries, all the learning based methods are significantly better than the Rule method. The ModAgg method is slightly better than all other methods. (2) However, for business name queries, only the ModAgg method can be significantly better than the Rule method, whereas the improvement of the Linear and Joint methods over the Rule method is not significant with respect to p-value < 0.01. One possible reason is that business name queries are relatively easy and all the methods have achieved high accuracy.

Overall, we can see that our learning methods are quite effective and the model aggregation method is the most stable one for both classes of queries.

Table 7.5 Evaluation of aggregation functions on ranking accuracy. Statistically significant differences (p-value < 0.01) compared to Rule are highlighted in bold.

	Category Queries	Business Name Queries
Rule	0.614	0.788
Ed-overall	0.575	0.841
Click	0.638	0.841
Linear	**0.750**	0.879
Joint	**0.760**	0.871
ModAgg	**0.769**	**0.917**

7.4.3.4 *Benefit of Multi-Aspect Relevance*

Table 7.5 also shows the benefit of our multi-aspect relevance formulation. We can see that Ed-overall performs much worse compared to the ModAgg method. The reason that Ed-overall performs worse is mainly due to the limited amount of training data. Click data performance is inferior, mainly because it is noisy. Our method leverages the aspect relevance and thus can utilize the small amount of Ed-overall data more effectively.

7.4.3.5 *Comparison of Aspect Importance*

The Linear, Joint, and ModAgg methods generate the weight vector ($w_{Matching}$, $w_{Distance}$, $w_{Reputation}$) for aspects as output. These weights indicate the relative importance of aspects in the overall relevance. For category queries, we have

$$w_{Matching} \gg w_{Reputation} \gg w_{Distance}.$$

For business name queries, we have

$$w_{Matching} \gg w_{Distance} > w_{Reputation}.$$

This result confirms our intuition that the reputation aspect is more important than the distance aspect for category queries, and vice versa, for business name queries. This finding shows that different types of queries work best with different aggregation functions.

In our current work, we mainly focus on two broad types of queries. These results show that there is probably much room for improvement if we can make our aggregation functions query-dependent or personalized. We leave these tasks as future work.

7.4.4 **Online Experimental Results**

Ranking functions can be compared in terms of pair accuracy or DCG in the offline setting, but they can also be compared in terms of how users interact with the search results in the online setting. In this section, we report our online results.

7.4.4.1 *Experiment Design*

In our online experiments, we conduct "bucket tests" for a certain period to compare different ranking algorithms. The bucket is created based on user cookies. A cookie is assigned to a fixed bucket in our test period. Each bucket corresponds to a small percentage of user population who use our local search engine. In different buckets, we show search results of different ranking algorithms. If one ranking algorithm is better than another, we would expect the user experience metric to be better.

We can see that online experiments are expensive and we cannot test many different algorithms. In our experiments, we were able to test only two functions during the same time period in our commercial local search engine. During two weeks, we compared

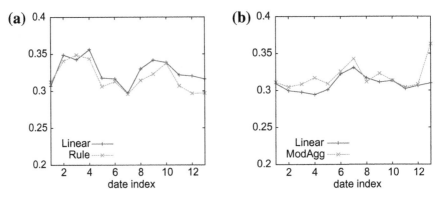

FIGURE 7.4

The clickthrough rate (CTR) comparisons based on online experiments for a commercial local search engine. CTRs are normalized not to show absolute values. Each comparison is done for a different test period due to online experiment constraints. (a) CTR5 comparison of Rule and Linear; (b) CTR5 comparison of Linear and ModAgg.

Rule and Linear. During another two weeks, we compared Linear and ModAgg. To compare two functions, we use CTR as our user experience metric. Specifically, we use CTR for top i positions and denote it as CTRi:

$$\text{CTR}i = \frac{\sum_{k=1}^{k=i} \text{clicks at position } k}{\sum_{k=1}^{k=i} \text{views at position } k}$$

For confidential reasons, we do not report the exact CTR, but we do report the normalized CTR over a fixed number.

7.4.4.2 *Results*

In Figure 7.4, we report the daily trends of the click-through rate (CTR) of ranking functions. The CTRs naturally fluctuate on different days. We can see that Linear is consistently better than Rule and ModAgg outperforms Linear during the whole period. The average CTR5s of Rule and Linear during the first test period are 0.315 and 0.325, respectively. The average CTR5s of Linear and ModAgg during the second test period are 0.308 and 0.314, respectively. These differences are statistically significant (p-value < 0.01).

This result is consistent with our offline experimental results and shows that our multi-aspect relevance framework outperforms a traditional one overall relevance scheme. In addition, it demonstrates that the model aggregation method is more effective than the label aggregation methods. Thus, using different ranking models for different aspects is more suitable for our multi-aspect relevance aggregation.

7.5 **Conclusions and Future Work**

The meaning of relevance in vertical searches is domain-specific and usually consists of multiple aspects. In this chapter, we proposed a multi-aspect relevance formulation for vertical searches in the learning-to-rank setting. In our formulation, the relevance between a query and a document is assessed with respect to each aspect, forming the multi-aspect relevance. To learn a ranking function, we studied two types of learning-based approaches, a label aggregation method and a model aggregation method, to estimate the tradeoff among these aspect relevancies. Then a ranking function is learned based on the multi-aspect relevance formulation. Since there are only a few aspects, a minimal amount of training data is needed to learn the tradeoff. We studied several methods to learn aggregation functions and conducted experiments on local search engine data. Our experimental results show that our multi-aspect relevance formulation is promising. The proposed aggregation approaches are very effective to learn the tradeoff among different aspects.

Our work can be extended as follows: First, we proposed to learn the ranking functions and aggregation functions separately in this chapter. Finding a way to learn them jointly is a promising direction. Second, our methods rely on manually identified aspects, and thus ways to automatically discover the aspects given a vertical are worth studying. Third, our multi-aspect relevance formulation provides a new base to study how to learn context-sensitive or personalized ranking functions. For example, it is possible to dynamically update our aggregation function based on short-term user interaction history.

Conclusions and Future Work

Aggregated Vertical Search

INTRODUCTION

Modern search portals such as Google, Bing, and Yahoo! provide access to a wide range of search services in addition to Web search. These search services, commonly referred to as *verticals*, include highly specialized search engines that focus on a particular type of media (e.g., *images*, *video*), search engines that focus on a particular type of search task (e.g., *news*, *local*), and applications that return a specific type of information (e.g., *weather*, *stock quotes*). In the most general sense, *aggregated search* is the task of providing integrated access to all these different vertical search services and to the core Web search engine within a common search interface via a single query box and a unified presentation of results.

Given a user's query, an aggregated search system must make a number of predictions. As one might expect, not every vertical is relevant to every query. If a user issues the query "nyc pizza restaurant locations," it is almost certain that the user wants local business information and not images. Thus, an important step for an aggregated search system is to present those verticals most likely to be relevant and to suppress those most likely to not be relevant. Moreover, queries are often ambiguous in terms of the user's actual intent. For example, if a user issues the query "New York style pizza" (Figure 8.1), it is unclear whether the user wants to find a place to eat (in which case local business results might be relevant) or wants to learn to cook New York-style pizza (in which case recipes, how-to videos, and/or images might be relevant). Thus, another important step for an aggregated search engine is to resolve contention between verticals and to present those more likely to be relevant in a more salient way.

Aggregated search might seem like a new technology, but it has its roots in a fairly mature subfield of information retrieval called *federated search*, where the goal is to provide automated search across multiple distributed collections or search engines. And, like most methods of federated search, most aggregated search methods approach the task in two subsequent steps: (1) predicting *which* verticals to present (*vertical selection*) and (2) predicting *where* to present them (*vertical presentation*). Vertical selection refers to the problem of selecting a subset of relevant verticals, given a query. One way to think about this is as the classification of verticals according to whether or not they should appear on the results page at all. Vertical

| new york style pizza | search |

New York-style pizza - Wikipedia, the free encyclopedia
en.wikipedia.org/wiki/New_York-style_pizza
New York-style pizza originated in **New York** City in the early 1900s, and in 1905, the first **pizza** establishment in the United States was opened in **New York**'s Little ...

New York Style Pizza | Serious Eats : Recipes
www.seriouseats.com/recipes/2010/10/new-york-style-pizza.html
1 hour before baking, adjust oven rack with **pizza** stone to middle position and preheat oven to 500°F. Turn single dough ball out onto lightly flour surface.

New York Style Pizza near North Carolina 27599

local

1. **NY Pizza** - (xxx) xxx-xxxx
   6458 Tryon Rd, Cary
   Directions – Menu

2. **NY Pizza** - (xxx) xxx-xxxx
   1831 N Harrison Ave, Cary
   Directions - Menu

New York Style Pizza Recipe - Allrecipes.com
allrecipes.com/Recipe/New York-Style Pizza
This is a no frills **New York Pizza** with heaps of mozzarella cheese and fresh basil. Use it as a base and add your favorite **pizza**

New York Style Pizza & Pasta
www.newyorkstylepizza.ca
New York Style Pizza & Pasta was established in 1991. Since then the restaurant has won restaurateur of the year awards five times and many other excellence awards...

Images for new york style pi

images

New york style pizza
www.yelp.com/search?find_desc=new+york+style+pizza&find_loc=New
Reviews on **New york style pizza** in **New** York: Rosa's **Pizza**, Lombardi's **Pizza**, Grimaldi's, John's Pizzeria, Keste **Pizza** & Vino, Bleecker Street **Pizza**, Joe's **Pizza** ...

News for new york style pizza
Photo Of The Day: New York Pizza
Gadling - 16 hours ago

news   There's lots of good food to be had in **New York** City. So much, in fact, that visitors must not forget to try...
NY man hopes to make world's fastest pizza
Wall Street Journal - 16 hours ago

FIGURE 8.1

Given the query "new york style pizza," an aggregated search system decides to blend results from the *local*, *images*, and *news* verticals into the core Web results.

presentation refers to the problem of interleaving this subset of verticals with the Web results.[1]

---

[1] This decomposition is primarily motivated by economics. Getting results from a vertical search engine often incurs some cost. This cost might be monetary if the aggregator is paying for access to a closed service. In the case of cooperative vertical search engines, this cost may be computational if the vertical search engine cannot support portal traffic. Therefore, vertical selection can be a method for reducing the overhead of an aggregator.

This chapter provides an overview of aggregated search techniques and methods for evaluation. As mentioned, an aggregated search system must make predictions about which vertical(s) are more likely to be relevant to a user's query. State-of-the-art approaches combine multiple types of evidence to make these decisions. Section 8.1 provides an overview of features used in aggregated search; Section 8.2 provides an overview of machine learning methods for combining features in order to make aggregated search predictions. Section 8.3 focuses on methods for evaluation and covers methods for test collection evaluation and online evaluation. Finally, Section 8.4 covers special topics in aggregated search. Among these, we focus on methods for sharing training data among verticals and methods for eliciting and exploiting implicit user feedback to improve future aggregated search predictions.

8.1 Sources of Evidence

There are many ways in which an aggregated search system might be able to determine that a vertical is relevant to a query. Consider, for example, the task of predicting when to present the *news* vertical in response to a user's request. If the query contains the term "news," this is a strong indication that the *news* vertical is relevant. That said, not every newsworthy query will contain the term "news." Consider, for example, the query "presidential debates." If many of the news articles currently in the news index contain these two query terms (or terms that are semantically related), this might also indicate *news* vertical intent. In this case, the underlying assumption is that content supply (i.e., an abundance of query-related content in the underlying vertical collection) can help predict content demand. A system might also consider content demand directly. In many cases, users can navigate and issue queries directly to a particular vertical search engine. In a cooperative environment, the aggregated search system might have access to this vertical-specific query stream. Thus, another source of evidence is the number of similar queries issued to the vertical in the recent past. Finally, if a vertical is presented in response to a query, the aggregated search system can keep track of the user's actions. Although implicit user feedback is subject to different types of bias, by averaging across many users, a system may be able to generate useful evidence for future impressions of the same query or similar queries.

Prior work shows that no single source of evidence can be used to predict that a particular vertical is relevant to a query [15,13,280]. Thus, state-of-the-art approaches to vertical presentation use machine learning to *combine* multiple types of predictive evidence as features. In this section, we provide an overview of the various types of features used in prior work.

8.1.1 Types of Features

In learning about different types of features, it helps to be aware of their similarities and differences. Broadly speaking, features can be organized along two dimensions. The first dimension relates to whether the value of the feature depends only on the query (is the same for all verticals), only on the vertical (is the same for all queries), or is unique to the vertical-query pair. The second dimension relates to whether the feature value can be generated without issuing the query to the vertical, must be generated after issuing the query to the vertical but before the vertical is presented to a user, or must be generated after the vertical is presented to a user.

With respect to the first dimension (i.e., the source of the feature value), there are three categories. *Query features* are generated from the query string and their values are independent of the candidate vertical. Examples include whether the query contains a particular term (e.g., "news," "pics," or "weather") or a particular named entity type (e.g., a person, location, or organization). *Vertical features* are generated from the candidate vertical and their values are independent of the query. Examples include the number of new documents added to the vertical collection or the number of queries issued directly to the vertical search engine in the recent past. Vertical features typically quantify bursts in vertical content supply or demand. Finally, *vertical-query features* are a function of both the query and the vertical in question. Examples include the number of hits in the vertical collection or the similarity between the query and the vertical's query stream.

With respect to the second dimension (i.e., the stage at which the feature value can be generated), there are also three categories. Pre-retrieval features can be generated without ever issuing the query to the vertical. Query features (generated from the query, independently from the vertical) and vertical features (generated from the vertical, independently from the query) tend to be pre-retrieval features. In most commercial environments, it is either impractical or impossible to issue every query to every vertical in order to decide which verticals to present and where. Thus, pre-retrieval features have received considerable attention in prior work. Post-retrieval features must be generated by issuing the query to the vertical. Examples include the average recency of the vertical's top results or the average retrieval score of the vertical's top results. Post-retrieval features are motivated by the fact that a vertical can be ultimately suppressed in light of poor post-retrieval evidence. For instance, if a vertical search engine retrieves an unusually low number of results, this may indicate that it is not relevant. Finally, *post-presentation* features are observed after the vertical is presented to a user and are typically derived from actions taken by the user. Post-presentations features typically consist of implicit feedback signals such as clicks and skips on the vertical results, which are thought to be positively or negatively correlated with vertical relevance. Post-presentation features are *retrospective*. As such, they allow self-assessment of presentation decisions and can be used to inform predictions during future impressions of the same query or similar queries. Figure 8.2 depicts the availability of different features at different stages of decision making.

Defining features as being pre-retrieval, post-retrieval, or post-presentation deserves additional clarification. One could imagine, for example, a system that caches post-retrieval and post-presentation features for future impressions of a query (Figure 8.3). Caching feature values is particularly useful for head queries, which are seen over and over. Caching post-retrieval and post-presentation feature values enables their use without having to issue the query to the vertical or having to present

$$\phi_{q,v_0}^{\text{pre-ret}} \qquad \phi_{q,v_0}^{\text{post-ret}} \qquad \phi_{q,v_0}^{\text{post-pres}}$$

$$\phi_{q,v_1}^{\text{pre-ret}} \longrightarrow \phi_{q,v_1}^{\text{post-ret}} \qquad \phi_{q,v_1}^{\text{post-pres}}$$

$$\vdots \qquad\qquad \vdots \qquad\qquad \vdots$$

$$\phi_{q,v_{k-1}}^{\text{pre-ret}} \qquad \phi_{q,v_{k-1}}^{\text{post-ret}} \qquad \phi_{q,v_{k-1}}^{\text{post-pres}}$$

$$\phi_{q,v_k}^{\text{pre-ret}} \longrightarrow \phi_{q,v_k}^{\text{post-ret}} \longrightarrow \phi_{q,v_k}^{\text{post-pres}}$$

FIGURE 8.2

Feature availability during different stages of decision making. Pre-retrieval features, $\phi_{q,v}^{\text{pre-ret}}$, are easy to compute, are available to all verticals, and help with vertical selection decisions. Post-retrieval features, $\phi_{q,v}^{\text{post-ret}}$, are computed only for those verticals from which we request results and are useful for making final presentation decisions. Post-presentation features, $\phi_{q,v}^{\text{post-pres}}$, are available only after the presentation decision has been made and is useful for evaluating performance and predicting the values of post-presentation features for future issuances of q. Features in gray are not computed or logged during an individual search session because of upstream decisions.

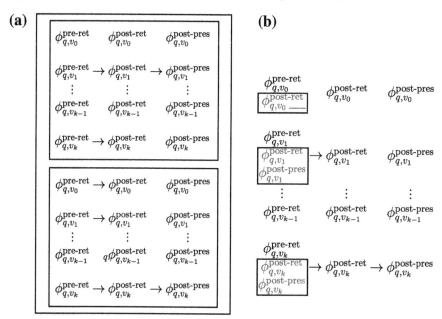

FIGURE 8.3

Feature caching. The left subfigure represents the logged features computed for previous issuances of q, including post-presentation features. The right subfigure represents the availability of cached feature values (red, in boxes) during runtime at the pre-retrieval stage. Note that these are approximations to downstream feature values and may be sensitive to corpus change or user differences.

the vertical to the user. However, based on the terminology used in this chapter, cached features are still considered post-retrieval and post-presentation features. The distinction lies in whether it is necessary to issue the query to the vertical or present the vertical to the user in order to generate the *exact* feature value for the current query. Vertical collections, vertical query streams, and vertical click behaviors are dynamic. Thus, while post-retrieval and post-presentation features can be cached for future impressions of a query, their values are likely to require periodic, and possibly online, updating.

8.1.2 Query Features

Query features are generated from the query string and not from any resource associated with a candidate vertical. As described in more detail in Section 8.2, a predictive relationship between query features and the relevance of a particular vertical must be either hardwired manually or learned using supervised machine learning.

Prior work has experimented with different types of query features. These include features that indicate the presence of a particular term (e.g., "photo," "weather," "stocks") [15,223], a particular named entity type (e.g., the name of a person, location, organization) [15], or a particular entry in a look-up table (e.g., a valid ZIP code or a valid ticker symbol) [15]. Such query features are typically binary-valued and implemented using rule-based triggers.

Query-term features such as those described here capitalize on the fact that certain keywords confidently predict vertical intent. The keyword "pics" suggests that the user wants images, the keyword "showtimes" suggests that the user wants movie times, and the keyword "directions" suggests that the user wants driving directions. Sometimes, however, a query might not have an explicit keyword. Thus, another type of query feature measures the degree of co-occurrence between the query terms and a set of manually identified vertical-specific keywords [13]. Co-occurrence statistics can be derived from the aggregated search system's own query log. So, for example, given the query "eiffel tower," the system might consider presenting the *images* vertical because "eiffel tower" tends to co-occur with terms such as "pics," "pictures," and "photos" in the system's query log.

Among the most successful query features investigated in prior work are query-category features, which measure the query's affinity to a set of predefined semantic categories [15,280]. Query-category features have been successful for several reasons. First, many verticals investigated in prior work have been topically focused—for example, *travel*, *health*, *games*, *music*, *autos*, and *sports* [15]. Second, query classification has been widely studied for purposes other than aggregated search (see, for example, [312,311,198]). Thus, aggregated search techniques can capitalize on these well-tested approaches for the purpose of feature generation. Finally, although general-purpose query categorization may require making a binary decision about the query's membership in a category, for the goal of aggregated search this is not required. Query-category features can be real-valued and be associated with the classifier's confidence values across the set of target categories. This gives the aggregated search model the flexibility of focusing on other types of features when query-category confidence values are *uniformly* low.

Query categorization is challenging because state-of-the-art classifiers tend to use a bag-of-words representation and queries are usually terse. However, a simple and effective solution is to categorize the query *indirectly*. That is, to issue the query to a search engine containing manually or even automatically labeled documents and to categorize the query based on the categories assigned to the top-ranked results [312,311]. Let C denote a set of predefined semantic categories (e.g., travel, health, sports, arts, movies, etc.). Given query q, the confidence value assigned to category $c \in C$ can be computed based on the average confidence value associated with the top-N results ($\mathcal{R}_N$) weighted by their retrieval score,

$$P(c|q) = \frac{1}{\mathcal{Z}} \sum_{d \in \mathcal{R}_N} P(c|d) \times \text{score}(d, q), \tag{8.1}$$

where $P(c|d)$ is the confidence value that document d belongs to category c, $\text{score}(d, q)$ is the retrieval score given to d in response to q, and normalizer $\mathcal{Z} = \sum_{c \in C} P(c|q)$.

8.1.3 **Vertical Features**

Vertical features are generated from the vertical, independent of the query. Therefore, their values are the same for all queries. There are two motivations for using vertical features in a model. First, some verticals are more popular than others, either because they satisfy a wider range of information needs (*news* vs. *stock quotes*) or because they satisfy more frequently occurring information needs (*weather* vs. *calculator*). Second, user demand for the same vertical is dynamic. A popular news event may trigger a burst in demand for the *news* vertical, unusual weather may trigger a burst in demand for the *weather* vertical, and a viral video may trigger a burst in demand for the *video* vertical.

As described in more detail later in Section 8.2, there are two ways that a model can learn to favor some verticals, irrespective of the query. The first way is to learn different models for different verticals. Most machine learning algorithms harness information about the target class distribution in the training data. The second way is to learn a single model for all verticals, but to add a set of features that signal the identity of the vertical in question. This can be done, for example, by adding one binary feature per candidate vertical. Then, given a query and a particular candidate vertical, the binary feature corresponding to that candidate can be set to 1, and the features corresponding to the other verticals can be set to 0.

In general, modeling bursts in vertical demand can be done in two ways. One way is to generate features directly correlated with vertical demand. To this end, one might generate features from the vertical's direct query traffic (provided, of course, that the vertical has direct search capabilities) or from clicks on recent presentations of the vertical (provided, of course, that the vertical is clickable). Detecting "bursty states" in a stream of events is a well-studied problem (see, for example, Kleinberg [203]), and such methods can be used to generate features that quantify the current demand for a particular vertical. The other method for modeling content demand is to model content supply, which may be correlated with demand. Such features might include the number of new results added to the vertical collection (e.g., *news*) or whether the vertical contains up-to-date information (e.g., *weather*).

8.1.4 Vertical-Query Features

Vertical-query features measure relationships between the vertical and the query and are therefore unique to the vertical-query pair. Vertical-query features can be classified into pre-retrieval, post-retrieval, and post-presentation features.

8.1.4.1 *Pre-Retrieval Vertical-Query Features*

Though it may seem counterintuitive, it is possible to generate vertical-query features without actually issuing the query to the vertical. One alternative is to generate vertical-query features from the vertical's query traffic. Such features consider the similarity between the query and those issued directly to the vertical by users. A simple similarity measure that has been effective in prior work is the query generation probability, given the vertical's query-log language model [15,100,16]. Let θ_v^{qlog} denote a language model constructed from vertical v's query log. The query generation probability is given by

$$P\left(q|\theta_v^{\text{qlog}}\right) = \prod_{w \in q} P\left(w|\theta_v^{\text{qlog}}\right).$$

(8.2)

Because queries have different lengths, it becomes important to normalize this value by $\mathcal{Z} = \sum_{v \in \mathcal{V}} P(q|\theta_v^{\text{qlog}})$.

This approach measures the similarity between the query and those issued to the vertical. A simpler alternative is to require an exact match. Diaz [98] used features that considered the proportion of vertical query traffic that corresponded to query q.

Other pre-retrieval features consider the similarity between the query and content from the vertical. As previously mentioned, aggregated search is related to *federated search*, where the objective is to provide integrated search across multiple *text-based* collections. It is often impractical to issue the query to every collection. Thus, the goal of *resource selection*, which is analogous to *vertical selection*, is to predict the existence of query-related content in a particular collection without issuing the query to the collection. Many different resource selection methods have been proposed in prior work. Two highly successful ones, which have been used as features during aggregated search, are Collection Retrieval Inference Network (CORI) [49] and RElevant Document Distribution Estimation (ReDDE) [315].

Both resource selection methods use sampled documents. In our case, if a particular vertical collection is accessible only via a search interface, query-based sampling [50] can be used. Query-based sampling is the iterative process of issuing a random query to the search engine, sampling documents from the results, selecting a new term from the current document sample to be used as new sampling query, and continuing until a large enough sample is collected. Usually, between 300–1,000 documents are sampled from each collection.

Of the two methods, CORI is perhaps the simplest. Let v_s denote the set of documents sampled from vertical v. Given k candidate verticals, CORI first constructs an index of k large documents, where the large document associated with vertical v is a concatenation of all documents in v_s. Then, given query q, CORI scores each vertical v according to the retrieval score associated with its large document. So, for example, under the query-likelihood retrieval model, the CORI score given to v in response to q would be

$$\phi_{q,v}^{\mathrm{cori}} = \prod_{w \in q} P(w|\theta_{v_s}), \tag{8.3}$$

where θ_{v_s} is the language model associated with v_s.

CORI tends to favor collections with the greatest *proportion* of query-related documents (presumably reflected in the sampled set). However, what we really want are the verticals with the greatest *absolute* number of query-related documents. ReDDE directly estimates the absolute number of query-related documents in a collection. Instead of turning each set v_s into a large document, ReDDE constructs an index of all individual documents within all sets of samples. This is referred to as the *centralized sample index*. Then, given query q, ReDDE conducts a retrieval from this index and scores vertical v according to

$$\phi_{q,v}^{\mathrm{redde}} = \frac{|v|}{|v_s|} \times \sum_{d \in \mathcal{R}_N} \mathcal{I}(d \in v_s), \tag{8.4}$$

where $\mathcal{R}_N$ denotes the top N results retrieved from the centralized sample index in response to q. ReDDE has an intuitive interpretation. Every document within $\mathcal{R}_N$ that originates from v represents $\frac{|v|}{|v_s|}$ *unobserved* query-related documents in v. Thus, the summation corresponds to the estimated total number of query-related documents in v.

8.1.4.2 *Post-Retrieval Vertical-Query Features*

In contrast with CORI and ReDDE, which predict the existence of relevant content without issuing the query to the vertical, post-retrieval features focus on the quality of the *actual* vertical results. Within IR, *retrieval effectiveness prediction* is the task of assessing the quality of a retrieval without human intervention—for example, based on observable properties of the top-ranked documents. Several methods for retrieval effectiveness prediction have been proposed. Such methods can be used to produce features that predict the quality of the vertical results. Based on these features, if the vertical results are predicted to be bad, a system might decide to suppress them.

Prior work on aggregated search investigated a retrieval effectiveness measure known as Clarity [79]. Clarity makes the assumption that in an effective retrieval, the top results should look different from the "average" document within the collection. Based on this assumption, Clarity [79] uses the Kullback-Leibler divergence to measure the difference between the language of the top N documents and the language of the entire vertical,

$$\phi_{q,v}^{\text{clarity}} = \sum_{w \in q} P(w|\theta_q) \log \left(\frac{P(w|\theta_q)}{P(w|\theta v)} \right), \tag{8.5}$$

where θ_q and θ_v are the query and vertical language models, respectively. The query language model can be estimated using the top N vertical results,

$$P(w|\theta_q) = \frac{1}{\mathcal{Z}} \sum_{d \in \mathcal{R}_N} P(w|\theta_d) P(q|\theta_d), \tag{8.6}$$

where $P(q|\theta_d)$ is the query likelihood score given d and $\mathcal{Z} = \sum_{d \in \mathcal{R}_N} P(q|\theta_d)$. Arguello *et al.* [15] used Clarity features for vertical selection. Different from the earlier description, however, the retrieval from the vertical was produced locally using sampled documents.

Other, perhaps simpler features that attempt to capture the quality of the vertical results are possible. One simple heuristic is to include the hit count (i.e., the number of results retrieved from the vertical). Notice that this is not necessarily equal to the number of results blended into the Web results if the vertical is presented. A vertical with an unusually low number of results is probably not relevant. The hit can be particularly informative when the vertical collection is highly dynamic. In prior work, Diaz [98] used the hit count as a feature in predicting *news* vertical relevance.

Alternatively, we can also include features that are highly vertical-specific and relate to the kinds of things users expect from good results. For instance, *news* results should be recent and from a reliable news source, *local* results should be about businesses that are nearby, *image* results should have a high picture quality, *video* results should have lots of views, *stock quote* and *weather* results should be up to date, and, finally, *shopping* results should be priced attractively. The possibilities here are vast. For example, any feature used by a vertical-specific ranker could potentially be included as a post-retrieval feature. These features characterize the quality of individual results. Thus, in cases where a vertical retrieves more than one result (e.g., not *weather* nor *finance*), these features can be computed by taking the average, minimum, and maximum values from the vertical's top N results.

Finally, for users to interact with vertical results, those results must be perceived as relevant. Thus, prior work has also considered features generated from the surrogate representation of the vertical results. Examples include number of query terms appearing in the surrogate title and the summary snippet or any other textual element of the surrogate representation [13]. Again, these features require combining the different values from the multiple results in the blended display. One possibility is to use the average, maximum, and minimum values.

8.1.4.3 *Post-Presentation Features*

Post-presentation features are derived from user actions on previous presentations of the vertical. These can be derived from previous presentations of the vertical for the *same query* (potentially from other users), previous presentations of the vertical for *similar queries* (potentially from other users), or previous presentations of the vertical for *same-session queries*.

The most commonly used post-presentation feature is the vertical-query *click-through rate* [280,279]. Let C_q^v denote the number of times vertical v was presented for query q and the user clicked on it, and let S_q^v denote the number of times v was presented for q and the user did not click on it. The vertical-query clickthrough rate is given by

$$\phi_{q,v}^{\text{click}} = \frac{C_q^v}{C_q^v + S_q^v}. \tag{8.7}$$

The main limitation with this formulation of CTR is that it requires an exact match between the current query and a previously observed query. Suppose a user issues a *previously unseen* query "ny style pizza" and the system needs to decide whether to present *local* results. Although the current query has no CTR, if it did it would probably have a CTR similar to that of the query "new york style pizza." For the purpose of feature generation, there are two ways to exploit clickthrough information from similar queries. One way is to take the average CTR from all previous queries weighted by the query-query similarity,

$$\phi_{q,v}^{\text{sim-click}} = \frac{1}{\mathcal{Z}} \sum_{q'} \text{sim}(q, q') \times \phi_{q,v}^{\text{click}}, \tag{8.8}$$

where q' denotes a previously seen query and $\mathcal{Z} = \sum_{q'} \text{sim}(q, q')$.

A second way of harnessing clickthrough evidence from similar queries is to build a language model from all previous queries associated with a click on the vertical (allowing duplicates queries) and then to compute the query-generation probability given this language model [13]:

$$\phi_{q,v}^{\text{click-lm}} = \prod_{w \in q} P\left(w | \theta_v^{\text{click}}\right), \tag{8.9}$$

where θ_v^{click} denotes the language model associated with the clicks on vertical v. Again, because queries have different lengths, it becomes important to normalize this value by $\mathcal{Z} = \sum_{v \in \mathcal{V}} \prod_{w \in q} P(w | \theta_v^{\text{click}})$.

Beyond clickthrough information, mouse movement can also be used as a source of post-presentation evidence. One challenge behind interpreting clickthrough data is that nonclicks do not necessarily indicate nonrelevance. It may be that the user did not notice the vertical. Maybe the vertical was presented below the fold, or maybe the user was satisfied by a result presented above it. Previous work shows that mouse hovers are correlated with eye gaze [168]. To date, mouse movement features have not been used in published work on vertical selection or presentation. However, one could imagine features that measure the number of times users hovered over previous presentations of the vertical but did not click on them. If effective, this type of evidence could be also extended to similar queries as described.

8.1.5 Implementation Details

At this point, it is important to take notice of two nuances associated with aggregated search features. First, not every feature will be available for every vertical. Consider, for example, ReDDE features, which use sampled vertical content to predict the quantity of query-related content in a vertical collection. A ReDDE feature does not make sense for a vertical that is not associated with a document collection (e.g., *calculator*). Likewise, some verticals do not have direct-search capabilities (e.g., *weather*). Thus, these verticals would not have features derived from the vertical query stream. As discussed in the next section, methods for combining evidence must accommodate the fact that different verticals will be associated with different sets of features. Second, some features (particularly query features) are likely to be correlated with relevance differently for different verticals. Consider, for example, a feature that indicates whether the query contains the term "news." This feature is likely to be positively predictive of the *news* vertical but negatively predictive of the *recipes* vertical. Thus, methods for combining evidence are likely to be more effective if they can learn a vertical-specific relation between features and vertical relevance.

Aggregated search requires combining *many* different types of features. In this section, we considered features derived from the query string, from the vertical query log, from sampled vertical content, from the actual vertical results, and from previous presentations of the vertical. In the next section, we present an overview of methods for combining features for making predictions.

8.2 Combination of Evidence

In Section 8.1, we described several signals believed to be correlated with vertical relevance. In this section, we describe how to combine those signals to make vertical selection and vertical presentation decisions.

8.2.1 Vertical Selection

The task of vertical selection refers to picking those verticals likely to appear on a good aggregated search results page. We can rephrase the task as follows: Given a query and a vertical, predict whether the vertical should be included on the search results page. Formally, let $\mathcal{V}$ be the set of k candidate verticals. We would like to learn a function that maps a query-vertical pair to relevance, $f : \mathcal{Q} \times \mathcal{V} \to \mathbf{R}$. Throughout this section, to maintain a general perspective, we remain agnostic about what we mean by functions, queries, and relevance. Nevertheless, when necessary, we adopt certain definitions that admit experimentally supported approaches.

8.2.1.1 *Training Data*

All of our algorithms require *training data* encoding examples of relevant and non-relevant query-vertical pairs, (q, v). There are two general methods for gathering training data. In a laboratory setting, assessors are provided with detailed relevance guidelines and then asked to judge the relevance of individual (q, v) pairs. The assessment might be query-driven (e.g., "for each query, request relevance judgments for all verticals") or vertical-driven (e.g., "for each vertical, request relevance judgments for many queries"). In query-driven assessment, editors are explicitly more aware of competing user intentions and may make judgments differently than they do with vertical-driven assessment. In either case, query sampling is crucial to training a model that can compute a reliable relevance grade for individual verticals and a calibrated relevance grade for comparison across verticals. To provide quality control, (q, v) pairs are usually judged by multiple assessors. Editorial assessment requires some overhead in terms of time (e.g., recruiting assessors, drafting guidelines, verifying labels) and money (e.g., paying assessors). Although crowdsourcing systems address some of these costs, editorial assessment also suffers because judgments are requested outside of a search context, resulting in relevance judgments that are only as good as the assessor's guess of the user intention. For example, local-intent queries almost always require an assessor with some familiarity about the hypothetical user's location; a naïve crowdsourced system may ask for a judgment from an assessor in a different city or country.

If we have access to a production aggregated search system, we can gather labels through *implicit feedback*. For example, if we have access to log data that includes vertical result presentation, we can hypothesize that a user click on a vertical result implies relevance. This allows us to collect a large set of tuples with no editorial cost. Data from implicit feedback carries its own issues. First, the labels are subject to bias effects from the layout constraints (i.e., not every vertical can be displayed for every query to the system), position (i.e., items higher in the page receive more clicks), or presentation (i.e., presentations such as images attract more clicks than other presentations). Furthermore, a click does not necessarily imply relevance; a user may have clicked accidentally or not found what they were looking for from the click. This effect can be mitigated by the large amount of data gathered in production systems.

Regardless of the source of training data, throughout this section we use the notation $\mathcal{D}$ to refer to the multiset of judged query-vertical pairs. Let the multisets $\mathcal{D}^+$ and $\mathcal{D}^-$ partition $\mathcal{D}$ into relevant and nonrelevant instances, respectively.

8.2.1.2 *Basic Models*

There are several ways we might construct the function f using $\mathcal{D}$. Perhaps the most straightforward way would be to manually enumerate which query-vertical pairs are likely to be relevant:

$$f_{\mathrm{MLE}}(q, v) = \frac{\left|\mathcal{D}^+_{(q,v)}\right|}{\left|\mathcal{D}_{(q,v)}\right|}, \tag{8.10}$$

where $\mathcal{D}_{(q,v)}$ is the subset of $\mathcal{D}$ containing (q, v). In other words, we are counting the fraction of presentations for that query that resulted in a relevant judgment with v. We refer to this figure as the *maximum likelihood estimate* of relevance for a query-vertical pair. Unfortunately, because we can never judge *every* query—even in a production setting—most of the queries we want to be able to make predictions on will not be in $\mathcal{D}$. Even if we gather a large amount of data in a production setting, the skewed query frequency distribution suggests that we will observe only a handful of impressions for most queries, resulting in a poor estimation of the relevance.

We can improve the coverage of the maximum likelihood estimate by exploiting the topical similarity between queries. Because queries can be represented as very sparse term vectors, any of the standard term-based similarity measures can be used [301]. Queries specifically have been studied in the literature and admit unique similarity measures [256,300,367]. Given such a similarity measure, we can compare a new query to those queries we have previously judged. For example, we can define a function

$$f_\kappa(q, v) = \sum_{(q',v)\in\mathcal{D}} \kappa(q, q') f_{\mathrm{MLE}}(q', v), \tag{8.11}$$

where $\kappa(q, q')$ is the similarity between two queries. In other words, we are smoothing the estimates from the maximum likelihood estimate using similar queries [99]. We refer to the result as the *kernel estimate* of relevance for a query-vertical pair. In this case, our coverage increases to include similar queries. However, depending on the robustness of our similarity measure, this may not be sufficient. For example, assume that we have hired editors to manually generate a set of relevant queries for an image vertical. If our image vertical contains a large number of cat pictures, but editors did not manage to label "cat" as a relevant query for the image vertical, our feline-inclined users will not discover these fascinating pictures. Therefore, it is important to understand that the effectiveness of f_κ is the topical nature of the query similarity. Nevertheless, techniques based on query similarity have been found to be a strong baseline [223].

We can address the issues with query similarity by using the signals described in Section 8.1. Specifically, our approach will be to learn f as a function from features of the query-vertical pair to relevance. That is,

$$f_\theta(q, v) = g(\phi_{q,v}, \theta_v), \tag{8.12}$$

where $\phi_{q,v}$ is the $m \times 1$ vector of m feature values described earlier and θ_v is a vector model parameter for that specific vertical. We have a set of model parameters for each vertical because the relationship between a feature and relevance is likely to be dependent on the vertical (e.g., the feature "query contains *picture*" is likely to be positively correlated with the image vertical but negatively with other verticals). We suspect that similar queries will have similar feature vectors; therefore, the behavior of f_κ is preserved. In addition, though, we can generalize to those queries with similar feature vectors but with potentially different topics. The function g has two arguments: features and model parameters. Features are often encoded as a vector of scalar and binary values according to the definitions in Section 8.1. We might use a subset of features—for example, only the pre-retrieval features—or all features, depending on the cost or availability. The model parameters represent the knobs used to tune the model, given some training data. The precise definition of θ_v depends on the functional form of g. If we are using logistic regression for g, then θ_v is a length m vector of feature weights and our functional form is the inner product between $\phi_{q,v}$ and θ_v,

$$g_{\log}(\phi_{q,v}, \theta_v) = \frac{\exp\left(\phi_{q,v}^{\mathsf{T}}\theta_v\right)}{1 + \exp\left(\phi_{q,v}^{\mathsf{T}}\theta_v\right)}. \tag{8.13}$$

Given a functional form, we tune θ_v such that classification errors on our training data are minimized. In the case of logistic regression, we minimize the logistic loss using an iterative technique such as the Newton-Raphson method. Many other functional forms exist in the machine learning literature. A full review is beyond the scope of this chapter.

Moving forward, we will adopt probabilistic versions of f. That is, we will adopt the notation

$$p_{(q,v)}^{\beta} = f(q, v) \tag{8.14}$$

to indicate that a score for a query-vertical pair (q, v) can be interpreted as a probability of relevance. More concretely, the probability p^{MLE} is the maximum likelihood probability of relevance, p^{κ} is the kernel density estimate of relevance, and p^{θ} is a parametric model of relevance. In principle, the techniques in the remainder of the chapter can be extended to nonprobabilistic paradigms.

8.2.1.3 *Advanced Models*

Each of the models presented in the previous section has advantages and disadvantages: p^{MLE} may be effective for judged query-vertical pairs, but the coverage is low; p^{κ} does not generalize to topics outside of $\mathcal{D}$, and p^{θ} may not capture topical similarity. In this section, we present one way of combining these approaches in a single framework [98].

Although p^{MLE} suffers from low coverage, for those queries where we have reliable judgements, performance is strong; Eq. 8.10 becomes more accurate with increasing data. On the other hand, our machine learned estimate p^{θ} provides an effective method when there is no data but does not change observed judgments (e.g., if the system presents that vertical to real users). One way to combine these two methods is with Bayesian updating. The intuition with Bayesian updating is that, in the absence of (enough) data for a specific query, we can use p^{θ} to estimate the relevance; after observing judgments from editors or from query logs, we can adjust this estimate. So, instead of modeling the precise probability of relevance, we are estimating a *distribution* over the value of the probability of relevance. Let p^{β} be this distribution. If we assume that the parametric form of this distribution is the beta distribution, then we can define it as

$$p_{(q,v)}^{\beta} \sim \mathrm{Beta}(a, b), \tag{8.15}$$

where we set the beta parameters such that

$$a = \mu p_{(q,v)}^{\theta} \qquad\qquad b = \mu\left(1 - p_{(q,v)}^{\theta}\right), \tag{8.16}$$

where μ is a hyperparameter of our model. That is, absent any data, the distribution over the probability of relevance is strictly a function of the $p^\theta_{(q,v)}$ and μ.

Assume that we have observed some positive and negative feedback for a query-vertical pair. Then, the posterior, given these data, is also a beta distribution,

$$p^\beta_{(q,v)} | \mathcal{D} \sim \text{Beta}\left(a + \left|\mathcal{D}^+_{(q,v)}\right|, b + \left|\mathcal{D}^-_{(q,v)}\right|\right), \tag{8.17}$$

and the posterior mean,

$$\hat{p}^\beta_{(q,v)} = \frac{\left|\mathcal{D}^+_{(q,v)}\right| + \mu p^\theta_{(q,v)}}{|\mathcal{D}_{(q,v)}| + \mu}. \tag{8.18}$$

Note here that we can gain an intuition for μ. For small values of μ, the model will be very sensitive to early feedback from the user. For large values, the model will rely on $p^\theta_{(q,v)}$ more than feedback.

The hypothesis underlying the kernel density estimate was that a query's probability of being relevant is related to the relevance of topically related queries. We can incorporate information from related queries as pseudo-judgments on the candidate query. Specifically, we can define the aggregated information for a query as

$$\tilde{\mathcal{D}}^+_{(q,v)} = \mathcal{D}^+_{(q,v)} + \sum_{q'} \kappa(q, q') \mathcal{D}^+_{(q',v)} \tag{8.19}$$

$$\tilde{\mathcal{D}}^-_{(q,v)} = \mathcal{D}^-_{(q,v)} + \sum_{q'} \kappa(q, q') \mathcal{D}^-_{(q',v)}. \tag{8.20}$$

We can use these modified counts in the same way we used the original counts in Eq. 8.18.

8.2.2 Vertical Presentation

Vertical presentation refers to deciding precisely where to place relevant verticals on the search results page. For simplicity, we constrain our discussion to a ranked list of Web documents interleaved with vertical results.

8.2.2.1 Pointwise Interleaving

According to Robertson, any ranked list of results to a user query should be ordered according each item's probability of relevance [291]. Since an aggregator interleaves vertical result blocks with Web documents, we can assert that the presentation problem reduces to estimating the probability of vertical relevance (Section 8.2.1.3). Let $p_{(q,d)}$ be the probability that Web document d is relevant to query q. If this probability is defined for all documents and we use a probabilistic vertical selection algorithm, then we can interleave items by the probabilities. The rank of v in the interleaved list is

$$\text{rank}_{(q,v)} = \left|\{d \in \mathcal{W} : p_{(q,d)} > p_{(q,v)}\}\right| + \left|\{v' \in \mathcal{V} : p_{(q,v')} > p_{(q,v)}\}\right|. \tag{8.21}$$

where $\mathcal{W}$ is our collection of Web documents. Because we are interested in estimating the probability of relevance of each vertical and document, we refer to this as *pointwise interleaving*.

Unfortunately, the assumptions underlying probabilistic interleaving are rarely satisfied. The scores returned by Web rankers are not guaranteed to be probabilities. For example, many modern learning-to-rank approaches rank documents by an arbitrary scalar value output by the ranking model. Even if Web document scores are probabilities, the values are unlikely to be well calibrated with the vertical selection scores, resulting in poor interleaving [142].

One strategy for comparing $p_{(q,v)}$ to a document retrieval score is to transform the original document score output by the Web search engine to a probability. If there are relevance labels available for (q, d) pairs, then we can learn a statistical model to do this transformation [7]. Specifically, we can learn a logistic regression model in the same way as in Eq. 8.13,

$$h_{\log}(\phi_{q,d}, \theta) = \frac{\exp\left(\phi_{q,d}^{\mathsf{T}}\theta\right)}{1 + \exp\left(\phi_{q,d}^{\mathsf{T}}\theta\right)}. \tag{8.22}$$

In this case, the features would, at a minimum, include the document score. Although we can add other features of the document, there is the temptation to begin adding large numbers of features to this model. There are two reasons to be cautious with feature addition. First, we want to avoid rebuilding a Web ranking algorithm; we only need to calibrate a score that, conceivably, has been independently and rigorously tested to predict relevance, albeit on a different scale. Second, feature computation, especially for Web documents, can be expensive if, for example, the value is stored in an index on a separate server. Furthermore, there is bandwidth overhead for the Web ranker to expose the entire feature vector used for core ranking.

In cases where interleaving decisions need to be made without knowledge of the Web document ranking scores, we can use position-based models to make interleaving decisions [280]. A position-based interleaving model is similar to the score transformation described in Eq. 8.22 except our only feature is the position of the document. As a result, we predict a fixed probability of relevance for each position in the ranking, regardless of the documents or their scores. Given probabilistic vertical selection scores, the vertical presenter can position each vertical according to

$$\mathrm{rank}_{(q,v)} = \sum_{i=0}^{|\mathcal{W}|} I(p_i > p_{(q,v)}) + \left|\{v' \in \mathcal{V} : p_{(q,v')} > p_{(q,v)}\}\right|, \tag{8.23}$$

where p_i is the predicted probability of relevance of rank position i.

8.2.2.2 *Pairwise Interleaving*

Given an accurate and calibrated probability of relevance for each document and vertical, pointwise interleaving should provide an optimal ranking. In reality, estimating the true probability of relevance is very difficult. In fact, estimating the probability of relevance may be an inappropriate target if we are only interested in the relative relevance of verticals and documents. The user is never exposed to the absolute probability of relevance and is only concerned that more relevant items are places above less relevant items. Therefore, we may want to focus our modeling effort on predicting users' preference users between pairs of items, given a query. Modeling the order of items instead of the absolute relevance is precisely the goal of *pairwise interleaving*.

Although the optimization target for pairwise interleaving differs from that for pointwise interleaving, many of the fundamentals are the same. Specifically, we are still interested in learning a function f_{LTR} with two differences. First, the domain includes the "web result" argument for determining the preference between a vertical and a Web result. This is similar to the task of estimating $p_{(q,d)}$ in the previous section. Second, for pairwise models, our range is the set of the reals. That is, we are only interested in a function that outputs a real value, unconstrained by modeling the exact probability of relevance. Our objective is to find f_{LTR} such that, given a query, the values for more relevant verticals or documents are larger than the values for less relevant verticals. The precise training of such models is studied in the field known as *learning to rank* (LTR) [227].

Casting pairwise interleaving as a learning-to-rank problem requires training a *single* model f_{LTR} to predict an item's rank, irrespective of its type (e.g., image, local, Web result). In our situation, this is problematic because different item types are associated with different features (i.e., some features may be specific to a handful of types, and some may be unique to a particular one). In addition, it is problematic because those features that are common to *multiple* types (e.g., whether the query contains a city name) may be predictive for some types more than others or even predictive for different types in the opposite direction. Next we propose three LTR variants that address these challenges in different ways. Each variant makes a different assumption about how features may be correlated with item relevance across item types.

8.2.2.2.1 Equally Correlated Features

One alternative is to assume that each feature is equally predictive of item relevance (in the same direction) independent of the item type:

$$\phi_{q,v}^{\text{shared}} = \left.\begin{bmatrix} \phi_{q,v}^{\text{pre-ret}} \\ \phi_{q,v}^{\text{post-ret}} \end{bmatrix}\right\} \text{ Shared features,} \qquad (8.24)$$

where $\phi_{q,v}^{\text{pre-ret}}$ is a column vector of pre-retrieval features and $\phi_{q,v}^{\text{post-ret}}$ is a column vector of post-retrieval features. The feature representation is as follows: Pre-retrieval features, $\phi_{q,v}^{\text{pre-ret}}$, are independent of the item. This model uses a *single* copy of each pre-retrieval feature. The values of post-retrieval features are item-specific (i.e., they are generated directly from the item or the item's search engine results). As with pre-retrieval features, this approach *also* uses a *single* copy of each post-retrieval feature in the subvector $\phi_{q,v}^{\text{post-ret}}$. If an item is not associated with a particular post-retrieval feature, then the feature is zeroed-out in that instance. Consider, for example, our post-retrieval features that determine the text similarity between the query and the summary snippets presented in the item. These features may only be associated with news and Web result items. Therefore, if the item is not one of these types, all these features are zeroed-out. This approach assumes that features are equally correlated with relevance irrespective of the item type. Once trained, model f_{LTR} will apply the *same* parameters to a feature independent of the instance's item type.

8.2.2.2.2 Uniquely Correlated Features

We can also assume that every feature—whether it is a pre- or post-retrieval feature—is uniquely correlated with relevance across different item types. The feature representation is as follows: We make a separate, item type-specific copy of each feature. So, for example, given $|\mathcal{V}| + 1$ item types, we make $|\mathcal{V}| + 1$ copies of each pre-retrieval feature (one per item type). Given an instance, all copies are zeroed-out except for those corresponding to the instance's item type. For post-retrieval features, we make one copy per item type for which the feature is available. That is,

$$
\phi_{q,v}^{\text{disjoint}} = \begin{bmatrix} 0 \\ 0 \\ \vdots \\ \phi_{q,v}^{\text{pre-ret}} \\ \phi_{q,v}^{\text{post-ret}} \\ \vdots \\ 0 \\ 0 \end{bmatrix} \begin{matrix} \left.\vphantom{\begin{matrix}0\\0\end{matrix}}\right\} \text{Non-}v \text{ features} \\ \\ \left.\vphantom{\begin{matrix}\phi\\\phi\end{matrix}}\right\} v \text{ features} \\ \\ \left.\vphantom{\begin{matrix}0\\0\end{matrix}}\right\} \text{Non-}v \text{ features} \end{matrix} \tag{8.25}
$$

Consider, for example, our temporal features, which are available for items from *blogs*, *community Q&A*, *news*, and *twitter*. We make four copies of each temporal feature.

This approach assumes that features are correlated differently with relevance depending on the item type. Once trained, model f_{LTR} will apply a *different* θ subset, depending on the instance's item type. Although this added flexibility may be advantageous, the increased number of features may introduce predictive noise and result in overfitting. Thus, this LTR variant may require more training data than the model described in the previous section.

8.2.2.2.3 Equally and Uniquely Correlated Features

The previous two approaches make opposite assumptions: Features are either equally correlated or uniquely correlated with relevance for different item types. A third alternative is to make neither assumption *a priori* but to give the algorithm the freedom to exploit both types of relationship using training data.

For this approach, we maintain a single copy of each pre- and post-retrieval feature that is shared across all item types. As before, if an instance's item type is not associated with a shared feature, the feature is zeroed-out for that instance. In addition to these shared features, we make one item type-specific copy of each pre- and post-retrieval feature. Given an instance, all copies corresponding to types other than the instance's item type are zeroed-out. That is,

$$
\phi_{q,v}^{\text{combined}} =
\begin{bmatrix}
\phi_{q,v}^{\text{pre-ret}} \\
\phi_{q,v}^{\text{post-ret}} \\
\vdots \\
0 \\
0 \\
\vdots \\
\phi_{q,v}^{\text{pre-ret}} \\
\phi_{q,v}^{\text{post-ret}} \\
\vdots \\
0 \\
0
\end{bmatrix}
\begin{array}{l}
\left.\vphantom{\begin{matrix}a\\a\end{matrix}}\right\}\ \text{Shared features} \\[1.2em]
\left.\vphantom{\begin{matrix}a\\a\end{matrix}}\right\}\ \text{Non-}v\ \text{features} \\[1.2em]
\left.\vphantom{\begin{matrix}a\\a\end{matrix}}\right\}\ v\ \text{features} \\[1.2em]
\left.\vphantom{\begin{matrix}a\\a\end{matrix}}\right\}\ \text{Non-}v\ \text{features}
\end{array}
\tag{8.26}
$$

The canonical feature representation for this approach is the union of features used by the previous two approaches.

This approach makes no assumption about how a feature is correlated with relevance across item types. If a feature is equally correlated across item types, the algorithm can assign a large (positive or negative) weight to the copy of the feature that is shared across types. Alternatively, if a feature is correlated differently for different item types, the algorithm can assign a large positive weight to some copies of the feature and a large negative weight to others. Of all three LTR variants, this one has the largest number of features and may therefore need the most training data to avoid overfitting.

8.3 Evaluation

Evaluation is essential to all subfields of information retrieval, and the same is true for aggregated search. In general, the goal of evaluation is to facilitate the objective comparison between different algorithms, different features, and different parameter settings. As previously mentioned, aggregated search is viewed as a two-step process: predicting which verticals to present (*vertical selection*) and predicting where in the Web results to present them (*vertical presentation*). In some situations, it is desirable to evaluate the vertical selection component in isolation. Given a query, the goal for the vertical selection component is to select those verticals that are relevant and suppress those verticals that are not relevant. In other situations, the goal is to evaluate the end-to-end aggregated search solution. In this case, the goal for the system is not only to select the relevant verticals but to present those verticals that are more likely to be relevant in a more salient way. In practice, this means presenting the most relevant verticals higher in the aggregated results. In the following sections, we present an overview of methods for aggregated search evaluation. First we focus on vertical selection evaluation, and then we focus on end-to-end evaluation.

8.3.1 Vertical Selection Evaluation

Vertical selection is the task of deciding which verticals to present along with the core Web results for a given query. From the perspective of evaluation, the best vertical selection system is the one that selects the relevant verticals and avoids selecting the ones that are not relevant. In this respect, vertical selection can be evaluated like any other multiclass classification problem, using metrics such as accuracy, which summarizes performance for all verticals, or precision and recall, which summarize performance for each vertical independently.

Let $\mathcal{Q}$ denote the set of evaluation queries and $\mathcal{V}$ denote the set of candidate verticals. Vertical selection evaluation requires knowing which verticals are *truly* relevant to each evaluation query $q \in \mathcal{Q}$. Let $\mathcal{V}_q$ denote the set of verticals that are *truly* relevant to query q, and let $\tilde{\mathcal{V}}_q$ denote the set of verticals that are *predicted* relevant to q. A commonly used evaluation metric for vertical selection evaluation is *accuracy*. Given a query q, a vertical selection component must make $|\mathcal{V}|$ predictions. That is, for each vertical v, it must decide whether to present the vertical or to suppress it. Accuracy measures the percentage of correct predictions and is computed as

$$\mathcal{A} = \frac{1}{|\mathcal{V}| \times |\mathcal{Q}|} \sum_{q \in \mathcal{Q}} \sum_{v \in \mathcal{V}} \left(\mathcal{I}(v \in \tilde{\mathcal{V}}_q \wedge v \in \mathcal{V}_q) \vee \mathcal{I}(v \notin \tilde{\mathcal{V}}_q \wedge v \notin \mathcal{V}_q) \right), \quad (8.27)$$

where $\mathcal{I}$ denotes the indicator function (equals 1 if its argument is true and 0 otherwise).

Other measures used in multiclass classification are also possible. For example, one can also calculate precision, recall, and f-measure with respect to each vertical and then possibly average across candidate verticals to obtain a single measure. Let $\mathcal{Q}_v$ denote the set of queries for which vertical v is *truly* relevant and $\tilde{\mathcal{Q}}_v$ denote the set of queries for which vertical v is *predicted* to be relevant. Precision, recall, and f-measure with respect to vertical v are given by

$$\mathcal{P}_v = \frac{1}{|\tilde{\mathcal{Q}}_v|} \sum_{q \in \tilde{\mathcal{Q}}_v} \mathcal{I}(q \in \mathcal{Q}_v) \qquad (8.28)$$

$$\mathcal{R}_v = \frac{1}{|\mathcal{Q}_v|} \sum_{q \in \mathcal{Q}_v} \mathcal{I}(q \in \tilde{\mathcal{Q}}_v) \qquad (8.29)$$

$$\mathcal{F}_v = \frac{2 \times \mathcal{P}_v \times \mathcal{R}_v}{\mathcal{P}_v + \mathcal{R}_v} \qquad (8.30)$$

In prior vertical selection evaluations, Arguello *et al.* [15] addressed the task of *single* vertical selection (a more simplified version of the full vertical selection task). During single vertical selection, the goal is to predict a single relevant vertical, if one exists, or to predict that no vertical is relevant. Let $\tilde{v}_q$ denote a system's single vertical prediction and $\tilde{v}_q = \emptyset$ denote the prediction that no vertical is relevant. In this work, accuracy was measured according to

$$\mathcal{A} = \frac{1}{|\mathcal{Q}|} \sum_{q \in \mathcal{Q}} \left(\mathcal{I}(\tilde{v}_q \in \mathcal{V}_q \wedge \mathcal{V}_q \neq \emptyset) \vee \mathcal{I}(\tilde{v}_q = \emptyset \wedge \mathcal{V}_q = \emptyset) \right). \qquad (8.31)$$

Li *et al.* [223] compared approaches to vertical selection by constructing interpolated precision-recall (PR) curves for each candidate vertical. Precision and recall for a vertical can be computed as described earlier, and different precision and recall operating points can be derived by sweeping the classifier's prediction confidence threshold. Usually, the higher the threshold, the higher the precision and the lower the recall. This evaluation method has the advantage of providing a more complete picture of the tradeoff between precision and recall for different approaches.

As previously mentioned, vertical selection evaluation requires knowing which verticals are relevant to each query. Arguello *et al.* [15] and Li *et al.* [223] used trained assessors. Assessors with expert knowledge about the various candidate verticals were given a set of queries (sampled from a commercial query log) and were asked to determine which verticals, if any, were likely to be relevant to each query. This method of assessment has two potential drawbacks. First, queries are often ambiguous. Therefore, it may be difficult for an assessor to determine the user's actual intent. Second, the assessments do not consider the vertical's relevance within the context of the core Web results.

Diaz [98] and König *et al.* [204] evaluated vertical selection for the *news* vertical in a production environment. The gold-standard data were collected using a commercial system, where a small fraction of query traffic was always presented the *news* vertical above the core Web results. Relevance judgments were derived from clickthrough data, and because the vertical was always presented, all *news* clicks and skips were observed. In other words, retrospectively, the data collection included queries for which the *news* vertical should not be selected based on observed skips. Features were generated and cached to allow repeated experimentation after the data collection phase. Evaluation was conducted using *accuracy*, defined here as the percentage of correctly predicted clicks and skips.

8.3.2 End-to-End Evaluation

Vertical selection evaluation is more clearly defined than end-to-end aggregated search evaluation. Consider, for example, the aggregated results shown in Figure 8.1. The basic end-to-end evaluation questions is: How good are these results? If the system presented *video* results instead of *image* results, would the presentation be better? And what about more subtle changes? For instance, what if the *local* vertical was presented above the first Web result? Would this be better? Would it really make a difference?

End-to-end aggregated search evaluation falls under three broad categories: test collection evaluation, online evaluation, and user study evaluation. Test collection evaluation builds on the Cranfield IR evaluation paradigm [73]. A test collection typically includes a set of queries, a set of systems (i.e., a set of verticals and core content providers) with responses to those queries, and a set of relevance judgements on the vertical and Web results. Given these three components, evaluation measures can be computed on any given aggregation of results. Online evaluation focuses on implicit user feedback from real users in an operational setting. Implicit feedback measures typically focus on clicks and skips, where clicks are usually treated as positive feedback and skips are usually treated as negative feedback. Finally, user study evaluation involves having users perform search tasks with different aggregated search systems in a controlled environment. Evaluation measures are derived from outcome measures thought to be correlated with a positive user experience or from responses to questions given to study participants.

All three evaluation methodologies have advantages and disadvantages and can be used to answer different types of research questions. Once a test collection is built, evaluation is basically free and results are reproducible. This makes test collection evaluation an attractive alternative for fine-tuning parameters. However, test collection evaluation assumes that collections are static and that relevance judgments from assessors are consistent with those made by real users. Online evaluation methods use real users in real situations. However, because evaluation measures are computed using implicit feedback signals, precision can be estimated more accurately than recall. That is, the operational system can observe false-positive mistakes but not false-negative mistakes. Finally, user study evaluation gives the researcher more control than online evaluation. For example, the researcher can learn about participants' backgrounds, can manipulate the higher-level search task, and can manipulate the search context. Such variables cannot be controlled and cannot be easily identified in an online setting. On the other hand, user studies are expensive and time consuming. For all these reasons, all three evaluation methodologies are important and all three are necessary to measure improvement and understand user behavior.

8.3.2.1   *Test Collection Evaluation*

Test collection evaluation follows the Cranfield evaluation paradigm [73] and has the following components: a static collection of retrievable items, a set of queries with topic descriptions that define what should and should not be considered relevant, a set of relevance judgments for all query-document pairs, and a suite of evaluation measures that operate on a ranking of known relevant/nonrelevant items. Usually, because collections are large and because most documents are not relevant, it is unnecessary (and often prohibitively expensive in terms of time and effort) for assessors to judge all documents for all queries. Instead, assessors typically judge only those documents most likely to be relevant. These can be determined using a method known as *pooling*. The basic idea is to take the union of top results from a wide range of systems. Documents within this set are judged, and documents outside of this set are automatically assumed to be not relevant.

With regard to aggregated search, test collection evaluation can deviate from the general Cranfield method in one respect. Depending on the formulation of the task, pooling results from the different systems being aggregated (i.e., from the set of candidate verticals and from the core Web search engine) may not be necessary. Most approaches to vertical selection and presentation assume that the top results from each vertical (those that would be presented if the vertical were selected) are fixed.

Thus far, two test collection evaluation methodologies have been proposed for aggregated search. The first was proposed by Arguello *et al.* [14]; the second was proposed by Zhou *et al.* [410]. The two methods have things in common. First, both impose constraints on the end-to-end aggregation task. For example, vertical results must be blended into the core Web results from top to bottom (i.e., verticals cannot be stacked horizontally), and if a vertical is presented, its results must be displayed in sequence. Second, both methods propose ways of collecting assessor relevance judgements on vertical results and on the core Web results for a given query. Finally, both methods propose evaluation measures that take as input a set of relevant judgments and can determine the quality of any possible aggregation of results (subject to the imposed constraints).

The approach from Arguello *et al.* [14] casts the aggregation task as *block ranking*. The first step is to impose a set of layout constraints. Most important, if a vertical is presented, then all its results must be presented together, and they must be presented within a set of predefined slots—for example, above the first Web result, between Web results three and four, or below the last Web result. Given such constraints, aggregated search can be viewed as a block ranking task whereby a block is defined as either a sequence of same-vertical results or a sequence of Web results that cannot be split.

Let $\mathcal{B}_q$ denote the set of blocks associated with query q. $\mathcal{B}_q$ includes one block for every vertical $v \in \mathcal{V}$ that retrieves a minimum number of results and one block for every sequence of Web results that cannot be split. Following the example constraints from earlier, Web Results 1–3 would form one block and Web Results 4–10 would form another block. Additionally, $\mathcal{B}_q$ includes an imaginary "end of SERP" block. Thus, the end-to-end goal for the system is to produce a ranking of all elements in $\mathcal{B}_q$, where the blocks ranked below the imaginary "end of SERP" block are suppressed and effectively tied. Given this formulation of the aggregated search task, the method proposed by Arguello *et al.* [14] is to derive an ideal or *reference* block ranking for each evaluation query q and to evaluate alternative block rankings for q based on their similarity or distance to the reference.

Given query q, let σ_q^* denote the ideal block ranking and σ_q denote a predicted block ranking. Two components are still missing. First, how do we derive σ_q^*, and second, how do we measure the similarity between σ_q and σ_q^*? In response the first question, Arguello *et al.* [14] collected preference judgments on all block pairs in $\mathcal{B}_q$ and derived the reference presentation σ_q^* by applying the Schulze voting method [305] to these preference judgments. In response to the second question, Arguello *et al.* [14] used a variant of Kendall's τ [206]. Although these were the particular solutions used in this work, other ways to construct σ_q^* and other ways of calculating the similarity between σ_q and σ_q^* are also possible.

The evaluation method proposed in Zhou *et al.* [410] takes a different approach. The main evaluation metric is defined as *utility*. Let σ_q still denote the output predicted by the system in response to query q. The output can still be viewed as a ranking of Web and vertical blocks. Zhou *et al.* define *utility* as the user's expected *gain* obtained from reading σ_q divided by the expected *effort* expended in reading σ_q:

$$\mathcal{U}(\sigma_q) = \frac{\sum_{b \in \sigma_q} E(b) \times G(b)}{\sum_{b \in \sigma_q} E(b) \times F(b)}. \tag{8.32}$$

Now let's consider the different components of this equation. Let $b \in \sigma_q$ denote a Web or vertical block presented in σ_q. The first component, $E(b)$, is defined as the probability that a user will examine block b. $E(b)$ can be derived in different ways; however, it should be a function of the block's position in the ranking as well as its visual salience. So, for example, all else being equal, a block of results from the *images* vertical should have a higher examination probability than a block of results from the *news* vertical. Image results are more salient than news results and are therefore more likely to be noticed and examined.

The second component, $G(b)$, is defined as the user's *gain* obtained from examining block b. One important distinction between this approach and the one proposed by Arguello *et al.* [14] is that this approach decouples the relevance of a system (i.e., the relevance of a vertical or the relevance of the Web search engine) from the relevance of the results retrieved by that system. Given a query, assessors are first asked to judge the relevance of a particular system, independent of any results. This is referred to as the query's *orientation*. Then assessors are asked to judge the items retrieved by each system based on topical relevance. Topical relevance is judged independently of the query's orientation. Finally, the gain associated with block b is given by the product of the total topical relevance of items within b (the sum of topical relevance grades associated with the items in b) and the query's orientation with respect to the system that produced b.

The third and final component, $F(b)$, is defined as the amount of *effort* required to assess the relevance of b. The idea here is that different types of results require different amounts of effort. For example, *images* require little effort because the surrogate is a faithful representation of the underlying result. On the other hand, *news* results require more effort because the user must read the summary snippet and possibly even navigate to the article. Finally, *video* results take a significant amount of effort because the user may need to view the entire video to assess its relevance. Thus, blocks from different systems can be assigned different weights based on different heuristics or assumptions.

The approach from Zhou *et al.* [410] is fairly general. One can imagine different browsing models for estimating the examination probability associated with a block ($E(b)$), different ways of measuring gain ($G(b)$), and different assumptions for modeling assessment effort ($F(b)$).

8.3.2.2 *Online Evaluation*

Online evaluation involves testing a system in an operational setting based on implicit user feedback. The basic idea is to have different subsets of users exposed to different systems and to compare between systems based on observable signals that are thought to be correlated with user satisfaction. To date, most online evaluations have focused on clicks and skips.

Online evaluation has two main advantages. First, the evaluation is conducted using real users in real situations. This facilitates the evaluation of methods that provide personalized results to different individuals and methods that harness evidence from the user's context—for example, their location. Second, the evaluation can be conducted using *lots* of people, ensuring that results generalize across users and situations.

That said, online evaluation also has some challenges. First and most important, implicit user feedback is noisy. Users tend to click on results that ranked higher and results that are visually salient—for example, results that show images. Moreover, when users do click, they do so based on *perceived* relevance. The underlying Web or vertical result may actually turn out to be not relevant. Skips are noisy as well. Users may satisfy their information need from the summary snippet, and in fact some verticals (e.g., *weather*) may not even be clickable. The second challenge is that online experiments are not repeatable. The users, the collections, and the queries will be different. That is not to say that online evaluation results cannot be trusted. The same comparison between approaches can be conducted multiple times to verify that the best system is still the best system. However, the exact outcome measures will be different. The dynamic nature of online evaluations makes it difficult to do debugging and error analysis, which often require changing one thing at a time.

One approach to online evaluation is to measure the *clickthrough* rate for each candidate vertical independently. Clickthrough rate answers the following question: Of the times the vertical was presented, how often was it clicked? The metric assumes that if a user did not click on a vertical that was presented, the vertical should not have been presented or should have been presented in a different location. Although clickthrough rate is an intuitive measure, it paints an incomplete picture. It measures precision but not recall. Suppose a system predicts a vertical relevant only when the system is *very* confident that it is relevant. Such a system would probably observe a very high clickthrough rate. However, what about the false negatives? In other words, how often did the system suppress a vertical that should have been presented?

To address this limitation, an evaluation based on clickthrough rate should also consider another measure, known as *coverage*. Coverage measures the percentage of queries for which the vertical was presented. Used in conjunction, a greater coverage and a higher clickthrough rate can be seen as an improvement. It means that the system made fewer false-negative *and* fewer false-positive mistakes. Although coverage is not equal recall, the measures are related. High coverage probably means high recall, but low coverage *does not* necessarily mean low recall.

Ponnuswami et al. [280] used clickthrough rate and coverage in conjunction to evaluate an end-to-end system in which verticals could be slotted into one of three positions: above the Web results, below the Web results, and in the middle. Clickthrough rate and coverage were measured independently for each vertical-slot pair.

In addition to the challenges mentioned online evaluation can also be time consuming and expensive. If the goal is to fine-tune an existing system, it might not be possible to conduct an online evaluation for every combination of parameter values. To address this limitation, a few recent studies have investigated methods for collecting online user-interaction data once and using these data to perform *multiple* rounds of offline testing [279,219]. These methods have some of the benefits of test collection evaluation. Namely, once the data are collected, evaluation is inexpensive and results are reproducible. The basic idea is to collect the user interaction data in a completely unbiased fashion, where every system output is *equally* probable. Then, given a particular model (with a particular parameter configuration), evaluation can be done by considering only the interaction data (e.g., the clicks and skips) associated with those outputs that are identical to what the system would have produced, given the same query. Results show that metrics computed in this offline fashion closely approximate those computed in an online setting using the same experimental system [279,219].

8.3.2.3 *User Study Evaluation*

User study evaluation involves exposing study participants to different systems and measuring their levels of task success or satisfaction. Compared to test collection evaluation and online evaluation, user study evaluation has a few advantages. First, participants can be asked questions that directly measure their level of satisfaction with the system. The evaluation does not rely on metrics that may be only weakly correlated with user satisfaction. Second, user studies can target specific user populations. For example, one can study differences in search behavior between experienced and inexperienced searchers. Third, because the experiment is conducted in a controlled setting, user studies can manipulate the higher-level task or the search context. Within aggregated search, user studies have been conducted to answer two basic questions: What do users want? and What are the factors that affect users' preferences or their behaviors?

Both test collection approaches discussed in Section 8.3.2.1 were validated by conducting user studies [14,410]. The goal was to compare the value of the proposed evaluation metric with user preferences between alternative presentations of aggregated results. The basic assumption is that a "good" metric should be consistent with user preferences. Both user studies consisted of showing participants pairs of aggregated results and comparing the metric score with the stated preference. Several common trends were observed. First, agreement between study participants was low. The Fleiss' Kappa agreement [122], which corrects for the expected agreement due to random chance, was about 20%. Given this low level of agreement between people, it would be unreasonable to expect any metric to agree with a user 100% of the time. Second, the agreement between the metric and the assessors was about 65%. Note that the expected agreement due to random chance is 50%. Finally, agreement between the metric and the assessors was greater (about 80%) on those presentation pairs where the value of the metric was drastically different. In other words, the proposed metrics were better at distinguishing between good and bad presentations than between pairs of good and pairs of bad presentations. Taken together, these three trends tell us that although perfect agreement between any metric and users' preferences is unlikely, there is room for improvement.

Preference behavior was also studied by Zhu and Carterette [413]. Again, participants were shown pairs of presentations for a given query and asked to state a preference. Different from the preference-based studies described earlier, however, this work only looked at the blending of the *image* vertical in different slots. The study found a strong preference for the *image* vertical ranked high for queries likely to have image intent.

Studies have also considered preference behavior over the course of an entire search session, not only on a query-by-query basis. Sushmita *et al.* [333] conducted a task-oriented user study with two types of interfaces: a tabbed interface, whereby users could only access different verticals using tabs, and an aggregated interface, where the top results from every vertical were blended into the core Web results. Participants were given a search task and asked to compile as much relevant content as possible. Two important trends were observed. First, the aggregated interface was associated with more clicks. Second, the amount of cross-vertical content compiled by participants was greater for the aggregated interface. Taken together, these two trends suggest that user engagement with vertical content is greater when the verticals are showcased in the main results.

The aggregated interface used in Sushmita *et al.* [333] was static—verticals were blended in fixed positions. In a later study, Sushmita *et al.* [334] investigated search behavior with a *dynamic* aggregated search interface. This study found two main results. First, users click more on verticals that are relevant to the task *and* verticals that are shown higher in ranking. In other words, aggregated search is not immune to positional bias. Users click more on verticals ranked higher, either because they scan results from top to bottom or because they trust that the top results are more relevant. Second, users click more on verticals that are more visually salient (in the case of this study, the *video* vertical). Thus, positional bias is not the only bias that affects clicks on vertical results.

Thus far, we have focused on user studies that investigate the question, What do users want? Users want a system that combines results from different sources in the main results and a system that makes the relevant verticals more salient. Next we focus on user studies that investigate factors that might affect user preference and search behavior.

As previously mentioned, an important advantage of user study evaluation is the ability to manipulate properties of the user's higher-level goal. Prior work shows that task complexity influences search behavior [173].[2] Among the differences in search behavior is the demand for *diverse* content. That is, during more complex tasks, users exhibit a greater demand for content that is more diverse (content from different sources or different types of media). Motivated by this finding, Arguello *et al.* [17] investigated the effect of task complexity on users' demand for vertical content,

---

[2] Here, task complexity refers to *cognitive* complexity, which relates to the amount of learning required for the user to complete the task.

operationalized using clicks on vertical results. The study looked at the interaction between two experimental variables: *task complexity* and *vertical aggregation*. Participants were given search tasks of varying degrees of complexity and used two different interfaces: a tabbed interface, in which vertical content was only *indirectly* accessible, and an aggregated interface, in which vertical results were also blended into the Web results. Results showed a greater number of vertical clicks for more complex tasks but only for the aggregated interface. However, the effect was only *marginally* significant. This result suggests that properties of the higher-level task may influence a user's demand for vertical results. Thus, session-level evidence, which can provide better hints about the higher-level task, may need to be considered in order to improve aggregated search.

During vertical selection, a false-negative mistake means that a nonrelevant vertical was presented alongside the core Web results. All evaluation methods for vertical selection and end-to-end aggregated search assume that all false-negative mistakes are *equally* bad. In other words, all instances where the system presents a nonrelevant vertical equally hurt the user's search experience. However, consider a user that issues the ambiguous query "jaguar" because she is looking for a list of a places in the world where jaguars can found in the wild. In this particular scenario, displaying the *images* vertical can be viewed as a false-negative mistake. The information need is more likely to be satisfied with Web results instead of image results. However, is the user experience equally affected if the images are all pictures of "jaguar" the automobile vs. pictures of "jaguar" the animal? Arguello and Capra [12] studied the effect of the query senses represented in the blended image results on user interaction with the Web results. They found that given an ambiguous query (e.g., "jaguar"), user interaction with the Web results, operationalized using Web clicks, is greater when the query senses represented in the image results (e.g., "jaguar" the animal or "jaguar" the car) are consistent with the intended query sense (e.g., "jaguar" the animal). This result suggests that in certain situations, a "spillover" effect can occur. In other words, depending on the vertical results, certain false-negative vertical predictions may have a stronger negative effect on the user's perception of *other* results presented on the SERP.

Such interaction effects between different components of a SERP, which include vertical results but also extend to components such as query suggestions and advertisements, motivate work on *whole-page* evaluation. The idea behind whole-page evaluation is that the relevance of a component may depend on *other* components presented on the SERP. For example, a relevant Web result presented at rank five may be less relevant if it contains information that is redundant with a Web result presented at rank one. Likewise, the quality of the SERP as a whole may be inferior if different components in the SERP (e.g, the Web results, the vertical results, and/or the query suggestions) focus on different query senses. Bailey *et al.* [23] proposed a whole-page evaluation methodology referred to as the Student Assignment Satisfaction Index (SASI). The evaluation methodology focuses on eliciting judgments from assessors on parts of the SERP within the context of the whole SERP. Bailey *et al.* [23] show that the SASI-style judgments on the whole page can be done surprisingly fast. A whole SERP can be evaluated in the time it takes an assessor to make two document-level relevance judgments in a test collection evaluation method. However, the main disadvantage of this evaluation method is that the judgments are purely retrospective. In other words, the judgments are based on the system's output and are therefore not reusable for future evaluations.

8.4 Special Topics

8.4.1 Dealing with New Verticals

Just as pages are constantly being added to and removed from the Web, verticals themselves appear as new subcollections are curated. Unfortunately, creating a new vertical requires training a new vertical selection model and requires new training data. As mentioned earlier, training data can be expensive to gather, so it would be attractive for a system to be able to exploit training data from existing verticals when training a new vertical selection model.

Let $y_v(q)$ denote the true relevance label of vertical v with respect to query q.[3] In the general vertical selection setting, the goal is to learn a function f that approximates y. In this section, we focus on the following scenario. Assume we have a set, S, of source verticals, each with labeled queries. Then suppose we are given a new (target) vertical t with no labeled data. The objective is to learn a function f that approximates y_t using *only* source-vertical training data. The quality of an approximation will be measured by some metric that compares the predicted and true query labels. We use notation

$$\mu(f, y_t, \mathcal{Q})$$

to refer to the evaluation of function f on query set $\mathcal{Q}$. This metric could be any of those discussed in Section 8.3.

A *portable* vertical selection model is defined as one that can make vertical relevance predictions with respect to any arbitrary vertical. In other words, a portable model is not specific to a particular vertical but rather is agnostic of the candidate vertical being questioned for relevance. For this reason, throughout this section, we adopt the shared feature representation ϕ^{shared} (Eq. 8.24).

Let us examine the distinction between a portable and nonportable vertical selection model with an example. Consider a single-evidence model that predicts a vertical relevant based on the number of times the users previously issued the query to the vertical. This type of evidence is likely to be positively correlated with the relevance of the vertical in question. In fact, it is likely to be positively correlated with vertical relevance irrespective of the particular candidate vertical. On the other hand, consider a model that predicts a vertical relevant if the query is classified as related to the *travel* domain. This model may be effective at predicting the relevance of a vertical that serves travel-related content. However, it is probably not effective on a vertical that focuses on a different domain. This model is less portable.

---

[3] This true label can be derived by thresholding of the training data, such as $\dfrac{\left|\mathcal{D}^+_{(q,v)}\right|}{\left|\mathcal{D}_{(q,v)}\right|} > \lambda$.

Most existing single-evidence resource selection models can be considered portable [316,315,314,308,345]. For example, ReDDE [315] prioritizes resources for selection based on the estimated number of relevant documents in the collection. This expectation is a function of the number of documents sampled from the collection that are predicted relevant and the estimated size of the original collection. The greater the expectation, the greater the relevance, irrespective of the particular resource.

8.4.1.1 *Basic Model*

The objective of a portable vertical selection model, $f_\star$, is to maximize the average performance across source verticals. Our assumption is that if $f_\star$ performs consistently well across S, then $f_\star$ will perform well on a new (target) vertical t. In general, the portability of a model is defined by a metric that quantifies performance for a vertical $s \in S$ and a function that aggregates performance across verticals in S.

For example, the portability, π, which uses the arithmetic mean of the metric, is defined by

$$\pi^{\text{avg}}(f_\star, y_S, Q_S) = \frac{1}{|S|} \sum_{s \in S} \mu(f_\star, y_s, Q_s), \qquad (8.33)$$

where Q_s is the set of training queries for source s and Q_S is the set of those sets; similarly, y_s provides labels for vertical s and y_S is the set of these functions. We refer to the model that optimizes π^{avg} as the *basic model*.

8.4.1.2 *Vertical Balancing*

In the basic model's training set, positive instances correspond to relevant query-vertical pairs from *all* source verticals. For this reason, we expect the basic model to focus on evidence that is consistently predictive of relevance across source verticals and hence predictive of the target vertical. In other words, vertical-specific evidence that is conflicting with respect to the positive class should be ignored. The challenge, however, is that the positive instances in the basic model's training pool may be skewed toward the more popular source verticals. This is problematic if these verticals are reliably predicted relevant using vertical-specific evidence, they are not likely to be predictive of the new target vertical. To compensate for this situation, we consider a *weighted* average of metrics across verticals. Specifically,

$$\pi^{\text{wavg}}(f_\star, y_S, Q_S) = \frac{1}{Z} \sum_{s \in S} w_s \mu(f_\star, y_s, Q_s), \qquad (8.34)$$

where $Z = \sum_{s \in S} w_s$. We use the simple heuristic of weighting a vertical with the inverse of its prior,

$$w_s = \frac{1}{p_s},$$

where p_s is the prior probability of observing a query with relevant vertical s. This value is approximated with the training data

$$p_s \approx \frac{\sum_{q \in \mathcal{Q}_s} y_s(q)}{|\mathcal{Q}_s|}.$$

The goal is to make training instances from minority verticals more influential and those from majority verticals less so.

8.4.1.3 *Feature Weighting*

An alternative to optimizing for a portable model is to find portable features and to train a model using only those. A *portable feature* is defined as a feature that is highly correlated with relevance across all verticals. Recall that, across verticals, all features are identically indexed. Let ϕ^i be a predictor based only on the value of feature i. In previous work, the effectiveness of features across verticals was shown to be very dependent on the vertical being considered. To address the expected instability of feature predictiveness across verticals, we adopt a harmonic average for our aggregation method:

$$\pi^{\mathrm{havg}}(\phi^i, y_{\mathcal{S}}, \mathcal{Q}_{\mathcal{S}}) = \frac{|\mathcal{S}|}{\sum_{s \in \mathcal{S}} \frac{1}{\mu(\phi_s^i, y_s, \mathcal{Q}_s)}} \tag{8.35}$$

Additionally, features on their own are not scaled to the label range, making the use of logistic loss difficult. Instead of constructing a mapping from a feature value to the appropriate range, we adopt a rank-based metric. In other words, for each feature, we rank queries by feature value and compute the harmonic mean average precision across verticals. Having computed the portability of each feature, we build a portable model by restricting our training to the most portable features.

8.4.1.4 *Adaptability*

Earlier we focused on ways of improving the portability of a model by influencing the model to ignore evidence that is vertical-specific. The argument is that a model that focuses heavily on vertical-specific evidence will not generalize well to a new target vertical.

Given access to target-vertical training data, previous work reveals two meaningful trends [15]. First, given a wide range of input features, most features contribute significantly to performance. In Arguello *et al.* [15], no small subset of features was solely responsible for effective vertical prediction. Second, the features that contributed the most to performance, which characterize the domain of the query, seem to be vertical-specific (assuming that verticals focus on different domains). Based on these observations, although ignoring vertical-specific evidence seems necessary to improve a model's portability, a model customized to a particular vertical is likely to benefit from it.

In the context of adaptation for Web search, Chen *et al.* [61] propose several ways to adapt an already-tuned model, given data in a new domain. Their approach, tree-based domain adaptation (TRADA), essentially consists of continuing the training process on labeled data from the target domain. Arguello *et al.* applied this technique to adapt predictions from a portable vertical selection model to a new vertical [16].

8.4.2 Explore/Exploit

The gathering training data in a production environment is limited by production constraints. We cannot show every vertical for every query and expect to gather training data, much less retain users. At the same time, if a production system only gathers data from existing presentation decisions, judgments on suppressed verticals will not be gathered. This is precisely the problem of balancing exploration (i.e., gathering training data with good coverage) and exploitation (i.e., providing users with a satisfying experience). That said, we may be able to gather a small amount of feedback without devastating system performance. Specifically, we would like to present a vertical display for a query, even though it is not predicted to be the display with the highest probability. As a result, our production system combines exploration (i.e., the random gathering of training data) with exploitation (i.e., the application of the trained model). Section 8.2 covers methods for exploitation. In this section, we discuss two methods for exploration.

Naïve exploration suggests randomly altering vertical-selection decisions as queries are submitted to the aggregated search system. Specifically, we can define a system sampling rate, ϵ, which determines whether the system decision will be perturbed. This approach is referred to as the ϵ-*greedy approach* [335].

The ϵ-greedy approach, though providing a control on the amount of sampling, does not incorporate any information from a query's feedback history. We may want to explore only when we have presented few displays. That is, we might make ϵ a function of $\mathcal{D}_{(q,v)}$. To achieve this goal, we can exploit the fact that Eq. 8.17 defines a distribution from which we can sample $p_{(q,v)}$. Using a random sample instead of the posterior mean results in a more data-driven policy than ϵ-greedy exploration. If we have seen few or no samples, the variance of the posterior will be high, resulting in samples unlike the posterior mean. As we accumulate samples, this variance falls, ensuring that samples will converge to the posterior mean. This process is similar to approaches used in reinforcement learning [329].

8.5 Conclusion

Although aggregated search is relatively new as a research topic, its foundation in distributed information retrieval has allowed rapid development of sophisticated models. In this chapter, we have outlined the fundamentals of developing an aggregated search system. These include features based on the distributed information retrieval literature as well as newer methods for training vertical selection and presentation systems.

Aggregated search will continue to develop as the online information landscape develops. New verticals will almost certainly necessitate revisiting feature development. At the same time, training algorithms will increasingly exploit more sophisticated user data to refine presentation decisions. Finally, as interfaces move away from traditional ranked lists, vertical presentation and interleaving frameworks will have to be modified.

Cross-Vertical Search Ranking

9

INTRODUCTION

Learning to rank represents an important class of supervised machine learning tasks with the goal of automatically constructing ranking functions from training data. As with many other supervised machine learning problems, the quality of a ranking function is highly correlated with the amount of labeled data used to train the function. Due to the complexity of many ranking problems, a large number of labeled training examples are usually required to learn a high-quality ranking function. In general, it is very expensive and time-consuming to acquire labeled data.

On the other hand, for modern vertical search engines, ranking over multiple related verticals or domains becomes a common situation. In some domains we may have a relatively large amount of training data, whereas in some other domains we can only collect very little. In those situations, making use of labeled data from related domains is a desirable direction to take to address the data scarcity in the target domain.

Besides ranking applications, this learning scenario is also popular for other applications; it has been studied as transfer learning in the literature. Existing transfer learning approaches mainly focus on knowledge transfer in the same feature space, i.e., the data from different domains are assumed in a common feature space. However, in practice, we often face the problem where the labeled data are scarce in their own feature space, whereas there may be a large amount of labeled heterogeneous data in another feature space. In fact, this problem arises frequently in vertical search systems. For example, a vertical search engine often conducts ranking learning tasks in various verticals (e.g., news search, blog search, product search, etc.); here, data from the *news* vertical may be helpful for blog search; these data usually exist in different feature spaces that are vertical-dependent. In international vertical search systems, there are also different language domains (e.g., English news search, Spanish news search, etc.). Here, data from an English language domain may be helpful for a Spanish language domain. However, the data usually exist in different feature spaces that are language dependent. Therefore, for a wide range of vertical search systems, it would be desirable to transfer the knowledge from heterogeneous domains to a target domain where we have relatively little training data available, since doing so provides a scalable and efficient solution for ranking learning for multiple verticals.

For homogeneous transfer learning, since the data are in a common feature space, the main challenge is to overcome the data distribution difference to learn domain correlation for knowledge transfer. On the other hand, for heterogeneous transfer learning, the domain difference is beyond distribution difference, since distributions from heterogeneous spaces are not even comparable. Therefore, in general, heterogeneous transfer learning is more challenging than homogenous transfer learning.

When it comes to ranking, the problem becomes *heterogeneous transfer ranking*, which is even more challenging due to the following facts. First, unlike in classification or regression, in ranking the labels (relevance scores) for different domains may not be comparable. For example, a domain can have five grade relevance scores; another domain can have binary relevance scores. In fact, since the relevance scores may be query-dependent, the absolute values are not important; the preference order between instances is more important. Therefore, heterogeneous transfer ranking needs to catch correlations between preference orders from different domains instead of the traditional label correlations in classification and regression. Second, in general, a ranking application needs thousands of (or millions of) training examples. It is important to develop a method that can scale well to large datasets.

In this chapter, we propose a general probabilistic model, the *pairwise cross-domain factor* (PCDF) model [419], for heterogeneous transfer ranking. The PCDF model is a feature-based transfer ranking model that learns common latent factors (features) to transfer knowledge across multiple heterogeneous ranking domains. PCDF assumes that (1) homogeneous features, heterogeneous features, and hidden relevance scores are generated conditioned on latent factors, and (2) preference orders are generated conditioned on hidden relevance scores. Through direct and indirect parameter sharing for the generative processes in different domains, the latent factors catch different types of domain correlations to extract the common knowledge for different domains.

9.1 The PCDF Model

9.1.1 Problem Formulation

For ease of exposition and to avoid notational clutter, we use the terms *target domain* and *source domain* to distinguish two given domains in a transfer learning task, though the discussions in this study are applicable to the situation that two domains are exchangeable and mutually helpful and can be easily extended to multiple domains.

We begin with notations. We consider that the target domain data exist in a $d_t + d_c$ dimension space and the source domain data exist in a $d_s + d_c$ dimension space, where d_c is the number of dimensions for their overlapped feature space (denoted as $\mathcal{S}^c$), and d_t and d_s are the number of dimensions for their dedicated feature spaces (denoted as $\mathcal{S}^t$ and $\mathcal{S}^d$), respectively. For traditional homogeneous transfer learning, all data are in the same feature space, i.e., $d_t = 0$ and $d_s = 0$. For totally heterogeneous transfer learning, the feature spaces for the different domains have no overlap, i.e., $d_c = 0$. In this study, we consider the most general case, partially overlapped heterogeneous feature spaces, which arises frequently in real applications.

We let n_t and n_s denote the numbers of instances in the target domain and the source domain, respectively. We let

$$X^{(t)} = [X^{(td)} X^{(tc)}]$$

denote the target domain data, where $X^{(td)} \in \mathbb{R}^{n_t \times d_t}$ denote the target domain data in its dedicated feature space, and $X^{(tc)} \in \mathbb{R}^{n_t \times d_c}$ denote target domain data in the common feature space. Similarly,

$$X^{(s)} = [X^{(sd)} X^{(sc)}]$$

denotes the source domain data, where $X^{(sd)} \in \mathbb{R}^{n_s \times d_s}$ denote the source domain data in its dedicated feature space, and $X^{(sc)} \in \mathbb{R}^{n_s \times d_c}$ denote the source domain data in the overlapped feature space. To denote the i-th data instance in the target domain or source domain, we use $X_{j.}^{(t)}$ or $X_{i.}^{(s)}$.

Furthermore, we let $R_{ij}^{(t)}$ denote the preference value between i-th instance and j-th instance in the target domain, such that

$$R_{ij}^{(t)} \begin{cases} > 0 & \text{if } i\text{-th instance is preferred over } j\text{-th instance,} \\ = 0 & \text{if } i\text{-th and } j\text{-th instance are equally preferred,} \\ < 0 & \text{if } j\text{-th instance is preferred over } i\text{-th instance.} \end{cases} \quad (9.1)$$

where $1 \leq i, j \leq n_t$ (however, it is not necessary that there is $R_{ij}^{(t)}$ for any pair of i and j in the data). In general $R_{ij}^{(t)} \in \mathbb{R}$. In the special case that only the preference order matters, $R_{ij}^{(t)} \in \{-1, 0, +1\}$. Note that even though the data are given with relevance labels or lists of ordered instances, they can be easily converted to the pairwise preferences. Similarly, we let $R_{ij}^{(s)}$ denote the preference value between the i-th instance and the j-th instance in the source domain.

In heterogeneous transfer ranking, given target domain data $X^{(td)}$, $X^{(tc)}$, and $R^{(t)}$ and source domain data $X^{(sd)}$, $X^{(sc)}$, and $R^{(s)}$, there are three types of domain difference to impede us from directly applying target domain data to the target domain: different feature distributions in the shared feature space; different dedicated feature spaces; and different distributions for pairwise preference values.

On the other hand, we need to catch three types of domain correlations for knowledge transfer. The first one is homogeneous feature correlation hidden in the overlapped feature space, i.e., correlation between $X^{(tc)}$ and $X^{(sc)}$, which is the focus of traditional homogeneous transfer learning. The second one is heterogeneous feature correlation hidden in the dedicated feature spaces, i.e., correlation between $X^{(td)}$ and $X^{(sd)}$. The third one is preference correlation, i.e., the correlation between $R^{(t)}$ and $R^{(s)}$.

9.1.2 Model Formulation

In this study we consider a generative model, in which features and pairwise preferences are generated conditioned on the latent variables.

9.1.2.1 *Feature Generating*

First we assume that the two domains' features are generated conditioned on the common latent factors with maximum domain correlations and minimum domain differences. In heterogenous transfer ranking, there are two types of feature correlations between the two domains, and intuitively it is difficult to catch them in one type of latent factor. Based on this observation, we propose the concept two-component latent factor. The two-component latent factors for the two domains are given as follows

$$Z^{(t)} = [Z^{(td)} Z^{(tc)}] \tag{9.2}$$

and

$$Z^{(s)} = [Z^{(sd)} Z^{(sc)}], \tag{9.3}$$

where $Z^{(t)} \in \mathbb{R}^{n_t \times (k_d + k_c)}$, $Z^{(td)} \in \mathbb{R}^{n_d \times k_c}$, $Z^{(tc)} \in \mathbb{R}^{n_t \times k_c}$, $Z^{(s)} \in \mathbb{R}^{n_s \times (k_c + k_d)}$, $Z^{(sd)} \in \mathbb{R}^{n_s \times k_d}$, $Z^{(sc)} \in \mathbb{R}^{n_s \times k_c}$, k_c is the dimension of latent factors for the common features, and k_d is the dimensions of latent factors for the dedicated features. In the target domain latent factor $Z^{(t)}$, the component $Z^{(td)}$ is to catch heterogeneous feature correlation and the component $Z^{(tc)}$ is to catch homogeneous feature correlation.

Then the common features in the overlapped feature space are generated according to the following probabilities

$$X^{(tc)} \sim p(X^{(tc)} \mid f(Z^{(tc)}; P^{(c)})) \tag{9.4}$$

$$X^{(sc)} \sim p(X^{(sc)} \mid f(Z^{(sc)}; P^{(c)})), \tag{9.5}$$

where $f(\cdot)$ is a link function and $P^{(c)}$ is the function parameter. Through the shared parameter $P^{(c)}$, the latent factors $Z^{(tc)}$ and $Z^{(sc)}$ catch common knowledge from the two domains' common features.

However, for the dedicated features $X^{(td)}$ and $X^{(sd)}$, since they are in the different feature spaces, in general direct knowledge transfer by sharing the link function parameter is not feasible. For example, if $X^{(td)}$ and $X^{(sd)}$ have different dimensions and we use the popular linear link function such that $f(Z; P) = ZP$, then it is not feasible for a shared parameter matrix $P^{(c)}$ to make the latent factor $Z^{(td)}$ and $Z^{(sd)}$ have the same dimension k_d. In other words, the parameter sharing is too strong an assumption for the heterogeneous features. On the other hand, it is more reasonable to learn the heterogeneous feature correlation indirectly through the interaction between different types of latent factors and interaction between latent factors and pairwise preferences (discussed in more detail later). Therefore, we assume that the dedicated features are generated with their own link function parameters as follows:

$$X^{(td)} \sim p(X^{(td)} \mid g(Z^{(td)}; P^{(td)})) \tag{9.6}$$

$$X^{(sd)} \sim p(X^{(sd)} \mid g(Z^{(sd)}; P^{(sd)})), \tag{9.7}$$

where $g(\cdot)$ is a link function and $P^{(td)}$ and $P^{(sd)}$ are the function parameters.

Furthermore, we assume prior distributions for $P^{(c)}$, $P^{(td)}$, and $P^{(sd)}$ to reduce overfitting,

$$P^{(c)} \sim p(P^{(c)}; \lambda_c) \tag{9.8}$$

$$P^{(td)} \sim p(P^{(td)}; \lambda_{td}) \tag{9.9}$$

$$P^{(sd)} \sim p(P^{(sd)}; \lambda_{sd}) \tag{9.10}$$

9.1.2.2 *Generating Pairwise Preferences*

To generate another observed variable, the pairwise preference score R_{ij}, we propose the concept of latent relevance score. We assume that each instance i has a latent relevance score y_i such that comparing a pair of y_i and y_j will give the between instance i and j.

In other words, we assume that Rij is generated conditioned on y_i and y_j for both domains

$$R_{ij}^{(t)} \sim p(R_{ij}^{(t)} \mid r(\mathbf{y}t_i, \mathbf{y}t_j)) \tag{9.11}$$

$$R_{ij}^{(s)} \sim p(R_{ij}^{(s)} \mid r(\mathbf{y}s_i, \mathbf{y}s_j)), \tag{9.12}$$

where r is a link function. An intuitive choice for r is the difference function, i.e., $r(a, b) = a - b$. For example, we can assume that the distribution of $\mathbb{R}_{ij}$ is the normal distribution with the difference of y_i and y_j as the mean such that

$$R_{ij} \mid y_i, y_j \sim \mathbf{N}(y_i - y_j, \sigma^2). \tag{9.13}$$

We further assume that the latent relevance score is generated conditioned on the latent factor:

$$\mathbf{y}t \sim p(\mathbf{y}t \mid h(Z^{(t)}; w)) \tag{9.14}$$

$$\mathbf{y}s \sim p(\mathbf{y}s \mid h(Z^{(s)}; w)), \tag{9.15}$$

where h (;) is a link function, $w \in \mathbb{R}^k$ is the function parameter, and $Z^{(t)}$ and $Z^{(s)}$ are defined as in Eqs. 9.2 and 9.3. Therefore, through the latent relevance scores and the shared parameter w, the latent factor is able to catch the pairwise preference correlation in addition to homogeneous feature correlation and heterogeneous feature correlation.

Similarly, we assume prior distributions for $P^{(w)}$ to reduce overfitting,

$$w \sim p(w; \lambda_w) \tag{9.16}$$

9.1.2.3 *PCDF and Its Variations*

Figure 9.1 summarizes the PCDF mode as a Bayesian network. From Figure 9.1, we can observe that the two domains share two parameters $P^{(c)}$ and w, which are bridges of knowledge transfer. Through the information propagation among the Bayesian network, the two-component latent factors catch the three types of domain correlations, i.e., the common knowledge crosses the two domains.

As a general model for heterogenous transfer ranking, PCDF can be easily modified to accommodate special cases.

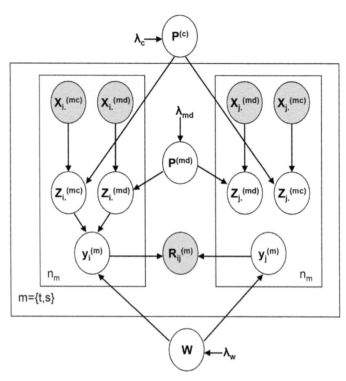

FIGURE 9.1

A PCDF Bayesian network.

First, it can be easily applied to homogeneous transfer ranking, i.e., two domains in a shared feature space. Figure 9.2 shows the PCDF model for homogenous data. From Figure 9.2, we observe that without the heterogeneous features and heterogeneous latent factors, the PCDF model is reduced to a new homogeneous transfer ranking model.

Second, with a little modification, the PCDF model can also be applied to the situation of data with absolute relevance scores. In such situations, yt and ys become observed variables and pairwise preferences are omitted. Hence, the PCDF model is reduced to a pointwise cross-domain factor model, which is shown in Figure 9.3. More interestingly, pointwise cross-domain factor model is beyond ranking applications, i.e., it can be directly applied to general regression and classification applications.

9.2 Algorithm Derivation

In this section, we derive the algorithm to learn the parameters for the PCDF model.

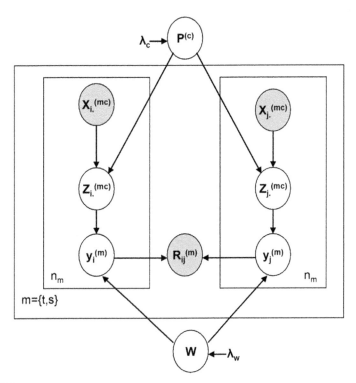

FIGURE 9.2

A PCDF model for homogeneous data.

9.2.1 Objective Specification

The likelihood function of the PCDF model is given in Eq. 9.17, in which D denotes observed data; Ω denotes all parameters; Φ^m denotes the set of observed pairwise preferences of instances i and j for domain m.

$$
p(D; \Omega) = \sum_{m=t,s} \Bigg(\sum_{(i,j)\in\Phi^m} \Big(p\Big(X_{i.}^{(mc)} \mid f\Big(Z_{i.}^{(mc)}; P^{(c)}\Big)\Big)
$$

$$
p\Big(X_{i.}^{(md)} \mid g\Big(Z_{i.}^{(md)}; P^{(md)}\Big)\Big) p\Big(\mathbf{y}m_i \mid h\Big(Z_{i.}^{(m)}; w\Big)\Big)
$$

$$
p\Big(X_{j.}^{(mc)} \mid f\Big(Z_{j.}^{(mc)}; P^{(c)}\Big)\Big) p\Big(X_{j.}^{(md)} \mid g\Big(Z_{j.}^{(md)}; P^{(md)}\Big)\Big)
$$

$$
p\Big(\mathbf{y}m_j \mid h\Big(Z_{j.}^{(m)}; w\Big)\Big)\Big) p\Big(R_{ij}^{(m)} \mid r\left(\mathbf{y}m_i, \mathbf{y}m_j\right)\Big)
$$

$$
p\Big(P^{(md)}; \lambda_{md}\Big)\Bigg) p\Big(P^{(c)}; \lambda_c\Big) p\left(w; \lambda_w\right), \tag{9.17}
$$

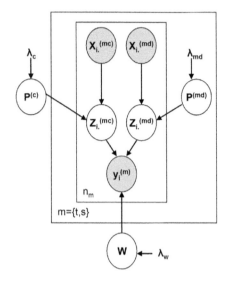

FIGURE 9.3

The pointwise cross-domain factor model.

Equation 9.17 is a general objective function. In this study, to instantiate Eq. 9.17, we adopt popular linear functions for the link functions f, g, and h, and we use an intuitive difference function for r. Furthermore, It has been observed in the literature [74] that maximizing likelihood under a certain distribution corresponds to minimizing distance under the corresponding distortion measure. For example, the normal distribution, Bernoulli distribution, multinomial distribution, and exponential distribution correspond to Euclidean distance, logistic loss, KL-divergence, and Itakura-Saito distance, respectively. Therefore, the problem of minimizing the negative log posterior of PCDF boils down to the following objective:

$$
\begin{aligned}
\min_{\Omega} \sum_{m=t,s} \Bigg(\sum_{(i,j)\in\Phi^m} & \Big(\alpha_{mc} l\left(X_{i.}^{(mc)}, Z_{i.}^{(mc)} P^{(c)}\right) \\
& + \alpha_{md} l\left(X_{i.}^{(md)}, Z_{i.}^{(md)} P^{(md)}\right) + \beta_m l\left(\mathbf{y}m_i, Z_{i.}^{(m)} w\right) \\
& + \alpha_{mc} l\left(X_{j.}^{(mc)}, Z_{j.}^{(mc)} P^{(c)}\right) \\
& + \alpha_{md} l\left(X_{j.}^{(md)}, Z_{j.}^{(md)} P^{(md)}\right) + \beta_m l\left(\mathbf{y}m_j, Z_{j.}^{(m)} w\right) \\
& + \gamma_m l\left(R_{ij}^{(m)}, \mathbf{y}m_i - \mathbf{y}m_j\right) \Bigg) + \lambda_{md}\omega\left(P^{(md)}\right) \\
& + \lambda_c \omega\left(P^{(c)}\right) + \lambda_w \omega(w),
\end{aligned}
\tag{9.18}
$$

where α, β, γ, and λ are tradeoff parameters; $l(.,.)$ are the loss functions (for convenience, we use l for all terms; in general, it could be different for different terms) corresponding to conditional distributions in Eq. 9.17; $\omega(.)$ is the regularization loss function corresponding to the prior distribution in Eq. 9.17.

The motivations for a computational framework instead of direct probabilistic inference are mainly twofold: First, the two formulations are somewhat equivalent, i.e., the conditional distributions can be encoded precisely through the choice of loss functions; likewise, the prior distributions over parameters could also be readily translated into the regularization penalties. Second, computational models allow more scalable algorithms, e.g., via stochastic gradient descent, whereas probabilistic reasoning often requires Monte Carlo sampling or quite nontrivial variational approximations.

9.2.2 Optimization and Implementation

In general, minimizing Eq. 9.19 is a nonconvex problem regardless of the choice of the loss functions and regularizers. Although there are convex reformulations for some settings, they tend to be computationally inefficient for large-scale problems; the convex formulations require the manipulation of a full matrix, which is impractical for anything beyond thousands of instances.

We established algorithms for distributed optimization based on the Hadoop MapReduce framework. The basic idea is to decompose the objective in Eq. 9.19 by optimizing with respect to each pairwise preference $R_{ij}^{(m)}$ and to combine the results for the parameters in the Reduce phase.

We briefly describe a stochastic gradient descent algorithm to solve the optimization of Eq. 9.19. The algorithm is computationally efficient and decouples different pairwise preferences. For a detailed discussion, see [416]. The algorithm loops over all the observations and updates the parameters by moving in the direction defined by a negative gradient. Specifically, for each observation $R_{ij}^{(m)}$, the algorithm performs the following sequence of updating. First, the hidden variables related to instance i are updated as follows:

$$\mathbf{y}m_i = \mathbf{y}m_i - \delta \left(\beta_m l' \left(\mathbf{y}m_i, Z_{i.}^{(m)} w \right) + \gamma_m l' \left(R_{ij}^{(m)}, \mathbf{y}m_i - \mathbf{y}m_j \right) \right); \qquad (9.19)$$

$$Z_{i.}^{(md)} = Z_{i.}^{(md)} - \delta \left(\alpha_{md} l' \left(X_{i.}^{(md)}, Z_{i.}^{(md)} P^{(md)} \right) \odot P^{(md)} \mathbf{1} \right.$$
$$\left. + \beta_m l' \left(\mathbf{y}m_i, Z_{i.}^{(md)} w^{(d)} \right) \odot w^{(d)} \right), \qquad (9.20)$$

$$Z_{i.}^{(mc)} = Z_{i.}^{(mc)} - \delta \left(\alpha_{mc} l' \left(X_{i.}^{(mc)}, Z_{i.}^{(mc)} P^{(c)} \right) \odot P^{(c)} \mathbf{1} \right.$$
$$\left. + \beta_m l' \left(\mathbf{y}m_i, Z_{i.}^{(mc)} w^{(c)} \right) \odot w^{(c)} \right), \qquad (9.21)$$

where δ is the learning rate, $\odot$ denotes elementwise multiplication, $\mathbf{1}$ denotes vector of 1s, and for convenience we write w into $\begin{bmatrix} w^{(d)} \\ w^{(c)} \end{bmatrix}$.

Second, the latent variables related to instance j are updated as follows:

$$\mathbf{ym}_j = \mathbf{ym}_j - \delta \left(\beta_m l' \left(\mathbf{ym}_j, Z_{j.}^{(m)} w \right) - \gamma_m l' \left(R_{ij}^{(m)}, \mathbf{ym}_i - \mathbf{ym}_j \right) \right); \quad (9.22)$$

$$
\begin{aligned}
Z_{j.}^{(md)} &= Z_{j.}^{(md)} - \delta \left(\alpha_{md} l' \left(X_{j.}^{(md)}, Z_{j.}^{(md)} P^{(md)} \right) \odot P^{(md)} \mathbf{1} \right. \\
&\quad \left. + \beta_m l' \left(\mathbf{ym}_j, Z_{j.}^{(md)} w^{(d)} \right) \odot w^{(d)} \right),
\end{aligned}
\quad (9.23)
$$

$$
\begin{aligned}
Z_{j.}^{(mc)} &= Z_{j.}^{(mc)} - \delta \left(\alpha_{mc} l' \left(X_{j.}^{(mc)}, Z_{j.}^{(mc)} P^{(c)} \right) \odot P^{(c)} \mathbf{1} \right. \\
&\quad \left. + \beta_m l' \left(\mathbf{ym}_j, Z_{j.}^{(mc)} w^{(c)} \right) \odot w^{(c)} \right),
\end{aligned}
\quad (9.24)
$$

Third, the parameters are updated as follows:

$$
\begin{aligned}
P^{(md)} &= P^{(md)} - \delta \left(\alpha_{md} l' \left(X^{(md)}, Z^{(md)} P^{(md)} \right) Z^{(md)} \right. \\
&\quad \left. + \lambda_{md} \omega' \left(P^{(md)} \right) \right),
\end{aligned}
\quad (9.25)
$$

$$
\begin{aligned}
P^{(c)} &= P^{(c)} - \delta \left(\sum_{m=t,s} \left(\alpha_{mc} l' \left(X^{(mc)}, Z^{(mc)} P^{(c)} \right) Z^{(mc)} \right) \right. \\
&\quad \left. + \lambda_c \omega' (P^{(c)}) \right),
\end{aligned}
\quad (9.26)
$$

$$
w = w - \delta \left(\sum_{m=t,s} \left(\beta_m l' \left(\mathbf{ym}, Z^{(m)} w \right) Z^{(m)} \right) + l w \omega' (w) \right). \quad (9.27)
$$

In summary, the algorithm loops over all instances of $R_{ij}^{(m)}$ to perform updating rules (Eqs. (9.21) through (9.27)) until it converges. In practice, the algorithm may not need to update parameters for each $R_{ij}^{(m)}$, since the changes of parameters may not be significant for one observation. Instead it could be more efficient to perform updating rules (Eqs. (9.25) through (9.27)) after performing updating rules (Eq. (9.19) through (9.24)) on a batch of observations. The general PCDF algorithm is summarized in Algorithm 1. Note that following the similar procedure, it is easy to derive the algorithms for the variations of the model in Figures 9.2 and 9.3, PCDF for homogenous data and pointwise (regression-based) cross-domain factor model.

Algorithm 1 General PCDF Algorithm

Input:$\{X^{(t)}, R^{(t)}, X^{(s)}, R^{(s)}\}$ and an integer b (number of instances for batch updating parameters).
Output:$\{P^{(td)}, P^{(sd)}, P^{(c)}, w\}$. **Method:**
  1: Initialize $\{Z^{(t)}, Z^{(s)}, \mathbf{y}t, \mathbf{y}s, P^{(td)}, P^{(sd)}, P^{(c)}, w\}$
  2: **repeat**
  3:   **for** m=t,d **do**
  4:     Randomly shuffle $R^{(m)}$
  5:     Let $count = 0$
  6:     **for** Each observed $R_{ij}^{(m)}$ **do**
  7:       Let $count = count + 1$
  8:       Perform updating rules (9.21)-(9.24).
  9:       Perform updating rules (9.26)-(9.29)
 10:       **if** count%b $== 0$ **then**
 11:         Perform updating rules (9.31)-(9.35)
 12:       **end if**
 13:     **end for**
 14:   **end for**
 15: **until** convergence

The proposed stochastic gradient descent-based algorithm has two desirable properties. First, it is ready for distributed optimization based on the Hadoop MapReduce framework, since it decouples different pairwise preference observations. Second, it is flexible to adopt different loss functions and regularization functions for different types of data with different distributions.

9.3 Experimental Evaluation

As a general heterogeneous ranking algorithm, PCDF can be applied to different ranking applications with different data distributions. In this section, we apply PCDF to Web search data to demonstrate the properties and effectiveness of PCDF.

Although the PCDF model is flexible in adopting different loss and regularization functions, in this study we evaluate PCDF with the most popular loss function, L2 loss, corresponding to normal distribution, i.e., we use L2 loss for all l in minimization (Eq. 9.19). For the regularization functions, we evaluate both L2 loss (normal distribution prior) and L1 loss (laplace distribution prior). We denote those two algorithms as *PCDF-n-he* and *PCDF-l-he* (n is for normal distribution prior; l is for laplace distribution prior; *he* is for heterogeneous ranking).

To our best knowledge, there is no existing transfer learning algorithm that is directly applicable to partially overlapped heterogeneous feature spaces. (However, we thank an anonymous reviewer for pointing out very recent works, such as [362], which may be modified to this learning situation.) In this study, we use two state-of-the-art homogeneous transfer learning algorithms, sparse coding (called *SC-ho*)

[285,212] and multitask feature learning (called *MTFL-ho*) [18], as comparisons. Furthermore, an intuitive way for heterogeneous transfer learning to occur is to treat one domain's dedicated features in another domain as missing values and apply existing homogeneous transfer learning to the data with missing values; hence we modify the sparse coding algorithm (it is difficult to modify MFLF for this) to handle missing values (called *SC-he*) to evaluate this idea. Finally, the baseline is using the original target domain training data only (called *TD*) for ranking learning.

We also evaluate algorithms for two PCDF variations in Figures 9.2 and 9.3 to gain deep understanding of PCDF itself. Similarly, we use L2 loss for all the loss functions, and L2 and L1 loss for the regularizer functions. For PCDF for homogeneous data in Figure 9.2, they are denoted as *PCDF-n-ho* and *PCDF-l-ho*, respectively; for the regression based cross-domain factor model in Figure 9.3, they are denoted *RCDF-n-he* and *RCDF-l-he*.

In summary, we compare 10 algorithms: TD, SC-ho, SC-he, MTFL-ho, PCDF-n-ho, PCDF-l-ho, RCDF-n-he, RCDF-n-he, PCDF-n-he, and PCDF-l-he.

9.3.1 Data

We use Web search data from a commercial search engine system, which conducts ranking learning tasks in various domains with different languages or different verticals. The source domain (denoted S0) is a general Web search for an English-speaking country, which has a relatively large amount of labeled data. The first target domain (denoted T1) is a general Web search for a Spanish-speaking country; the second target domain (denoted T2) is a news article search for the same country as S0; the third target domain (denoted T3) is an answer search (providing a text search for a knowledge-sharing community) for another non-English-speaking country.

In the data, each query-document example is represented by a feature vector. Those query-document examples in domain S and T1 are originally labeled using a five-grade labeling scheme, and those in domain T1 and T2 are originally labeled using a four-grade labeling scheme. We then transform them into pairwise preference data.

The features generally fall into the following three categories: Query features comprise features dependent on the query only and have constant values across all the documents—for example, the number of terms in the query, whether or not the query is a person's name, and so on. Document features comprise features dependent on the document only and have constant values across all the queries—for example, the number of inbound links pointing to the document, the amount of anchor texts in bytes for the document, and the language identity of the document. Query-document features comprise features dependent on the relation of the query with respect to the document d—for example, the number of times each term in the query appears in the document d, the number of times each term in the query appears in the anchor texts of the document, a.

The four domains have an overlapped feature space consisting of text match features, which describes various aspects of text match between a query and a document,

Table 9.1   Data summary for one source domain and three target domains.

Dataset	S0	T1	T2	T3
Number of examples	50,121	5,112	5,087	5,124
Number of preference pairs	325,684	26,534	25,332	26,898
Overlapped features	67	67	67	67
Dedicated features	121	81	93	76

such as title match and body match. Each domain has its own dedicated feature space. For example, all domains have their own dedicated features related to term segmentation in a query that is language dependent; T2 has its dedicated features related to news articles, freshness. Table 9.1 summarizes the data information for four domains. In our experiments, 20% of data for each target domain are used as training data (i.e., labeled data are very scarce in target domains); 80% of them are used as test data to make evaluation robust. All the source domain data are used as training data to help the target domains.

9.3.2 Experimental Setting

To evaluate those transfer learning algorithms, first the new latent features and parameters are learned by the algorithms; then source domain and target domain training data with the new latent features are used by a base ranking learner to train a ranking model. Third, the ranking models are tested on the test data of the target domain, which are also projected into the new feature space.

For the base ranking learner, we use the gradient-boosting decision tree (GBDT) [130]. For performance measure of the ranking models, we adopt the widely used discounted cumulative gain (DCG). Specifically, we use DCG-k, since users of a search engine are only interested in the top k results of a query rather than a sorted order of the entire document collection. In this study, we select k as 5 and 1. For every experimental setting, 10 runs are repeated, and the average DCG of 10 runs is reported for each experiment setting.

The gradient of L1 regularization function is the discontinuous sign function. We approximate it by a steep soft-sign function $l(x) = \frac{1-\exp(-\theta x)}{1+\exp(-\theta x)}$, where θ is a positive number controlling the ramp of $l(x)$ (we use $\theta = 100$).

For the dimension of the latent factor, in our preliminary experiments we observe that the performance is not sensitive to it as long as it is not too small. In this study, we simply set $k_c = 20$ and $k_d = 20$. Other parameters, such as the learning rate, are selected by cross-validation.

9.3.3 Results and Discussions

The relative weight of source domain data with respect to the target domain data controls how much the source domain affects the target domain. It is very important because it directly affects the efficiency of the knowledge transfer. For example, the low weight will impede the knowledge transfer no matter how close the two domains are.

We evaluate the effects of relative weights of the source domain data for PCDF-n-he and PCDF-l-he algorithms to illustrate this important aspect. Figure 9.4 shows the effects of relative weights of source domain data on DCG5 performance for all three target domains. From Figure 9.4, we observe that the algorithms perform best at weight 0.6 for target domain T1, weight 0.5 for target domain T2, and weight 0.4 for target domain T3. The results imply that T1 is the closest to the source domain, T2 is the second closest, and T3 is the third closest. This is consistent with our domain knowledge about the four domains. Note that it is flexible for PCDF algorithms to adopt the optimal relative weights that can be decided by cross-validation.

The DCG5 and DCG1 comparisons of the 10 algorithms are shown in Figures 9.5 and 9.6. From these figures, we observe the following interesting facts:

- TD performs worst in all settings. This is due to insufficient training data for the target domains and confirms the basic motivation of transfer ranking: to improve poor ranking performance in domains with insufficient training data.
- Overall, PCDF-l-he performs best and PCDF-n-he performs second. This shows that PCDF can effectively catch domain correlations in both overlapped and heterogeneous feature spaces to improve learning in the target domain.
- PCDF-n-he and PCDF-l-he perform better than RCDF-n-he and RCDF-l-he. The possible reason is that PCDF catches correlations from preference orders, which matters more for ranking applications than absolute scores.
- PCDF-n-he and PCDF-l-he perform better than PCDF-n-ho and PCDF-l-ho, since PCDF-n-ho and PCDF-l-ho can use only features in the overlapped space and miss the knowledge transfer in the heterogenous feature spaces.
- PCDF-n-ho and PCDF-l-ho perform better than SC-ho and MTFL-ho. This shows that PCDF helps not only common knowledge learning across heterogeneous feature spaces but also in the same feature space, i.e., PCDF also provides an effective homogeneous transfer ranking model.
- The MTFL algorithm performs better than SC algorithms. The possible reason for this is that as a supervised learning algorithm, MTFL learns the more informative latent features by making use of label information.
- SC-he does not perform better than SC-ho, even though SC-he uses both overlapped features and heterogeneous features. This implies that simply treating one domain's dedicated features in another domain as missing values cannot effectively catch the heterogeneous feature correlation.
- Overall, the L1 regularization algorithms perform better than L2 regularization algorithms. This shows that the choice of the regularization functions could have significant impact on performance, and hence it is desirable for an algorithm to be flexible to adopt different regularization functions.

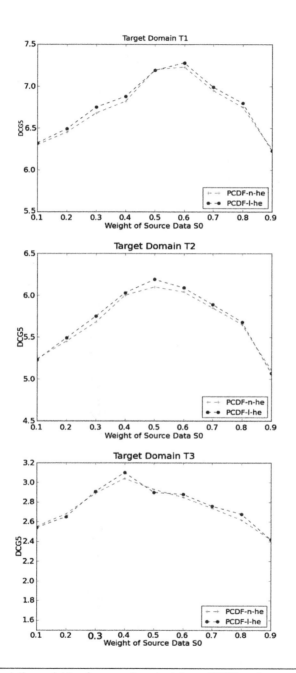

FIGURE 9.4

The effects of relative weights of source domain data on DCG5 performance.

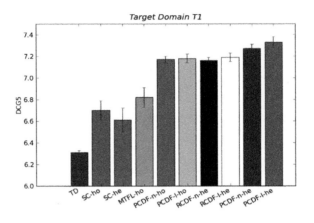

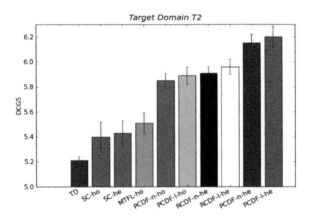

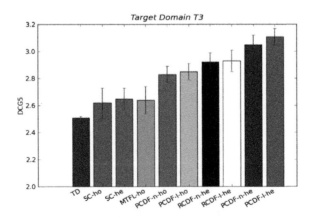

FIGURE 9.5

DCG5 comparisons of 10 algorithms on the three target domains.

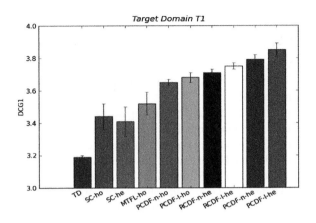

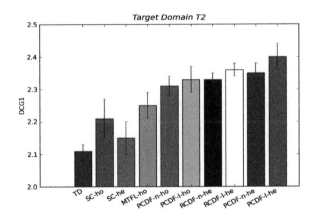

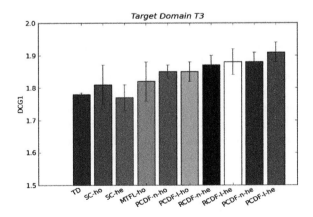

FIGURE 9.6

DCG1 comparisons of 10 algorithms on the three target domains.

9.4 **Related Work**

Cross-domain ranking is the overlapping field of ranking and transfer learning. Since ranking literature is extensitively covered in other chapters of this book, here we focus on transfer learning-related work.

Historically, special cases of transfer learning have been explored in the literature under different names, including sample selection bias [155], class imbalance [174], and covariate shift [313]. Those studies mainly address the difference between training and testing data distribution. For example, class imbalance assumes that the density of input variables conditioned on output variables is the same for train and test data, whereas the marginal density of output variables is different for training and test data.

Transfer learning approaches can be mainly categorized into three classes [275]: A popular class of transfer learning methods is instance-based [31,85,224,34,167, 90,332], which assumes that certain parts of the data in the source domain can be reused for the target domain by reweighting. [179] proposed a heuristic method to remove "misleading" training instances from the source domain so as to include "good" instances from labeled source-domain instances and unlabeled target-domain instances. [85] introduced a boosting algorithm, TrAdaBoost, which assumes that the source and target domain data use exactly the same set of features and labels, but the distributions of the data in the two domains are different. In addition, TrAdaBoost assumes that due to the difference in distributions between the source and the target domains, some of them could be useful in learning for the target domain, but some of them may not and could even be harmful. Therefore, TrAdaBoost attempts to iteratively reweight the source domain data and target domain data to reduce the effect of the "bad" source data while encouraging the "good" source data to contribute more for the target domains. [31] proposed a framework to simultaneously reweight the source domain data and train models on the reweighted data with a kernel logistic regression classifier. The studies have shown the promising results of data reweighting for many applications, such as NLP [179], and special learning tasks such as binary classification [85,89].

Another category can be viewed as model-based approaches [306,210,116,39]. These assume that the source tasks and the target tasks share some parameters or priors of their models. An efficient algorithm MT-IVM [210], which is based on the Gaussian process (GP), was proposed to handle multidomain learning cases. MT-IVM tries to learn parameters of GP over multiple tasks by assigning the same GP prior to the tasks. Similarly, hierarchical Bayes (HB) is used with GP for multitask learning [306]. [116] borrowed the idea of [306] and used SVMs for multidomain learning. The parameters of SVMs for each domain are assumed to be separable into two terms: a common term across tasks and a task-specific term. [244] proposed a consensus regularization framework for transfer learning from multiple source domains to a target domain.

The third category of transfer learning approaches are feature based. [35,285,84,11, 18,19,213], where a feature representation is learned for the target domain and used to transfer knowledge across domains. A structural correspondence learning (SCL) algo-rithm [35] is proposed to use unlabeled data from the target domain to extract features so as to reduce the difference between source and target domains. A simple kernel mapping function, introduced in [88], maps the data from both domains to a high-dimensional feature space. [285] proposed to apply sparse coding, an unsupervised feature construction method, to learning higher-level features across domains. On the other hand, heterogeneous transfer learning starts to attract attention very recently. We notice that [382] extends PLSA to a specific application, using social Web data to help image clustering; [362] proposes a manifold alignment-based approach for heterogeneous domain adaptation; [150] formulates heterogeneous transfer learning as multitask and multiview learning and proposes a graph-based solution; and [148] focus on single-task learning with multiple outlooks, which is also related to hetero-geneous transfer learning.

The fourth category of approaches is based on relational knowledge transfer [258,91,257]. [257] proposed the algorithm TAMAR, which transfers relational knowl-edge with Markov logic networks (MLNs) across relational domains. MLNs combines the compact expressiveness of first-order logic with the flexibility of prob-ability. TAMAR was later extended to the single-entity-centered setting of transfer learning [258], where only one entity in the target domain is available. [91] proposed an approach to transferring relational knowledge based on a form of second-order Markov logic. In summary, those approaches assume that some relationships among the data in the source and target domains are similar.

Another related field is semisupervised learning [36,415,183,268], which mainly addresses the problem that the labeled data are too few to build a good classifica-tion/regression function by making use of a large amount of unlabeled data and a small amount of labeled data. Co-training [36,415], which trains two learners for two views by iteratively including unlabeled data, is closely related to transfer learning. The major difference is that in co-training, we have one set of instances with fea-tures partitioned into two "views." In transfer learning, we use different sets of data instances from different domains.

A few studies have been applied to the idea of transfer learning for the learning-to-rank problem. Zha et al. [399] uses multitask learning techniques to incorporate query difference, where each query is regarded as a task. However, the objective of this work is to learn a single ranking function instead of multiple functions for multiple tasks. TransRank [60] considers cross-domain information to attack transfer learning problems for ranking, which utilizes the labeled data from a source domain to enhance the learning-of-ranking function in the target domain with augmented fea-tures. However, this approach does not make use of unlabeled data. Gao et al. [134] explore several model adaptation methods for Web search ranking. They trained two ranking functions separately, then interpolated the two functions for the final result, and their experiments show that the simple model interpolation method achieves the best results. Similarly, heterogeneous transfer ranking is rarely touched in the literature. We notice that [361] proposes a regularized framework to addresses rank-ing cross-heterogeneous domains. It simultaneously minimizes two loss functions corresponding to two related domains by mapping each domain onto a shared latent space.

Among those transfer learning approaches generally instance-based and model-based approaches generally depend on the assumption of homogeneous features more strongly than do feature-based approaches. Another advantage of feature-based approaches is their flexibility of adopting different base ranking learners in real applications, i.e., after the common latent features learned from different domains, it is flexible to use any ranking learner on the new training data with common latent features to train ranking functions. Those motivate us to focus on deriving a feature-based model in this study.

9.5 Conclusions

In this chapter, we proposed a novel probabilistic model, PCDF, for cross-domain (vertical) ranking. The proposed model learns latent factors for multidomain data in partially overlapped heterogeneous feature spaces. The model is capable of learning homogeneous feature correlation, heterogeneous feature correlation, and pairwise preference correlation for cross-domain knowledge transfer. We also derive two PCDF variations to address two important special cases. Under the PCDF model, we derive a stochastic gradient-based algorithm, which facilitates distributed optimization and is flexible in adopting different loss functions and regularization functions to accommodate different data distributions. The extensive experiments on real Web search datasets demonstrate the effectiveness of the PCDF model and algorithms.

References

[1] Google Local: <http://local.google.com/>.

[2] TREC: <http://trec.nist.gov/>.

[3] Yahoo Local: <http://local.yahoo.com/>.

[4] Benitez AB, Beigi M, Chang S-F. Using relevance feedback in content-based image metasearch. IEEE Internet Comput 1998;2:59–69.

[5] Agarwal D, Chen B-C, Elango P, Wang X. Click shaping to optimize multiple objectives. In: KDD; 2011. p. 132–40.

[6] Agarwal D, Chen B-C, Elango P, Wang X. Personalized click shaping through lagrangian duality for online recommendation. In: SIGIR; 2012. p. 485–94.

[7] Agarwal D, Gabrilovich E, Hall R, Josifovski V, Khanna R. Translating relevance scores to probabilities for contextual advertising. Proceedings of the 18th ACM conference on information and knowledge management, CIKM '09. New York, NY, USA: ACM; 2009. p. 1899–902.

[8] Agichtein E, Brill E, Dumais S, Ragno R. Learning user interaction models for predicting web search result preferences. In: SIGIR; 2006.

[9] Amati G, van Joost C, Rijsbergen C. Probabilistic models of information retrieval based on measuring the divergence from randomness. ACM Trans Inf Syst 2002;20:357–89.

[10] Amin A, Townsend S, Ossenbruggen J, Hardman L. Fancy a drink in canary wharf?: A user study on location-based mobile search. In: INTERACT '09; 2009. p. 736–49.

[11] Ando RK, Zhang T. A high-performance semi-supervised learning method for text chunking. In: Proceedings of the 43rd annual meeting on association for computational linguistics. Morristown, NJ, USA: Association for Computational Linguistics; 2005. p. 1–9.

[12] Arguello J, Capra R. The effect of aggregated search coherence on search behavior. In: Proceedings of the 21st ACM international conference on information and knowledge management, CIKM '12. New York, NY, USA: ACM; 2012. p. 1293–302.

[13] Arguello J, Diaz F, Callan J. Learning to aggregate vertical results into web search results. Proceedings of the 20th ACM international conference on information and knowledge management, CIKM '11. New York, NY, USA: ACM; 2011. p. 201–10.

[14] Arguello J, Diaz F, Callan J, Carterette B. A methodology for evaluating aggregated search results. Proceedings of the 33rd European conference on advances in information retrieval, ECIR'11. Berlin, Heidelberg, Germany: Springer-Verlag; 2011. p. 141–52.

[15] Arguello J, Diaz F, Callan J, Crespo J-F. Sources of evidence for vertical selection. Proceedings of the 32nd international ACM SIGIR conference on research and development in information retrieval; 2009. p. 315–22.

[16] Arguello J, Diaz F, Paiement J-F. Vertical selection in the presence of unlabeled verticals. Proceedings of the 33rd international ACM SIGIR conference on research and development in information retrieval, SIGIR '10. New York, NY, USA: ACM; 2010. p. 691–8.

[17] Arguello J, Wu W-C, Kelly Diane, Edwards Ashlee. Task complexity, vertical display and user interaction in aggregated search. Proceedings of the 35th international ACM SIGIR conference on research and development in information retrieval, SIGIR '12. New York, NY, USA: ACM; 2012. p. 435–44.

[18] Argyriou A, Evgeniou T, Pontil M. Multitask feature learning. In: Advances in neural information processing systems: proceedings of the 2006 conference. MIT Press; 2007. p. 41.

[19] Argyriou A, Micchelli CA, Pontil M, Ying Y. A spectral regularization framework for multi-task structure learning. Adv Neural Inf Process Syst 2008:20.

[20] Arikan I, Bedathur S, Berberich K. Time will tell: leveraging temporal expressions in ir. WSDM 2009.

[21] Baeza-Yates R, Ribeiro-Neto B et al. Modern information retrieval, vol. 463. New York, NY, USA: ACM; 1999.

[22] Baeza-Yates R, Saint-Jean F, Castillo C. Web dynamics, age and page quality. In: String processing and information retrieval; 2002. p. 453–61.

[23] Bailey P, Craswell N, White RW, Chen L, Satyanarayana A, Tahaghoghi SMM. Evaluating whole-page relevance. Proceedings of the 33rd international ACM SIGIR conference on research and development in information retrieval, SIGIR '10. New York, NY, USA: ACM; 2010. p. 767–8.

[24] Belew RK. Finding out about. Cambridge University Press; 2000.

[25] Berberich K, Vazirgiannis M, Weikum G. Time-aware authority rankings. Internet Math 2005;2(3):301–32.

[26] Berberich K, König AC, Lymberopoulos D, Zhao P. Improving local search ranking through external logs. In: SIGIR '11; 2011. p. 785–94.

[27] Berg TL, Forsyth DA. Animals on the web. Proceedings of IEEE conference on computer vision and pattern recognition; 2006. p. 1463–70.

[28] Berger AL, Pietra SAD, Pietra VJD. A maximum entropy approach to natural language processing. Comput Linguist 1996;22(1):39–71.

[29] Bertheir R-N, Richard M. A belief network model for IR. In: Proceedings of ACM special interest group on information retrieval; 1996.

[30] Jiang B, Yi C. A taxonomy of local search: semi-supervised query classification driven by information needs. In: CIKM '11; 2011. p. 2425–28.

[31] Bickel S, Brückner M, Scheffer T. Discriminative learning for differing training and test distributions. Proceedings of the 24th international conference on machine learning. New York, NY, USA: ACM; 2007. p. 81–8.

[32] Bing: <www.bing.com>.

[33] Blei DM, Ng AY, Jordan MI. Latent Dirichlet allocation. J Mach Learn Res 2003;3:993–1022.

[34] Blitzer J, Crammer K, Kulesza A, Pereira F, Wortman J. Learning bounds for domain adaptation. Adv Neural Inf Process Syst 2008:20.

[35] Blitzer J, McDonald R, Pereira F. Domain adaptation with structural correspondence learning. Proceedings of the empirical methods in natural language processing (EMNLP); 2006.

[36] Blum A, Mitchell T. Combining labeled and unlabeled data with co-training. Proceedings of the eleventh annual conference on computational learning theory. New York, NY, USA: ACM; 1998. p. 92–100.

[37] Blumenthal D. Stimulating the adoption of health information technology. New Engl J Med 2009;360(15):1477–9.

[38] Bonacich P. Factoring and weighting approaches to clique identification. J Math Sociol 1972;2:113–20.

[39] Bonilla EV, Chai KMA, Williams CKI. Multi-task gaussian process prediction. Adv Neural Inf Process Syst 20:153–60.

[40] Boulos MNK. A first look at HealthCyberMap medical semantic subject search engine. Technol Health Care 2004;12(1):33–41.

[41] Box GEP, Cox DR. An analysis of transformations. J R Stat Soc B 1964;26(2): 211–52. [Methodological].

[42] Bremner D, Demaine E, Erickson J, Iacono J, Langerman S, Morin P, et al. Output-sensitive algorithms for computing nearest-neighbor decision boundaries. Discrete Comput Geom 2005;33(4):596–604.

[43] Brill E. Transformation-based error-driven learning and natural language processing: a case study in part of speech tagging. Comput Linguist 1995.

[44] Brin S, Page L. The anatomy of a large-scale hypertextual web search engine. In: Proceedings of international conference on world wide web; 1998.

[45] Broder A. A taxonomy of web search. ACM Sigir forum, vol. 36. ACM; 2002. p. 3–10.

[46] Brown PF, deSouza PV, Mercer RL, Pietra VJD, Lai JC. Class-based n-gram models of natural language. Comput Linguist 1992;18(4):467–79.

[47] Burges C, Shaked T, Renshaw E, Lazier A, Deeds M, Hamilton N, et al. Learning to rank using gradient descent. In: Proceedings of the 22nd international conference on machine learning; 2005. p. 89–96.

[48] Burges CJC, Shaked T, Renshaw E, Lazier A, Deeds M, Hamilton N, et al. Learning to rank using gradient descent. In: ICML; 2005. p. 89–96.

[49] Callan JP, Lu Z, Bruce Croft W. Searching distributed collections with inference networks. Proceedings of the 18th annual international ACM SIGIR conference on research and development in information retrieval, SIGIR '95. New York, NY, USA: ACM; 1995. p. 21–8.

[50] Jamie C, Margaret C. Query-based sampling of text databases. ACM Trans Inf Syst 2001;19(2):97–130.

[51] Can AB, Baykal N. MedicoPort: a medical search engine for all. Comput Methods Programs Biomed 2007;86(1):73–86.

[52] Cannon J, Lucci S. Transcription and EHRs. Benefits of a blended approach. J AHIMA 2010;81(2):36.

[53] Cao Y, Wang C, Zhang L, Zhang L. Edgel index for large-scale sketch-based image search. In: Proceedings of IEEE international conference on computer vision and pattern recognition; 2011. p. 761–8.

[54] Cao Z, Qin T, Liu TY, Tsai MF, Li H. Learning to rank: from pairwise approach to listwise approach. In: ICML. ACM; 2007. p. 129–36.

[55] Carr N. Real-time search. Commun ACM 2010. Available from: <www.technologyreview.com/computing/25079/>.

[56] Chakrabarti K, Cauduri S, won Hwang S. Automatic categorization of query results. In: Proceedings of SIGMOD 2004; 2004.

[57] Chang S-F, Ma W-Y, Smeulders A. Recent advances and challenges of semantic image/video search. Proceedings of IEEE international conference on acoustics, speech, and signal processing, vol. 4; 2007. p. 1205–8.

[58] Chapelle O, Zhang Y. A dynamic bayesian network click model for web search ranking. Proceedings of the 18th international conference on world wide web (WWW); 2009. p. 1–10.

[59] Olivier C, Yi C. Yahoo! learning to rank challenge overview. J Mach Learn Res - Proc Track 2011;14:1–24.

[60] Chen D, Yan J, Wang G, Xiong Y, Fan W, Chen Z. TransRank: A novel algorithm for transfer of rank learning. In: IEEE ICDM workshops. 2008.

[61] Chen K, Zhang Y, Zheng Z, Zha H, Sun G. Adapting ranking functions to user preference. ICDE workshops. 2008. p. 580–7.

[62] Chen Y, Wang JZ. Image categorization by learning and reasoning with regions. J Mach Learn Res 2004;5:913–39.

[63] Chen Y, Cao H, Mei Q, Zheng K, Xu H. Applying active learning to supervised word sense disambiguation in medline. J Am Med Inform Assoc 2013.

[64] Cheng T, Yan X, Chuan C, Chang K. Entityrank: searching entities directly and holistically. In: International conference on very large databases (VLDB); 2007. p. 387–98.

[65] Chernoff H, Lehmann EL. The use of maximum likelihood estimates in χ^2 tests for goodness of fit. Ann Math Stat 1954:579–86.

[66] Cho J, Roy S, Adams R. Page quality: in search of an unbiased web ranking. In: Proceedings of ACM SIGMOD conference; 2005.

[67] Tom C, Anders G. Instant availability of patient records, but diminished availability of patient information: A multi-method study of gp's use of electronic patient records. BMC Med Inform Decis Mak 2008;8(1):12.

[68] Chuang GC-H, Jay Kuo C-C. Wavelet descriptor of planar curves: theory and applications. IEEE Trans Image Process 1996;5(1):56–70.

[69] Church K, Oliver N. Understanding mobile web and mobile search use in today's dynamic mobile landscape. In: MobileHCI '11; 2011. p. 67–76.

[70] Church K, Smyth B. Understanding the intent behind mobile information needs. In: IUI '09; 2009. p. 247–56.

[71] Church K, Smyth B, Cotter P, Bradley K. Mobile information access: a study of emerging search behavior on the mobile internet. ACM Trans Web 2007:1.

[72] Cilibrasi RL, Vitanyi PMB. The google similarity distance. IEEE Trans Knowledge Data Eng 2007;19(3):370–83.

[73] Cleverdon CW. The ASLIB cranfield research project on the comparative efficiency of indexing systems. ASLIB Proc 1960;12(12):421–31.

[74] Collins M, Dasgupta S, Reina R. A generalization of principal component analysis to the exponential family. In: NIPS'01; 2001.

[75] Cortes C, Vapnik V. Support-vector networks. Mach Learn 1995;20:273–97.

[76] Cossock D, Zhang T. Statistical analysis of Bayes optimal subset ranking. IEEE Trans Inf Theory 2008;54(11):5140–54.

[77] Crammer K, Singer Y. Pranking with ranking. In: Advances in neural information processing systems. 2001.

[78] Craswell N, Robertson S, Zaragoza H, Taylor M. Relevance weighting for query independent evidence. In: SIGIR '05; 2005. p. 416–23.

[79] Cronen-Townsend S, Zhou Y, Croft WB. Predicting query performance. Proceedings of the 25th annual international ACM SIGIR conference on research and development in information retrieval, SIGIR '02, New York, NY, USA; 2002. p. 299–306.

[80] Cui J, Wen F, Tang X. IntentSearch: interactive on-line image search re-ranking. In: Proceedings of ACM multimedia; 2008. p. 997–8.

[81] Cui J, Wen F, Tang X. Real time google and live image search re-ranking. In: Proceedings of ACM multimedia; 2008. p. 729–32.

[82] Cui Y, Roto V. How people use the web on mobile devices. In: WWW '08; 2008. p. 905–14.

[83] Dai N, Shokouhi M, Davison BD. Learning to rank for freshness and relevance. In: SIGIR; 2011. p. 95–104.

[84] Dai W, Xue GR, Yang Q, Yu Y. Co-clustering based classification for out-of-domain documents. In: Proceedings of the 13th ACM SIGKDD international conference on knowledge discovery and data mining. New York, NY, USA: ACM; 2007. p. 210–9.

[85] Dai W, Yang Q, Xue GR, Yu Y. Boosting for transfer learning. In: Proceedings of the 24th international conference on Machine learning. New York, NY, USA: ACM; 2007. p. 193–200.

[86] Das Sarma A, Das Sarma A, Gollapudi S, Panigrahy R. Ranking mechanisms in twitter-like forums. In: Proceedings of the third ACM international conference on Web search and data mining, WSDM; 2010. p. 21–30.

[87] Datta R, Joshi D, Li J, Wang JZ. Image retrieval: ideas, influences, and trends of the new age. ACM Comput Surv 2008;40(65).

[88] Daumé H. Frustratingly easy domain adaptation. In: Annual meeting—association for computational linguistics, vol. 45. 2007. p. 256.

[89] Daumé H. Cross-task knowledge-constrained self training. In: Proceedings of the 2008 conference on empirical methods in natural language processing. Honolulu, Hawaii, USA: Association for Computational Linguistics; 2008. p. 680–8.

[90] Daumé H, Marcu D. Domain adaptation for statistical classifiers. Journal of Artif Intell Res 2006;26:101–26.

[91] Davis J, Domingos P. Deep transfer via second-order markov logic. In: AAAI workshop: transfer learning for complex tasks. 2008.

[92] DeBenedet AT, Saini SD, Takami M, Fisher LR. Do clinical characteristics predict the presence of small bowel angioectasias on capsule endoscopy?. Dig Dis Sci 2011;56(6):1776–81.

[93] Deerwester S et al. Improving information retrieval with latent semantic indexing. In: Proceedings of the 51st annual meeting of the American society for information science; 1988. p. 36–40.

[94] Del Corso GM, Gulli A, Romani F. Ranking a stream of news. In: Proceedings of WWW conference; 2005.

[95] Demartini G, Firan CS, Iofciu T, Krestel R, Nejdl W. A model for ranking entities and its application to Wikipedia. In: Latin American web conference (LA-WEB); 2008.

[96] Jia D, Wei D, Richard S, Li LJ, Li K, Fei-fei L. Imagenet: a large-scale hierarchical image database. In: Proceedings of IEEE international conference on computer vision and pattern recognition; 2009.

[97] Dhillon I, Modha D. Concept decomposition for large sparse text data using clustering. Mach Learn 2001;1(42):143–75.

[98] Diaz F. Integration of news content into web results. In: Proceedings of the second ACM international conference on web search and data mining (WSDM); 2009. p. 182–91.

[99] Fernando D. Regularizing ad hoc retrieval scores. CIKM '05: proceedings of the 14th ACM international conference on information and knowledge management. New York, NY, USA: ACM; 2005. p. 672–9.

[100] Diaz F, Arguello J. Adaptation of offline vertical selection predictions in the presence of user feedback. In: SIGIR 2009; 2009.

[101] Ding H, Liu J, Lu H. Hierarchical clustering-based navigation of image search results. In: Proceedings of ACM multimedia; 2008. p. 741–4.

[102] Docteur E, Berenson R. How will comparative effectiveness research affect the quality of health care? Timely analysis of immediate health policy issues. 2010.

[103] Doing-Harris KM, Zeng-Treitler Q. Computer-assisted update of a consumer health vocabulary through mining of social network data. J Med Internet Res 2011;13(2).

[104] Dom B. An information-theoretic external cluster-validity measure. In: UAI; 2002. p. 137–45.

[105] Dom B. Q_3 and Q_4: a *Complete*-coding refinement to an information-theoretic external clustering validity measure. Technical report TBD, yahoo! Labs.

[106] Dong A, Chang Y, Zheng Z, Mishne G, Bai J, Zhang R, et al. Toward recency ranking in web search. In: WSDM; 2010. p. 11–20.

[107] Dou Z, Song R, Wen J-R. A large-scale evaluation and analysis of personalized search strategies. In: WWW '07; 2007. p. 581–90.

[108] Radu D, Paula P, Christina L, Birger L, Jørgensen HL, Cox IJ, et al. Findzebra: a search engine for rare diseases. Int J Med Inform 2013.

[109] Dumais S. Latent semantic analysis. ARIST Rev Inf Sci Technol 2004:38.

[110] Dupret G, Liao C. Cumulated relevance: a model to estimate document relevance from the click through logs of a web search engine. In: Proceedings of the third international ACM conference on web search and data mining (WSDM); 2010.

[111] Dwork C, Kumar R, Naor M, Sivakumar D. Rank aggregation methods for the web. Proceedings of the 10th international conference on world wide web, WWW '01; 2001. p. 613–22.

[112] Edinger T, Cohen AM, Bedrick S, Ambert K, Hersh W. Barriers to retrieving patient information from electronic health record data: Failure analysis from the trec medical records track. In: AMIA Annu Symp Proc; 2012. p. 180.

[113] Mathias E, Kristian H, Tamy B, Marc A. Sketch-based image retrieval: benchmark and bag-of-features descriptors. IEEE Trans Visual Comput Graphics 2011;17:1624–36.

[114] Elsas JL, Arguello J, Callan J, Carbonell JG. Retrieval and feedback models for blog feed search. Proceedings of the 31st annual international ACM SIGIR conference on research and development in information retrieval; 2008. p. 347–54.

[115] Etheredge LM. A rapid-learning health system. Health Aff 2007;26(2):w107–18.

[116] Evgeniou T, Pontil M. Regularized multitask learning. Proceedings of the tenth ACM SIGKDD international conference on knowledge discovery and data mining. New York, NY, USA: ACM; 2004. p. 109–17.

[117] Facebook: <www.facebook.com>.

[118] Christos F, Ron B, Myron F, Jim H, Wayne N, Dragutin P, et al. Efficient and effective querying by image content. J Intell Inf Syst 1994;3:231–62.

[119] Fang H, Tao T, Zhai CX. A formal study of information retrieval heuristics. In: SIGIR '04; 2004. p. 49–56.

[120] Fei-Fei L, Perona P. A Bayesian hierarchical model for learning natural scene categories. In: Proceedings of IEEE conference on computer vision and pattern recognition; 2005. p. 524–31.

[121] Jing F, Li M, Zhang H-J, Zhang B. An efficient and effective region-based image retrieval framework. IEEE Trans Image Process 2004;13(5):699–709.

[122] Fleiss JL. Measuring nominal scale agreement among many raters. Psychol Bull 1971;76(5):378–82.

[123] Flickr. <www.flickr.com>.

[124] Long F, Zhang H-J, Feng DD. Fundamentals of content-based image retrieval, chapter. In: Feng DD, Siu WC, Zhang H-J. editors. Multimedia information retrieval and management technological fundamentals and applications. Berlin, Heidelberg, Germany, 2003.

[125] Fox EA, Sharat S. A comparison of two methods for soft boolean interpretation in information retrieval. Technical report TR-86-1. Virginia Tech, Department of Computer Science. 1986.

[126] Jennifer F, Longhurst CA, Sutherland SM. Evidence-based medicine in the EMR era. N Engl J Med 2011;365(19):1758–9.

[127] Freund Y, Schapire RE. Large margin classification using the perceptron algorithm. Mach Learn 1999;37(3):277–96.

[128] Friedman CP, Wong AK, Blumenthal D. Achieving a nationwide learning health system. Science Translational Medicine 2010;5:7.

[129] Friedman JH. Stochastic gradient boosting. Comput Stat Data Anal 2002;38:367–78.

[130] Friedman JH. Greedy function approximation: a gradient boosting machine. Ann Statist 2001;29:1189–232.

[131] Friedman JH, Hastie T, Tibshirani R. Additive logistic regression: a statistical view of boosting. Ann Statist 2000;28(2):337–407.

[132] Froehlich J, Chen MY, Smith IE, Potter F. Voting with your feet: an investigative study of the relationship between place visit behavior and preference. In: Ubicomp'06; 2006. p. 333–50.

[133] Ganesan K, Zhai CX. Opinion-based entity ranking. In: Information Retrieval; 2011.

[134] Gao J, Wu Q, Burges C, Svore K, Su Y, Khan N, et al. Model adaptation via model interpolation and boosting for Web search ranking. In: Proceedings of the 2009 conference on empirical methods in natural language processing; Aug. 2009. p. 505–13.

[135] Gelgi F, Davulcu H, Vadrevu S. Term ranking for clustering web search results. In: Proceedings of tenth international workshop on the web and databases (WebDB 2007), Beijing, China. 2007.

[136] Geng B, Yang L, Xu C, Hua X.-S. Content-aware ranking for visual search. In: Proceedings of IEEE international conference on computer vision and pattern recognition; 2010.

[137] Gerard S, Fox EA, Wu H. Extended, boolean information retrieval. Commun ACM 1983:26.

[138] Gevers T, Smeulders AWM. Image search engines: an overview. In: Medioni G, SBK. editors. Emerging topics in computer vision. 2004.

[139] Ghamrawi N, McCallum A. Collective multi-label classification. In: CIKM; 2005. p. 195–200.

[140] Ghose A, Goldfarb A, Han SP. How is the mobile internet different?: search costs and local activities. In: ICIS; 2011.

[141] Google: <www.google.com>.

[142] Gordon MD, Lenk PJ. When is the probability ranking principle suboptimal?. J Am Soc Inf Sci 1992;43(1):1–14.

[143] Gregg W, Jirjis J, Lorenzi NM, Giuse D. StarTracker: an integrated, web-based clinical search engine. AMIA annual symposium proceedings, vol. 2003. American Medical Informatics Association; 2003. p. 855.

[144] Grünwald PD. The minimum description length principle. MIT Press; 2007.

[145] Hanauer DA. Emerse: the electronic medical record search engine. AMIA Annual Symposium Proceedings, vol. 2006. American Medical Informatics Association; 2006. p. 941.

[146] Hanauer DA, Englesbe MJ, Cowan JA, Campbell DA. Informatics and the american college of surgeons national surgical quality improvement program: automated processes could replace manual record review. J Am Coll Surg 2009;208(1):37.

[147] Hanauer DA, Liu Y, Mei Q, Manion FJ, Balis UJ, Zheng K. Hedging their mets: The use of uncertainty terms in clinical documents and its potential implications when sharing the documents with patients. AMIA Annual Symposium Proceedings, vol. 2012. American Medical Informatics Association; 2012. p. 321.

[148] Harel M, Mannon S. Learning from multiple outlooks. In: Lise G, Tobias S, editors. Proceedings of the 28th international conference on machine learning (ICML-11), ICML '11. New York, NY, USA: ACM; 2011. p. 401–8.

[149] Hartzband P, Groopman J et al. Off the record–avoiding the pitfalls of going electronic. N Engl J Med 2008;358(16):1656–7.

[150] He J, Lawrence R. A graph-based framework for multi-task multi-view learning. In: Getoor L, Scheffer T, editors. Proceedings of the 28th international conference on machine learning (ICML-11), ICML '11. New York, NY, USA: ACM; 2011. p. 25–32.

[151] He J, Li M, Zhang H-J, Tong H, Zhang C. Manifold-ranking-based image retrieval. In: Proceedings of ACM international conference on multimedia; 2004.

[152] He X, Baker M. XHRank: ranking entities on the semantic web. International semantic web conference (ISWC); 2007. p. 387–98.

[153] Hearst MA, Pedersen JO. Reexamining the cluster hypothesis: scatter/gather on retrieval results. SIGIR '96: proceedings of the 19th annual international ACM SIGIR conference on research and development in information retrieval. New York, NY, USA: ACM; 1996. p. 76–84.

[154] Hearst MA, Pedersen JO. Reexamining the cluster hypothesis: scatter/gather on retrieval results. In: SIGIR '96; 1996. p. 76–84.

[155] Heckman JJ. Sample selection bias as a specification error. Econometrica: J Economet Soc 1979:153–61.

[156] Herbrich R, Graepel T, Obermayer K. Large margin rank boundaries for ordinal regression. 2000.

[157] Hersh WR. Adding value to the electronic health record through secondary use of data for quality assurance, research, and surveillance. Clin Pharmacol Ther 2007;81:126–8.

[158] Hersh WR. Information retrieval: a health and biomedical perspective. Springer; 2009.

[159] Hilligoss B, Zheng K. Chart biopsy: an emerging medical practice enabled by electronic health records and its impacts on emergency department-inpatient admission handoffs. J Am Med Inform Assoc 2013;20(2):260–7.

[160] Hirschtick RE. Copy-and-paste. JAMA: J Am Med Assoc 2006;295(20):2335–6.

[161] Hofmann T. Probabilistic latent semantic indexing. In: SIGIR '99; 1999. p. 50–7.

[162] Hollink L, Schreiber G, Wielinga BJ. Patterns of semantic relations to improve image content search. J Web Semant 2007;5(3):195–203.

[163] Hoque E, Strong G, Hoeber O, Gong M. Conceptual query expansion and visual search results exploration for web image retrieval. In: Atlantic web intelligence conference; 2011. p. 73–82.

[164] Hsu W, Kennedy L, Chang S-F. Video search re-ranking through random walk over document-level context graph. In: Proceedings of the ACM multimedia; 2007. p. 971–80.

[165] Hsu W, Kennedy LS, Chang S-F. Video search re-ranking via information bottleneck principle. In: Proceedings of the ACM multimedia; 2006. p. 35–44.

[166] Hu Y, Yu A, Li Z, Li M. Image search result clustering and reranking via partial grouping. In: IEEE international conference on multimedia & expo; 2007. p. 603–6.

[167] Huang J, Smola AJ, Gretton A, Borgwardt KM, Scholkopf B. Correcting sample selection bias by unlabeled data. Adv Neural Inf Process Syst 2007;19:601.

[168] Huang J, White R, Buscher G. User see, user point: gaze and cursor alignment in web search. Proceedings of the 2012 ACM annual conference on human factors in computing systems, CHI '12. New York, NY, USA: ACM; 2012. p. 1341–50.

[169] Zitouni H, Sevil S, Ozkan D, Duygulu P. Reranking of web image search results using a graph algorithm. In: Proceedings of international conference on pattern recognition; 2008.

[170] Ide NC, Loane RF, Demner-Fushman D. Essie: a concept-based search engine for structured biomedical text. J Am Med Inf Assoc 2007;14(3):253–63.

[171] Indyk P, Motwani R. Approximate nearest neighbors: towards removing the curse of dimensionality 1998:604–13.

[172] Jain V, Varma M. Learning to re-rank: Query-dependent image re-ranking using click data. In: Proceedings of the 20th international conference on world wide web; 2011. p. 277–86.

[173] Jain V, Varma M. Learning to re-rank: query-dependent image re-ranking using click data. In: Proceedings of the 20th international conference on world wide web; 2009. p. 1–20.

[174] Japkowicz N, Stephen S. The class imbalance problem: a systematic study. Intell Data Anal 2002;6(5):429–49.

[175] Jarvelin K, Kekalainen J. Cumulated gain-based evaluation of IR techniques. ACM Trans Inf Syst 2002;20:422–46.

[176] Järvelin K, Kekäläinen J. Cumulated gain-based evaluation of IR techniques. ACM TOIS 2002;20(4):422–46.

[177] Jarvelin K, Kekalainen J. IR evaluation methods for retrieving highly relevant documents. In: SIGIR; 2000. p. 41–8.

[178] Järvelin K, Kekäläinen J. Cumulated gain-based evaluation of IR techniques. ACM Trans Inf Syst 2002;20:422–46.

[179] Jiang J, Zhai C. Instance weighting for domain adaptation in NLP. In: Annual meeting—association for computational linguistics, vol. 45. 2007. p. 264.

[180] Jin Y, Matsuo Y, Ishizuka M. Ranking entities on the web using social network mining and ranking learning. In: World wide web conference (WWW).

[181] Jing Y, Baluja S. PageRank for product image search. In: Proceedings of international world wide web conference; 2008. p. 307–16.

[182] Jing YS, Baluja S. VisualRank: applying PageRank to large-scale image search. Trans Pattern Anal Mach Intell 2008:1877–90.

[183] Joachims T. Transductive inference for text classification using support vector machines. In: Sixteenth international conference on machine learning; 1999.

[184] Joachims T. Optimizing search engines using click through data. In: KDD; 2002. p. 133–42.

[185] Joachims T. Optimizing search engines using clickthrough data. In: Proceedings of ACM conference on knowledge discovery and data mining; 2002.

[186] Joachims T, Granka L, Pan B, Hembrooke H, Radlinski F, Gay G. Evaluating the accuracy of implicit feedback from clicks and query reformulations in web search. ACM Trans Inf Syst (TOIS) 2007;25(2).

[187] Joachims T. Optimizing search engines using clickthrough data. KDD '02: proceedings of the eighth ACM SIGKDD. New York, NY, USA: ACM; 2002. p. 133–42.

[188] Joachims T, Granka L, Pan B, Hembrooke H, Gay G. Accurately interpreting clickthrough data as implicit feedback. In: SIGIR; 2005. p. 154–61.

[189] Joachims T, Granka L, Pan B, Hembrooke H, Gay G. Accurately interpreting click-through data as implicit feedback. In: Proceedings of ACM SIGIR 2005. New York, NY, USA: ACM; 2005. p. 154–61.

[190] Joachims T, Granka L, Pan B, Hembrooke H, Radlinski F, Gay G. Evaluating the accuracy of implicit feedback from clicks and query reformulations in web search. ACM Trans Inf Syst 2007:25.

[191] Forney GDJr. The viterbi algorithm. Proc IEEE 1973;61:268–78.

[192] Smith JR, Jaimes A, Lin C-Y, Naphade M, Natsev AP, Tseng B. Interactive search fusion methods for video database retrieval. Proceedings of IEEE international conference on image processing, vol. 1; 2003.

[193] Kamvar M, Baluja S. A large-scale study of wireless search behavior: google mobile search. In: CHI '06; 2006. p. 701–9.

[194] Kamvar M, Baluja S. Deciphering trends in mobile search. Computer Aug. 2007;40:58–62.

[195] Kang B-Y, Kim D-W, Kim H-J. Fuzzy information retrieval indexed by concept identification. Berlin, Heidelberg, Germany: Springer; 2005.

[196] Kang C, Lee J, Chang Y. Predicting primary categories of business listings for local search. In: CIKM '12; 2012. p. 2591–4.

[197] Kang C, Wang X, Chen J, Liao C, Chang Y, Tseng B, et al. Learning to rerank web search results with multiple pairwise features. In: Proceedings of the fourth ACM international conference on web search and data mining; 2011. p. 735–44.

[198] Kang I-H, Kim GC. Query type classification for web document retrieval. Proceedings of the 26th annual international ACM SIGIR conference on research and development in information retrieval, SIGIR '03. New York, NY, USA: ACM; 2003. p. 64–71.

[199] Kanhabua N, Nrvåg K. Determining time of queries for reranking search results. Research and advanced technology for digital libraries 2010:261–72.

[200] Karlsson F. Constraint grammar as a framework for parsing running text. In: Proceedings of the 13th international conference of computational linguistics; 1990. p. 168–73.

[201] Kennedy L, Chang S-F. A reranking approach for context-based concept fusion in video indexing and retrieval. In: Proceedings of ACM international conference on image and video retrieval; 2007. p. 333–40.

[202] King B, Wang L, Provalov I, Zhou J. Cengage learning at TREC 2011 medical track. In: Proceedings of the 20th Text Retrieval Conference; 2011.

[203] Kleinberg J. Bursty and hierarchical structure in streams. Proceedings of the eighth ACM SIGKDD international conference on knowledge discovery and data mining, KDD '02. New York, NY, USA: ACM; 2002. p. 91–101.

[204] König AC, Gamon M, Wu Q. Click through prediction for news queries. Proceedings of SIGIR; 2009. p. 347–54.

[205] Kraaij W. Variations on language modeling for information retrieval. Ph.D. thesis. University of Twente. 2004.

[206] Kumar R, Vassilvitskii S. Generalized distances between rankings. Proceedings of the 19th international conference on world wide web, WWW '10. New York, NY, USA: ACM; 2010. p. 571–80.

[207] Kummamuru K, Lotlikar R, Roy S, Singal K, Krishnapuram R. A hierarchical monothetic document clustering algorithm for summarization and browsing search results. WWW '04: proceedings of the 13th international conference on world wide web. New York, NY, USA: ACM; 2004. p. 658–65.

[208] Lancaster FW, Fayen EG. Information retrieval on-line. Los Angeles, CA, USA: Melville Publishing; 1973.

[209] Lane ND, Lymberopoulos D, Zhao F, Campbell AT. Hapori: context-based local search for mobile phones using community behavioral modeling and similarity. In: Ubicomp '10; 2010. p. 109–18.

[210] Lawrence ND, Platt JC. Learning to learn with the informative vector machine. In: Proceedings of the 21st international conference on machine learning. New York, NY, USA: ACM; 2004.

[211] Lee D, Seung S. Learning the parts of objects by nonnegative matrix factorization. Nature 1999;401:788–91.

[212] Lee H, Battle A, Raina R, Ng AY. Efficient sparse coding algorithms. In: NIPS; 2007. p. 801–8.

[213] Lee SI, Chatalbashev V, Vickrey D, Koller D. Learning a meta-level prior for feature relevance from multiple related tasks. In: Proceedings of the 24th international conference on machine learning. New York, NY, USA: ACM; 2007. p. 489–96.

[214] Lew MS, Sebe N, Djeraba C, Jain R. Content-based multimedia information retrieval: state of the art and challenges. ACM Trans Multimedia Comput Commun Appl 2006;2:1–19.

[215] Li B, Ma S. On the relation between region and contour representation. In: Proceedings of the IEEE international conference on pattern recognition; 1994. p. 352–5.

[216] Li CE, Li B, Li CS. Learning image query concepts via intelligent sampling. In: IEEE international conference on multimedia & expo; 2001. p. 961–4.

[217] Li J, Chang S-F, Lesk M, Lienhart R, Luo J, Smeulders AWM. New challenges in multimedia research for the increasingly connected and fast growing digital society. In: Proceedings of ACM SIGMM international workshop on multimedia information retrieval, USA. 2007.

[218] Li L, Chu W, Langford J, Wang X. Unbiased offline evaluation of contextual-bandit-based news article recommendation algorithms. Proceedings of the fourth ACM WSDM '11; 2011. p. 297–306.

[219] Li L, Chu W, Langford J, Wang X. Unbiased offline evaluation of contextual-bandit-based news article recommendation algorithms. Proceedings of the fourth ACM international conference on web search and data mining, WSDM '11. New York, NY, USA: ACM; 2011. p. 297–306.

[220] Li SZ, Hou XW, Zhang H, Cheng Q. Learning spatially localized, parts-based representation. CVPR 2001;1:207–12.

[221] Li X, Liu B, Yu P. Time sensitive ranking with application to publication search. In: Proceedings of eighth IEEE international conference on data mining; 2008. p. 893–8.

[222] Li X, Wang D, Li J, Zhang B. Video search in concept subspace: a text-like paradigm. In: Proceedings of international conference on image and video retrieval; 2007.

[223] Li X, Wang Y-Y, Acero A. Learning query intent from regularized click graphs. SIGIR '08: proceedings of the 31st annual international ACM SIGIR conference on research and development in information retrieval. New York, NY, USA: ACM; 2008. p. 339–46.

[224] Liao X, Xue Y, Carin L. Logistic regression with an auxiliary data source. Machine learning-international workshop/conference, vol. 22; 2005. p. 505.

[225] Liu J, Lai W, Hua X-S, Huang Y, Li S. Video search reranking via multi-graph propagation. In: Proceedings of ACM multimedia; 2007. p. 208–17.

[226] Liu T-Y. Learning to rank for information retrieval. Found Trend Inf Retrieval 2009;3(3):225–331.

[227] Liu T-Y. Learning to rank for information retrieval. Springer; 2011.

[228] Liu T-Y, Mei T, Hua X-S. CrowdReranking: exploring multiple search engines for visual search reranking. In: Proceedings of ACM special interest group on information retrieval; 2009. p. 500–7.

[229] Liu Y, Mei T, Tang J, Wu X, Hua X-S. Graph-based pairwise learning to rank for video search. In: Proceedings of international multi-media modelling conference; 2009.

[230] Liu Y, Mei T, Wu X, Hua X-S. Optimizing video search reranking via minimum incremental information loss. In: Proceedings of ACM international workshop on multimedia information retrieval. 2008. p. 253–9.

[231] Liu Y-T, Liu T-Y, Qin T, Ma Z-M, Li H. Supervised rank aggregation. Proceedings of the 16th international conference on world wide web; 2007. p. 481–90.

[232] Liu Y, Mei T. Optimizing visual search reranking via pairwise learning. IEEE Trans Multimedia 2011;13(2):280–91.

[233] Liu Y, Mei T, Hua X-S, Tang J, Wu X, Li S. Learning to video search rerank via pseudo preference feedback. In: Proceedings of IEEE international conference on multimedia & expo; 2008.

[234] Liu Y, Mei T, Hua X-S, Wu X, Li S. Multi-graph-based query-independent learning for video search. IEEE Trans Circuit Syst Video Technol 2009;19(12):1841–50.

[235] Liu Y, Mei T, Qi G, Xiuqing W, Hua X-S. Query-independent learning for video search. In: Proceedings of IEEE international conference on multimedia & expo; 2008.

[236] Lovins JB. Development of a stemming algorithm. Mech Transl Comput Linguistics 1968;11:22–31.

[237] Lowe DG. Distinctive image features from scale-invariant keypoints. Int J Comput Vision 2004;60(2):91–110.

[238] Lowe HJ, Ferris TA, Hernandez PM, Weber SC. Stride: a an integrated standards-based translational research informatics platform. AMIA Annual Symposium Proceedings, vol. 2009. American Medical Informatics Association; 2009. p. 391.

[239] Lu Y, Peng F, Wei X, Dumoulin B. Personalize web search results with user's location. In: SIGIR; 2010. p. 763–4.

[240] Luo G. Design and evaluation of the iMed intelligent medical search engine. IEEE 25th International Conference on Data Engineering, ICDE'09. IEEE; 2009. p. 1379–90.

[241] Luo G. Lessons learned from building the iMed intelligent medical search engine. Engineering in medicine and biology society, 2009. EMBC 2009. Annual international conference of the IEEE. IEEE; 2009. p. 5138–42.

[242] Luo G, Tang C, Yang H, Wei X. MedSearch: a specialized search engine for medical information. In: Proceedings of the 16th international conference on world wide web. ACM; 2007. p. 1175–6.

[243] Luo G, Tang C, Yang H, Wei X. MedSearch: a specialized search engine for medical information retrieval. In: Proceedings of the 17th ACM conference on Information and knowledge management. ACM; 2008. p. 143–52.

[244] Luo P, Zhuang F, Xiong H, Xiong Y, He Q. Transfer learning from multiple source domains via consensus regularization. CIKM '08: proceeding of the 17th ACM conference on information and knowledge management. New York, NY, USA: ACM; 2008. p. 103–12.

[245] Lv Y, Zhai C. Positional language models for information retrieval. In: Proceedings of ACM special interest group on information retrieval; 2009.

[246] Lv Y, Lymberopoulos D, Wu Q. An exploration of ranking heuristics in mobile local search. In: SIGIR '12; 2012. p. 295–304.

[247] Lv Y, Zhai CX. Lower-bounding term frequency normalization. In: CIKM '11; 2011. p. 7–16.

[248] Lymberopoulos D, Zhao P, König AC, Berberich K, Liu J. Location-aware click prediction in mobile local search. In: CIKM '11; 2011.

[249] Macdonald C, Ounis I, Soboroff I. Overview of the TREC 2009 blog track. 2009.

[250] Manning CD, Raghavan P, Schütze H. An introduction to information retrieval. Cambridge University Press; 2009.

[251] Marlin B. Modeling user rating profiles for collaborative filtering. In: Thrun S, Saul L, Schölkopf B, editors. Advances in neural information processing systems, vol. 16. Cambridge, MA, USA: MIT Press; 2004.

[252] McEntyre J, Lipman D. PubMed: bridging the information gap. Can Med Assoc J 2001;164(9):1317–9.

[253] Mediapedia: <http://mediapedia.nla.gov.au/>.

[254] Mehtre BM, Kankanhalli MS, Lee WF. Shape measures for content based image retrieval: a comparison. Inf Process and Manage 1997;33(3):319–37.

[255] Mei T, Hua X-S, Lai W, Yang L, et al. MSRA-USTC-SJTU at TRECVID 2007: high-level feature extraction and search. In: TREC video retrieval evaluation online proceedings; 2007.

[256] Metzler D, Dumais ST, Meek C. Similarity measures for short segments of text. In: ECIR; 2007. p. 16–27.

[257] Mihalkova L, Huynh T, Mooney RJ. Mapping and revising markov logic networks for transfer learning. Proceedings of the national conference on artificial intelligence, vol. 22; 2007. p. 608.

[258] Mihalkova L, Mooney RJ. Transfer learning by mapping with minimal target data. In: Proceedings of the AAAI-08 workshop on transfer learning for complex tasks. 2008.

[259] Moon T, Smola A, Chang Y, Zheng Z. IntervalRank-isotonic regression with listwise and pairwise constraints. In: Proceedings of the ACM international conference on web search and data mining; 2010.

[260] Moss J, Andison M, Sobko H. An analysis of narrative nursing documentation in an otherwise structured intensive care clinical information system. AMIA Annual Symposium Proceedings, American Medical Informatics Association, vol. 2007; 2007. p. 543.

[261] Mutalik PG, Deshpande A, Nadkarni PM. Use of general-purpose negation detection to augment concept indexing of medical documents: a quantitative study using the UMLS. J Am Med Inform Assoc 2001;8(6):598–609.

[262] Naphade M, Smith JR, Tesic J, Chang S-F, Hsu W, Kennedy L, et al. Large-scale concept ontology for multimedia. IEEE Multimedia 2006;13(3):86–91.

[263] Natarajan K, Stein D, Jain S, Elhadad N. An analysis of clinical queries in an electronic health record search utility. Int J Med Inform 2010;79(7):515–22.

[264] Natsev A, Haubold A, Tešić J, Xie L, Yan L. Semantic concept-based query expansion and re-ranking for multimedia retrieval. In: Proceedings of ACM multimedia; 2007. p. 991–1000.

[265] Neo S-Y, Zhao J, Kan M-Y, Chua T-S. Video retrieval using high level features: exploiting query matching and confidence-based weighting. In: ACM international conference on image and video retrieval; 2006.

[266] Ngo C-W, Jiang Y-G, Wei X-Y, Zhao W, Liu Y, Wang J, et al. VIREO/DVMM at TRECVID 2009: high-level feature extraction, automatic video search, and content-based copy detection. In: TREC video retrieval evaluation online proceedings; 2009.

[267] Nie Z, Zhang Y, Wen JR, Ma WY. Object-level ranking: bringing order to web objects. In: World wide web conference (WWW); 2005.

[268] Nigam K, McCallum AK, Thrun S, Mitchell T. Text classification from labeled and unlabeled documents using EM. Mach Learn 2000;39(2):103–34.

[269] Nunes S. Exploring temporal evidence in web information retrieval. In: BCS IRSG symposium: future directions in information access. 2007.

[270] Oberg R, Rasmussen L, Melski J, Peissig P, Starren J. Evaluation of the Google search appliance for patient cohort discovery. In: AMIA: annual symposium proceedings/AMIA symposium; 2008. p. 1104.

[271] Osinski S. Improving quality of search results clustering with approximate matrix factorisations. In: Proceedings of the 28th European conference on IR research (ECIR 20 06). London, UK, Berlin, Germany: Springer; 2006.

[272] Osinski S, Stefanowski J, Weiss D. Lingo: search results clustering algorithm based on singular value decomposition. Advances in soft computing, intelligent information processing and web mining, proceedings of he international IIS: IIPWM 20 04 conference, Zakopane, Poland; 2004. p. 359–68.

[273] Ounis I, Macdonald C, de Rijke M, Mishne G, Soboroff I. Overview of the TREC 2006 blog track. In: TREC; 2006.

[274] Palchuk MB, Fang EA, Cygielnik JM, Labreche M, Shubina M, Ramelson HZ, et al. An unintended consequence of electronic prescriptions: prevalence and impact of internal discrepancies. J Am Med Inform Assoc 2010;17(4):472–6.

[275] Pan, SJ., Yang Q. A survey on transfer learning. Technical report HKUST-CS08-08. Department of Computer Science and Engineering, Hong Kong University of Science and Technology: Hong Kong, China, November; 2008.

[276] Pandey S, Roy S, Olston C, Cho J, Chakrabarti S. Shuffling a stacked deck: the case for partially randomized ranking of search engine results. VLDB 2005.

[277] Pasca M. Towards temporal web search. ACM SAC 2008.

[278] Pass G, Zabih R. Comparing images using joint histograms. Multimedia Syst 1999;7(3):234–40.

[279] Ponnuswami AK, Pattabiraman K, Brand D, Kanungo T. Model characterization curves for federated search using click-logs: predicting user engagement metrics for the span of feasible operating points. Proceedings of the 20th international conference on world wide web, WWW '11. New York, NY, USA: ACM; 2011. p. 67–76.

[280] Ponnuswami AK, Pattabiraman K, Wu Q, Gilad-Bachrach R, Kanungo T. On composition of a federated web search result page: using online users to provide pairwise preference for heterogeneous verticals. Proceedings of the fourth ACM international conference on web search and data mining, WSDM '11. New York, NY, USA: ACM; 2011. p. 715–24.

[281] Ponte JM, Croft WB. A language modeling approach to information retrieval. Proceedings of the 21st annual international ACM SIGIR conference on research and development in, information retrieval; 1998. p. 275–81.

[282] Porter MF. An algorithm for suffix stripping. Program 1980;14(3):130–7.

[283] Pound J, Mika P, Zaragoza H. Ad-hoc object retrieval in the web of data. In: WWW; 2010. p. 771–80.

[284] Zisserman A, Fergus R, Perona P. A visual category filter for google images. In: Proceedings of European conference on computer vision; 2004.

[285] Raina R, Battle A, Lee H, Packer B, Ng AY. Self-taught learning: transfer learning from unlabeled data. In: Proceedings of the 24th international conference on machine learning. New York, NY, USA: ACM; 2007. p. 759–66.

[286] Reis S, Church K, Oliver N. Rethinking mobile search: towards casual, shared, social mobile search experiences. In: Searching 4 fun! 2012 workshop at ECIR '12. 2012.

[287] Ricardo B-Y, Berthier R-N. Modern information retrieval. Addison Wesley; 2009.

[288] Rissanen J. Information and complexity in statistical modeling. Information science and statistics. Springer; 2007.

[289] Robertson SE, Jones KS. Relevance weighting of search terms. J Am Soc Inf Sci 1976;27:129–46.

[290] Robertson SE, Walker S. Some simple effective approximations to the 2-poisson model for probabilistic weighted retrieval. In: SIGIR '94; 1994. p. 232–41.

[291] Robertson S. The probability ranking principle. J Doc 1977.

[292] Robertson S, Zaragoza H, Taylor M. Simple BM25 extension to multiple weighted fields. In: ACM international conference on information and knowledge management. New York, NY, USA: ACM; 2004. p. 42–9.

[293] Robertson SE, Walker S. Some simple effective approximations to the 2-poisson model for probabilistic weighted retrieval. In: SIGIR; 1994. p. 232–41.

[294] Rodriguez M, Posse C, Zhang E. Multiple objective optimization in recommender systems. Proceedings of the sixth ACM conference on recommender systems, RecSys'12; 2012. p. 11–8.

[295] Roelleke T, Wang J. Probabilistic logical modelling of the binary independence retrieval model. In: Proceedings of international conference on theory in information retrieval; 2007.

[296] Sarukkai R. Video search: opportunities and challenges. In: Proceedings of ACM international workshop on multimedia information retrieval. 2005.

[297] Rui Y, Huang TS, Chang S-F. Image retrieval: current techniques, promising directions and open issues. J Visual Commun Image Represent 1999;10(1):39–62.

[298] Rui Y, She A, Huang T. Modified fourier descriptors for shape representation: a practical approach. In: Proceedings of international workshop on image databases and multimedia search. 1996.

[299] Safran C, Bloomrosen M, Hammond WE, Labkoff S, Markel-Fox S, Tang PC, et al. Toward a national framework for the secondary use of health data: an American medical informatics association white paper. J Am Med Inform Assoc 2007;14(1):1–9.

[300] Sahami M, Heilman TD. A web-based kernel function for measuring the similarity of short text snippets. Proceedings of the 15th international conference on world wide web, WWW '06. New York, NY, USA: ACM; 2006. p. 377–86.

[301] Salton G, Wong A, Yang CS. A vector space model for automatic indexing. Commun ACM 1975;18(11):613–20.

[302] Sanderson M. Test collection-based evaluation of information retrieval systems. Found Trend Inf Retrieval 2010;4(4):247–375.

[303] Boyd S, Vandenberghe L. Convex optimization. Cambridge University Press; 2004.

[304] Schroff F, Criminisi A, Zisserman A. Harvesting image databases from the web. In: Proceedings of IEEE international conference on computer vision; 2007.

[305] Schulze M. A new monotonic, clone-independent, reversal symmetric, and condorcet-consistent single-winner election method. Soc Choice Welfare 2011;36:267–303.

[306] Schwaighofer A, Tresp V, Yu K. Learning Gaussian process kernels via hierarchical Bayes. Adv Neural Inf Process Syst 2005;17:1209–16.

[307] Thamarai Selvi R, George Dharma Prakash Raj E. Information retrieval models: a survey. Int J Res Rev Inf Sci 2012;2(3).

[308] Seo J, Croft BW. Blog site search using resource selection. In: CIKM 2008. ACM; 2008. p. 1053–62.

[309] Seyfried L, Hanauer DA, Nease DA, Albeiruti R, Kavanagh J, Kales HC. Enhanced identification of eligibility for depression research using an electronic medical record search engine. Int J Med Inform 2009;78(12):e13–8.

[310] Sharma D. Stemming algorithms: a comparative study and their analysis. Int J Appl Inf Syst Found Comput Sci 2012;4(3):7–12.

[311] Shen D, Sun J-T, Yang Q, Chen Z. Building bridges for web query classification. Proceedings of the 29th annual international ACM SIGIR conference on research and development in information retrieval, SIGIR '06. New York, NY, USA: ACM; 2006. p. 131–8.

[312] Shen X, Tan B, Zhai CX. Context-sensitive information retrieval using implicit feedback. In: SIGIR '05; 2005. p. 43–50.

[313] Shimodaira H. Improving predictive inference under covariate shift by weighting the log-likelihood function. J Stat Plan Infer 2000;90(2):227–44.

[314] Shokouhi M. Central rank-based collection selection in uncooperative distributed information retrieval. In: ECIR 2007; 2007. p. 160–72.

[315] Si L, Callan J. Relevant document distribution estimation method for resource selection. In: SIGIR 2003. ACM; 2003. p. 298–305.

[316] Si L, Jin R, Callan J, Ogilvie P. A language modeling framework for resource selection and results merging. In: CIKM 2002. ACM; 2002. p. 391–7.

[317] Singhal A, Buckley C, Mitra M. Pivoted document length normalization. In: SIGIR '96; 1996. p. 21–9.

[318] Sivic J, Zisserman A. Video Google: a text retrieval approach to object matching in videos. In: Proceedings of IEEE international conference on computer vision; 2003. p. 1470–7.

[319] Skowron M, Araki K. Effectiveness of combined features for machine learning based question classification. Inf Media Technol 2006;1(1):461–81.

[320] Smeulders AWM, Worring M, Santini S, Gupta A, Jain R. Content-based image retrieval at the end of the early years. IEEE Trans Pattern Anal Mach Intell 2000;22(12):1349–80.

[321] Smith JR, Chang S-F. VisualSeek: a fully automated content-based image query system. In: Proceedings of ACM international conference on multimedia; 1996. p. 87–98.

[322] Smith JR, Chang S-F. Automated binary texture feature sets for image retrieval. Proceedings of the IEEE international conference on acoustics, speech, and signal processing; 1996. p. 2239–42.

[323] Smith JR, Chang S-F. Tools and techniques for color image retrieval. In: Storage and retrieval for image and video databases. 1996. p. 426–37.

[324] Cees GM, Snoek M, Jan W, van Gemert C, Geusebroek JM, Smeulders AWM. The challenge problem for automated detection of 101 semantic concepts in multimedia. Proceedings of the ACM international conference on multimedia, Santa Barbara, CA, USA; 2006.

[325] Snoek CG, Worring M. Are concept detector lexicons effective for video search?. In: Proceedings of IEEE international conference in multimedia & expo; 2007.

[326] Sohn T, Li KA, Griswold WG, Hollan JD. A diary study of mobile information needs. In: CHI '08; 2008. p. 433–42.

[327] Stearns MQ, Price C, Spackman KA, Wang AY. Snomed clinical terms: overview of the development process and project status. In: Proceedings of the AMIA symposium. American Medical Informatics Association; 2001. p. 662.

[328] Tong S, Chang E. Support vector machine active learning for image retrieval. In: Proceedings of ACM international conference on multimedia; 2001. p. 524–31.

[329] Strens MJA. A bayesian framework for reinforcement learning. ICML '00: proceedings of the seventeenth international conference on machine learning. San Francisco, CA, USA: Morgan Kaufmann; 2000. p. 943–50.

[330] Stricker M, Orengo M. Similarity of color images. In: Storage and retrieval for image and video databases. 1995. p. 381–92.

[331] Sugiyama K, Hatano K, Yoshikawa M. Adaptive web search based on user profile constructed without any effort from users. In: WWW '04; 2004. p. 675–84.

[332] Sugiyama M, Nakajima S, Kashima H, von Bunau P, Kawanabe M. Direct importance estimation with model selection and its application to covariate shift adaptation. Adv Neural Inf Process Syst 2008:20.

[333] Sushmita M, Joho H, Lalmas M. A task-based evaluation of an aggregated search interface. Proceedings of the 16th international symposium on string processing and information retrieval, SPIRE '09. Berlin, Heidelberg, Germany: Springer-Verlag; 2009. p. 322–33.

[334] Sushmita S, Joho H, Lalmas M, Villa R. Factors affecting clickthrough behavior in aggregated search interfaces. Proceedings of the 19th ACM international conference on information and knowledge management, CIKM '10. New York, NY, USA: ACM; 2010. p. 519–28.

[335] Sutton R, Barto A. Reinforcement learning. MIT Press; 1998.

[336] Svore KM, Volkovs M, Burges CJC. Learning to rank with multiple objective functions. In: WWW; 2011. p. 367–76.

[337] Wei S, Zhao Y, Zhu Z, Liu N. Multimodal fusion for video search re-ranking. IEEE Trans Knowledge Data Eng 2009.

[338] Indyk P, Haveliwala TH, Gionis A. Scalable techniques for clustering the web. In: Proceedings of the WebDB workshop. 2000. p. 129–34.

[339] Tan B, Shen X, Zhai CX. Mining long-term search history to improve search accuracy. In: KDD '06; 2006. p. 718–23.

[340] Tange HJ, Schouten HC, Kester ADM, Hasman A. The granularity of medical narratives and its effect on the speed and completeness of information retrieval. J Am Med Inf Assoc 1998;5(6):571–82.

[341] Taylor M, Guiver J, Robertson S, Minka T. SoftRank: optimising non-smooth rank metrics. In: Proceedings of international ACM conference on web search and data mining; 2008.

[342] Tešsić J, Natsev A, Smith J-R. Cluster-based data modeling for semantic video search. In: Proceedings of international conference on image and video retrieval; 2007.

[343] Tešsić J, Natsev A, Xie L, Smith J-R, Yan R. Data modeling strategies for imbalanced learning in visual search. In: IEEE international conference on multimedia & expo; 2007.

[344] Teevan J, Karlson A, Amini S, Bernheim Brush AJ, Krumm J. Understanding the importance of location, time, and people in mobile local search behavior. In: MobileHCI '11; 2011. p. 77–80.

[345] Thomas P, Shokouhi M. Sushi: scoring scaled samples for server selection. In: SIGIR 2009. ACM; 2009.

[346] Tian M, Yang L, Wang L, Yang Y, Wu X, Hua X-S. Bayesian video search reranking. In: Proceedings of the ACM multimedia. p. 131–140.

[347] Xinmei T, Dacheng T, Xian-Sheng H, Xiuqing W. Active reranking for web image search. IEEE Trans Image Process 2010;19(3):805–20.

[348] Mei T, Rui Y. Image Similarity, Chapter. In: Ling L, Tamer Ozsu M, editors. Encyclopedia of database systems. Springer; 2009.

[349] Toda H, Kataoka R. A search result clustering method using informatively named entities. WIDM '05: proceedings of the 7th annual ACM international workshop on web information and data management. New York, NY, USA: ACM; 2005. p. 81–6.

[350] TRECVID: <www-nlpir.nist.gov/projects/trecvid/>.

[351] Tsatsaronis G, Panagiotopoulou V. A generalized vector space model for text retrieval based on semantic relatedness. Proceedings of the 12th conference of the European chapter of the association for computational linguistics; 2009. p. 70–8.

[352] Turchin A, Shubina M, Breydo E, Pendergrass ML, Einbinder JS. Comparison of information content of structured and narrative text data sources on the example of medication intensification. J Am Med Inform Assoc 2009;16(3):362–70.

[353] Özlem U, Ira G, Yuan L, Isaac K. Identifying patient smoking status from medical discharge records. J Am Med Inform Assoc 2008;15(1):14–24.

[354] van Zwol R, Pueyo LG, Muralidharan M, Sigurbjörnsson B. Machine learned ranking of entity facets. In: SIGIR; 2010. p. 879–80.

[355] van Zwol R, Garcia Pueyo L, Muralidharan M, Sigurbjörnsson B. Ranking entity facets based on user click feedback. In: Fourth IEEE international conference on semantic computing (IEEE ICSC2010), Pittsburgh, PA, USA; 2010.

[356] van Zwol R, Sigurbjörnsson B, Adapala R, Garcia Pueyo L, Katiyar A, Kurapati K, et al. Faceted exploration of image search results. In: WWW; 2010. p. 961–70.

[357] Venetis P, Gonzalez H, Jensen CS, Halevy AY. Hyper-local, directions-based ranking of places. PVLDB 2011;4(5):290–301.

[358] Vercoustre A-M, Thom JA, Pehcevski J. Entity ranking in Wikipedia. SAC '08: proceedings of the 20 08 ACM symposium on Applied computing. New York, NY, USA: ACM; 2008. p. 1101–6.

[359] Voorhees EM, Hersh W. Overview of the TREC 2012 medical records track. In: Proceedings of the 21st Text REtrieval conference; 2012.

[360] Voorhees EM. The TREC question answering track. Nat Lang Eng 2001;7(4):361–78.

[361] Wang B, Tang J, Fan W, Chen S, Yang Z, Liu Y. Heterogeneous cross domain ranking in latent space. Proceeding of the 18th ACM conference on information and knowledge management, CIKM '09; 2009. p. 987–96.

[362] Wang C, Mahadevan S. Heterogeneous domain adaptation using manifold alignment. In: IJCAI; 2011. p. 1541–6.

[363] Wang D, Li X, Li J, Zhang B. The importance of query-concept-mapping for automatic video retrieval. In: Proceedings of ACM multimedia; 2007.

[364] Wang J, Hua X-S. Interactive image search by color map. ACM Trans Intell Syst Technol 2011;3(12).

[365] Weiner M, Stump TE, Callahan CM, Lewis JN, McDonald CJ. Pursuing integration of performance measures into electronic medical records: beta-adrenergic receptor antagonist medications. Qual Saf Health Care 2005;14(2):99–106.

[366] Welch LR. Hidden markov models and the baum-welch algorithm. IEEE Inf Theor Soc Newsletter 2003;53(4).

[367] Wen J-R, Nie J-Y, Zhang H-J. Clustering user queries of a search engine. Proceedings of the 10th international conference on world Wide Web, WWW '01. New York, NY, USA: ACM; 2001. p. 162–8.

[368] Wikipedia: <www.wikipedia.org>.

[369] Wilcox AB, Chen Y-H, Hripcsak G. Minimizing electronic health record patient-note mismatches. J Am Med Inform Assoc 2011;18(4):511–4.

[370] Wilson ML, Elsweiler D. Casual-leisure searching: the exploratory search scenarios that break our current models. In: 4th international workshop on human-computer interaction and information retrieval, New Brunswick, NJ, USA. Aug. 2010.

[371] Wong SKM, Ziarko W, Wong PCN. Generalized vector spaces model in information retrieval. Proceedings of ACM special interest group on information retrieval, New York, NY, USA; 1985. p. 18–25.

[372] Wu Q, Burges CJC, Svore K, Gao J. Ranking, boosting, and model adaptation. Technical report MSR-TR-2008-109. Microsoft research. 2008.

[373] Wu Y, Tian Q, Huang T. Discriminant-em algorithm with application to image retrieval. In: Proceedings of IEEE conference on computer vision and pattern recognition; 2000. p. 155–62.

[374] Xia F, Liu TY, Wang J, Zhang W, Li H. Listwise approach to learning to rank: theory and algorithm. In: Proceedings of international conference on machine learning; 2008.

[375] Xu B, Bu J, Chun C, Deng C, Xiaofei H, Wei L, et al. Efficient manifold ranking for image retrieval. In: Proceedings of ACM special interest group on information retrieval; 2011. p. 525–34.

[376] Xu H, Jingdong W, Xian-Sheng H, Shipeng L. Image search by concept map. In: Proceedings of ACM special interest group on information retrieval; 2010. p. 275–82.

[377] Yahoo: <www.yahoo.com>.

[378] Yan R. Probabilistic models for combining diverse knowledge sources in multimedia retrieval. PhD thesis. Carnegie Mellon University. 2006.

[379] Yan R, Hauptmann A, Jin R. Multimedia search with pseudo-relevance feedback. In: ACM international conference on image and video retrieval; 2003. p. 238–47.

[380] Yanagawa A, Chang S-F, Kennedy L, Hsu W. Columbia university's baseline detectors for 374 LSCOM semantic visual concepts. In: Columbia University ADVENT Technical Report ♯222-2006-8. March 2007.

[381] Yang L, Mei Q, Zheng K, Hanauer DA. Query log analysis of an electronic health record search engine. AMIA annual symposium proceedings, vol. 2011. American Medical Informatics Association; 2011. p. 915.

[382] Yang Q, Chen Y, Xue G-R, Dai G-R, Yu Y. Heterogeneous transfer learning for image clustering via the social web. In: ACL '09; 2009. p. 1–9.

[383] Wang C, Li Z, Zhang L, Cao Y, Wang H, Zhang L. MindFinder: interactive sketch-based image search on millions of images. In: Proceedings of ACM multimedia; 2010.

[384] Yao T, Mei T, Ngo C-W. Co-reranking by mutual reinforcement for image search. In: ACM international conference on image and video retrieval; 2010.

[385] Yao T, Ngo C-W, Mei T. Circular reranking for visual search. IEEE Trans Image process 2013;22(4):1644–55.

[386] Yee K-P, Swearingen K, Li K, Hearst M. Faceted metadata for image search and browsing. In: CHI; 2003. p. 401–8.

[387] Yi J, Maghoul F, Pedersen J. Deciphering mobile search patterns: a study of yahoo! Mobile search queries. In: WWW '08; 2008. p. 257–66.

[388] Yi X, Raghavan H, Leggetter C. Discovering users' specific geo intention in web search. In: WWW; 2009. p. 481–90.

[389] Gaffney S, Zhou Y, Nie L. Surface form resolution based on Wikipedia. In: Proceedings of COLING; 2010.

[390] YouTube: <www.youtube.com>.

[391] Rubner Y, Tomasi C, Guibas LJT. The earth mover's distance as a metric for image retrieval. Int J Comput Vision 2000;40(2):99–121.

[392] Rui Y, Huang TS, Ortega M, Mehrotra S. Relevance feedback: a power tool for interactive content-based image retrieval. IEEE Trans Circuits Syst Video Technol 1998;8:644–55.

[393] Yue Y, Finley T, Radlinski F, Joachims T. A support vector method for optimizing average precision. In: Proceedings of ACM special interest group on information retrieval; 2007.

[394] Zadrozny S, Nowacka K. Fuzzy information retrieval model revisited. Fuzzy Sets Syst 2009;160:2173–91.

[395] Zahn CT, Roskies RZ. Fourier descriptors for plane closed curve. IEEE Trans Comput 1972;21:269–81.

[396] Zamir O, Etzioni O. Web document clustering: A feasibility demonstration. In: Proceedings of SIGIR 1998; 1996. p. 46–84.

[397] Zavesky E, Chang. S-F. CuZero: embracing the frontier of interactive visual search for informed users. In: Proceedings of ACM multimedia information retrieval; 2008. p. 237–44.

[398] Zeng H-J, He Q-C, Chen Z, Ma W-Y, Ma J. Learning to cluster web search results. In: SIGIR. New York, NY, USA: ACM; 2004. p. 210–7.

[399] Zha H, Zheng Z, Fu H, Sun G. Incorporating query difference for learning retrieval functions in world wide web search. In: Proceedings of the 15th ACM CIKM conference; 2006.

[400] Zhai C, Lafferty J. A study of smoothing methods for language models applied to ad hoc information retrieval. In: SIGIR; 2001. p. 334–42.

[401] Zhai CX, Lafferty J. A study of smoothing methods for language models applied to ad hoc information retrieval. In: Proceedings of ACM SIGIR 2001; 2001. p. 334–42.

[402] Zhang D, Mao R, Li H, Mao J. How to count thumb-ups and thumb-downs: user-rating based ranking of items from an axiomatic, perspective. In: ICTIR'11; 2011. p. 238–49.

[403] Zhang L, Lin F, Zhang B. Support vector machine learning for image retrieval. Proceedings of the IEEE international conference on image processing; 2001. p. 721–4.

[404] Zhang L, Zhang Y. Interactive retrieval based on faceted feedback. In: Proceeding of the 33rd international ACM SIGIR; 2010. p. 363–70.

[405] Zheng K, Mei Q, Hanauer DA. Collaborative search in electronic health records. J Am Med Inform Assoc 2011;18(3):282–91.

[406] Zheng Z, Chen K, Sun G, Zha H. A regression framework for learning ranking functions using relative relevance judgments. In: SIGIR; 2007. p. 287–94.

[407] Zheng Z, Zha H, Zhang T, Chapelle O, Chen K, Sun G. A general boosting method and its application to learning ranking functions for web search. Advances in neural information processing systems, vol. 20. MIT Press; 2008. p. 1697–704.

[408] Zhou D, Bousquet O, Lal T, Weston J, Scholkopf B. Learning with local and global consistency. In: Proceedings of advances in neural information processing system; 2003. p. 321–8.

[409] Zhou D, et al. Ranking on data manifolds. In: Advances in neural information processing systems. 2004.

[410] Zhou K, Cummins R, Lalmas M, Jose JM. Evaluating aggregated search pages. Proceedings of the 35th international ACM SIGIR conference on research and development in information retrieval, SIGIR '12. New York, NY, USA: ACM; 2012. p. 115–24.

[411] Zhou L, Tao Y, Cimino JJ, Chen ES, Liu H, Lussier YA, et al. Terminology model discovery using natural language processing and visualization techniques. J Biomed Inform 2006;39(6):626–36.

[412] Zhou XS, Huang TS. Relevance feedback for image retrieval: a comprehensive review. Multimedia Syst 2003;8(6):536–44.

[413] Zhu D, Carterette B. An analysis of assessor behavior in crowdsourced preference judgements . In: SIGIR workshop on crowdsourcing for search evaluation. New York, NY, USA: ACM; 2010. p. 21–6.

[414] Zhu D, Carterette B. Exploring evidence aggregation methods and external expansion sources for medical record search. In: Proceedings of the 21st text retrieval conference; 2012.

[415] Zhu X. Semisupervised learning literature survey. Computer science. University of Wisconsin-Madison. 2006.

[416] Zinkevich M, Weimer M, Smola A, Li L. Parallelized stochastic gradient descent. In: Lafferty J, Williams CKI, Shawe-Taylor J, Zemel RS, Culotta A. editors. Advances in neural information processing systems 23. 2010. p. 2595–603.

[417] Scheufele EL, Housman D, Wasser JS, Pauker SG, Palchuk MB. i2b2 and keyword search of narrative clinical text. In: AMIA annual symposium proceedings; 2011. 1950.

[418] Kang C, Vadrevu S, Zhang R, van Zwol R, Pueyo LG, Torzec N, et al. Ranking related entities for web search queries. In: Proceedings of the 20th international world wide web conference (WWW); 2011. p. 67–8.

[419] Long B, Chang Y, Dong A, He J. Pairwise cross-domain factor model for heterogeneous transfer ranking. In: Proceedings of the fifth ACM international conference on web search and data mining. WSDM '12, Seattle, Washington, USA. New York, NY, USA: ACM; 2012. p. 113–22.

Author Index

Subject Index

233

Printed and bound by CPI Group (UK) Ltd, Croydon, CR0 4YY

03/10/2024

01040324-0010